After the First Death

*An Anthology of Wales and War
in the Twentieth Century*

After the First Death

*An Anthology of Wales and War
in the Twentieth Century*

Edited by Tony Curtis

seren

Seren is the book imprint of
Poetry Wales Press Ltd,
57 Nolton Street, Bridgend,
CF31 3AE, Wales
www.seren-books.com

For individual contributions see Acknowledgments pages

A CIP record for this title is available from
the British Library CIP Office

ISBN 978-1-85411-450-1

*The publisher acknowledges the financial support of the
Arts Council of Wales*

Cover painting by Charles Burton

Printed in Plantin by Bell & Bain, Glasgow

Contents

The Thirties

The Second World War

Post-War, Cold War, New Wars

Introduction

The writers and readers of this anthology will have led much of their lives or have their roots in the twentieth century, a century, like most others, of war. The two World Wars challenged, broke and shaped political borders, traditions, societies, individuals and their beliefs more profoundly than the wars of previous centuries. While few of us now living have had direct experience of war, in uniform or as civilians, it is likely that the wars our families fought or suffered in, and more recently the fear of nuclear war or terrorism, will have been a significant factor in our lives.

Wales was last invaded in what is reported as music hall fashion by dispirited French troops at the end of the eighteenth century. Whether they were convinced that the marching townsfolk of Fishguard and their women's tall hats were Grenadier guards or not, it makes a reassuring story about the island security we have enjoyed. Not since the landing at Dale of Henry Tudor, later Henry IV, had Wales been the gateway to England. Not since the castle sieges of the English Civil War in the seventeenth century had ordnance been fired in anger in Wales.

Wales had enlisted men for the Crimea and the Boer War, but in 1914 Wales, in common with the rest of Britain, was caught up in a wave of patriotic fervour: as many men served in that conflict as worked in the essential mining industry which fuelled the fleet and the factories. From the Somme, at Mametz Wood and through Paschendale, up to the armistice in November 1918, Welsh regiments and divisions served widely and suffered greatly on the Western Front. It is surely part of most of our families' histories. My Pembrokeshire grandmother's cousin James Charles Thomas had been a member of the Pembrokeshire Yeomanry and served in the Middle East before being transferred to the Machine Gun Corps; he was killed in the German counter-offensive at Cambrai in December 1917. His body was not recovered until the following January. Some corner of the village of Caudry is forever Tallyhoo Farm, Llangwm.

In the Second World War Wales, particularly the south Wales docks, was heavily bombed by the Luftwaffe. When Dylan Thomas made his *Return Journey to Swansea* he found ghosts and insecure memories in the rubble. In 1942 my mother came back to the land of her father and generations of Williamses to serve as a Land Army girl; there she met my father who served on coastal defences around Milford Haven. I memorialised that in a poem 'Land Army Photographs', which conflates events and coincidences to make its point. Now, after further questioning, I know that they met at the end of the war and could never have both looked up, she at her flax gathering and he at the gun emplacement, and seen "the white belly of that flying boat / Cut into the Haven". Writing about war, as writing about most things, will be subject to the vagaries of memory and the indulgences of the imagination. This anthology is not a history book; it does, however, collect letters and autobiography as well as poems and fiction.

Every town and city in Wales has a war memorial; I remember marching with the Scouts to parade before the one outside the hospital in Carmarthen, on 11th November 1958. At Manorbier where my mother lives there is a memorial outside the gates of Gerald of Wales' castle. It has the names of the dead from the two World Wars: in the Great War four pairs of brothers are listed from that small village. They include the sons of the Viscount St. David: the Hon. Arnold who died in 1915 and is buried at Aveluy on the Somme and the Hon. Roland who died in 1916 and whose name is on the Menin Gate and whose body, therefore, must have remained undiscovered. The upper classes went over the top first and died first.

On the Ypres memorial are also listed Arthur Owen Phillips who served with the Canadian Mounted Rifles and George Williams who was with the Saskatchewan regiment. Like my grandmother's cousin from Jeffreyston, these men had been seduced by the promise of land to take up the challenges of free, grim acres in Canada, but had returned to fight for their homeland. This was truly a world war: the war to end wars. And then there was another: my mother's cousin David White from Vancouver, whose mother Leah Williams had also emigrated to Canada from Bangor at the turn of the century, is buried beneath Monte Cassino where he died on 23rd May 1944. He was a Lance Sergeant in the Seaforth Highlanders of Canada. Two women related by marriage to my Williams family in Bangor were victims of German bombs which were jettisoned over the Bethesda area on a raid on Liverpool in 1941: Ellen Davies and Nancy Pritchard are listed on the Bethesda war memorial underneath the names of the men. The two World Wars shaped us whether or not we know about or remember our losses.

The town where I live, Barry, has just renovated its King's Square; there in 1917 the first American 'Dough Boys' lined up before going off to the Western Front; across from my house was the camp of the Lancashire Fusiliers. The inhabitants of Lydstep and Manorbier are currently protesting against the MOD's night firing of missiles from Skrinkle Point; they need to practice. The artist Arthur Giardelli, who came to Merthyr in the war as a CO, lives on the edge of the

Castlemartin artillery range. NATO tanks pound that Pembrokeshire peninsula from the other side of his thorn hedge. The Men from Hereford and others tramp at night over Pen-y-Fan. Ghurkhas and their families live next door to Christopher Meredith in Brecon. Tornadoes scream over Snowdonia and Powys on low-level practice sorties. My wife taught Anthony Keeble, a young Welsh Guards soldier from Cowbridge killed in 1982 in the Falklands on the *Sir Galahad*. Our local papers profile the casualties in Iraq and Afganistan. The wars still come back to Wales and affect us all.

The present anthology began as a manuscript of over five hundred pages. There is a wealth of material relating to warfare and Wales in the twentieth century; much editing and many losses were incurred in the process of producing the book in your hands. I regret the loss of further letters and poems by Edward Thomas and Alun Lewis; extracts of fiction from Siân James and Emyr Humphreys; more letters from Lloyd George, more poems and fictions, and many moving remembrances from those who actually fought in the trenches – raw, honest unliterary works. I have indicated sources for some of these in my bibliography.

The companion volume to this – *Wales and War in the Twentieth Century: A Collection of Critical Essays* – pays attention to the significant writers and artists of the century. Readers will find references to writers and books which have contributed to this anthology as well as those for whom there was not room. Each volume supports the other. I was persuaded by Jeremy Hooker's work to include poems by Wilfred Owen; Owen was the outstanding poet of the Great War and perhaps the greatest poet of any war. He recognised his Welsh ancestry, as did the London Welshman Edward Thomas. Robert Graves and Siegfried Sassoon are included as they were commissioned in Welsh regiments. Other colleagues made the case for the inclusion of writers and works, but the final selection is solely my responsibility.

Tony Curtis

R.S. Thomas
Welsh History

We were a people taut for war; the hills
Were no harder, the thin grass
Clothed them more warmly than the coarse
Shirts our small bones.
We fought, and were always in retreat,
Like snow thawing upon the slopes
Of Mynydd Mawr; and yet the stranger
Never found our ultimate stand
In the thick woods, declaiming verse
To the sharp prompting of the harp.

Our kings died, or they were slain
By the old treachery at the ford.
Our bards perished, driven from the halls
Of nobles by the thorn and bramble.

We were a people bred on legends,
Warming our hands at the red past.
The great were ashamed of our loose rags
Clinging stubbornly to the proud tree
Of blood and birth, our lean bellies
And mud houses were a proof
Of our ineptitude for life.

We were a people wasting ourselves
In fruitless battles for our masters,
In lands to which we had no claim,
With men for whom we felt no hatred.

We were a people, and are so yet.
When we have finished quarrelling for crumbs
Under the table; or gnawing the bones
Of a dead culture, we will arise,
Armed, but not in the old way.

The Great War 1914-1918

The Great War for me

Wilfred Owen
Anthem for Doomed Youth

What passing-bells for these who die as cattle?
– Only the monstrous anger of the guns.
Only the stuttering rifles' rapid rattle
Can patter out their hasty orisons.
No mockeries now for them; no prayers nor bells;
Nor any voice of mourning save the choirs, –
The shrill, demented choirs of wailing shells;
And bugles calling for them from sad shires.

What candles may be held to speed them all?
Not in the hands of boys but in their eyes
Shall shine the holy glimmers of good-byes.
The pallor of girls' brows shall be their pall;
Their flowers the tenderness of patient minds,
And each slow dusk a drawing-down of blinds.

Edward Thomas
'Recruits'

Probably there are two kinds of patriot; one that can talk or write, and one that cannot; though I suspect that even the talkers and writers often come down in the end to 'I do not understand. I love.' It must happen more than once or twice that a man who can say why he ought to fight for his country fails to enlist. The very phrase, 'to fight for one's country', is a shade too poetical and conscious for any but non-combatants. A man enlists for some inexplicable reason which he may translate into simple, conventional terms. If he has thought a good deal about it, he has made a jump at some point, beyond the reach of his thought. The articulate and the inarticulate are united in the ranks at this moment by the power to make that jump and come to the extreme decision. I heard a mother trying to persuade – pretending she was trying to persuade – a young man against enlisting. She said: 'I would not risk my life for anybody. It isn't yours, for one thing. Think of Mary. I would sooner go to America ...' She found a hundred things to say, few of them quite genuine, since it was her desire to overpower him, not to express herself. In argument he was overpowered. His reasons he could not give. Nevertheless, if he passed the doctor he was going; if the doctor rejected him, he rather hoped some girl would taunt him – she would have to produce a champion to justify her. Had the eleven or twelve thousand recruits from Birmingham written down their reasons, I dare say they would not have been worth much more than the pen, ink, and paper. That is, assuming they included no poets, and I do not see that they were more likely to prove poets than the men, women, and children who made haste to send in their verses to the papers. Out of the crowd at Newcastle the dissatisfied one spoke best. If any at Coventry or elsewhere were kept waiting so long outside the recruiting office that they changed their minds and went away, they might speak better still. Some men of spirit may have kept back to spite their interfering persuaders. Why, the lowest slut in the town, fetching her beer at eleven-thirty, would look after a procession of recruits and say: 'So they ought to. Lord! look what a lot of fellows hang about the corners. They ought to fight for their country.'

There was really no monotony of type among these recruits, though the great majority wore dark clothes and caps, had pale faces tending to leanness, and stood somewhere about five foot seven. It was only the beginning, some thought, of a wide awakening to a sense of the danger and the responsibility. Clean and dirty – some of them, that is, straight from the factory – of all ages and features, they were pouring in. Some might be loafers, far more were workers. I heard that of one batch of two hundred and fifty at Newcastle, not one was leaving less than two pounds a week. Here and there a tanned farm labourer with lighter-coloured, often brownish, clothes, chequered the pale-faced dark company. The streets never lacked a body of them or a tail disappearing. Their tents, their squads drilling this way and that, occupied the great bare Town Moor above Newcastle. The town was like a vast fair where men were changing hands instead of cattle. The ordinary racket of tramcar and crowd was drowned by brass instruments, bagpipes, drums and tin boxes beaten by small boys, men in fifties and in hundreds rounding a corner to the tune of 'It's a long, long way to Tipperary'. Thousands stood to watch them. With crowds on the kerbstones, with other crowds going up and down and across, with men squatting forward on the pavement, it was best to have no object but to go in and out. The recruits were the constant, not the only attraction. The newest ones marching assumed as military a stiff uprightness as possible. The older ones in uniform were slacker. Some stood at corners talking to girls; others went in and out of 'pubs' attended by civilians; more and more slouched, or staggered, or were heavy-eyed with alcohol. Everyone was talking, but the only words intelligible were 'Four o'clock winner' and 'It's a long, long way to

Tipperary'. At nightfall the boys who beat the drums and tins began to carry around an effigy and to sing 'The Kaiser, the Kaiser', or

> And when we go to war
> We'll put him in a jar,
> And he'll never see his daddy any more.

Companies of recruits were still appearing. Perhaps their faces were drawn and shining with drink, fatigue, and excitement, but they remained cheerful even when a young officer with a dry, lean face and no expression said 'Good night' without expression and rode off. His was the one expressionless, dead calm face in the city, the one that seemed to have business of its own, until I crossed the river and saw the women on the doorsteps of the steep slum, the children on pavement and in gutter. They were not excited by the fever in Clayton Street and Market Street, any more than by St. Mary's bells banging away high above slum and river, or by the preacher at the top of Church Street bellowing about 'the blessed blood of Jesus Christ'. In an almost empty tavern a quiet old man was treating a lad in a new uniform, and giving him advice: 'Eat as much as you can, and have a contented mind.' It was a fine warm evening. But what could the great crowd do to spend its excitement? As a crowd, nothing. In a short time it was doubled. For at nine o'clock the public-houses had to be emptied and shut. The burly bell of St. Nicholas tolled nine over thousands with nothing to do. Those who had not taken time by the forelock and drunk as much as they would normally have done by eleven, stood about aimlessly. A man took his stand in Bigg Market and sang for money. It was not what people wanted. Several youths got together at a short distance and tried to bawl down the singer. Even that was not what people wanted. Even the temperance man was only half pleased when he reflected that what he had long agitated for in vain had been done by one stroke of the military pen. There was nothing to be done but to go to bed and wait for the morning papers.

Siân James
'Church and State'

Lowri's grandfather sat by the fire, squat and black and unsmiling. His daughter-in-law had put him in his chapel coat that morning and polished his face with a piece of flannel. He was still angry. He spat into the fire from time to time. Josi took over the tin of tobacco he'd brought for him. At Lowri's request.

'Are you going to the war?' the old man asked, puzzled by the gift.

'Too old, man,' Josi said.

'Too old?' The old man cleared his throat noisily.

'You think I should fight, do you?' Josi asked, amiably.

'For the bloody English. No.' The little man spat squarely into the flames. 'They wanted me to fight once; against the Russians, I think, or the Turks. Not I. My family fight against the bloody English, not for them. My father burnt his ricks in the tithe war, ready to starve rather than pay the tithes.'

'It was the church you were fighting then.'

'Same thing, church and state. My grandfather was one of 'Becca's maidens in the hungry forties. They were fighters if you like. Pulled down all the bloody toll gates. Dressed as ladies, but it couldn't hide their men's hearts. Toll gates. Bloody English.'

'Lloyd George is a good little man to my way of thinking,' Josi said peaceably, 'and he's one of the English now.'

'Turn-coat from the North.'

'Good little man to my way of thinking,' Josi said again. 'Not my business, though. Not today.'

The old man spun round to face him, the light of understanding in his eyes at last.

'You're the bridegroom, are you?'

'Aye,' Josi said. 'That's right.'

'You old ram.'

Bertrand Russell
Letter to Lady Ottoline Morrell, July 1916

Central Hotel, Merthyr, Sunday evg.

My Darling – I found your letter when I arrived this morning ...

We had another terrible Comm^{ee} yesterday. I don't know how it will work out. I came down as far as Cardiff late last night & on here this morning. I spoke here at 2.30 a *wonderful* meeting, as they had promised. The Chief Constable even is friendly here – I had some talk with him afterwards. I find the police short-hand writer who takes down every word I say is getting his orders from London, not the local police. There were between 2000 & 3000 people, quite unanimous – it was very inspiring.

I want a *great* fuss made about my not being allowed to go to America. I left it to Allen to arrange the fuss. Probably he will have spoken to you about it. Trinity is going to consider on Tuesday whether to dismiss me for 'grave moral obloquy' but no doubt I have incurred that.

I did have hopes the war would end this year but now I have practically none. Apparently Kitchener's 3 years will be right.

Tuesday mg. Port Talbot.

... The state of feeling here is quite astonishing. This town subsists on one enormous steel works, the largest in S. Wales; the men are starred, & earning very good wages. They are not suffering from the war in any way. Yet they seem all to be against it. On Sunday afternoon I had an open-air meeting on a green: there were two Chapels on the green, & their congregations came out just before I began. They stayed to listen. A crowd of about 400 came – not like open-air meetings in the South where people stay a few minutes out of curiosity & then go away – they all stayed the whole time, listened with the closest attention, & seemed unanimously sympathetic. The man who has been organising for me here works 12 hours every day except Sunday in the steel works. Their energy is wonderful.

Sunday evening I spoke at Briton Ferry – a really wonderful meeting – the hall was packed, they were all at the highest point of enthusiasm – they inspired me & I spoke as I have never spoken before. We put a resolution in favour of immediate peace negotiations, which was carried unanimously. (I did not notice any abstentions, tho' presumably the two plainclothes men who had come to take notes must have abstained). Those who had not already signed the peace petition signed it in large numbers. One needs no prudent reticences – no humbug of any sort – one can just speak out one's whole mind. I thought the great offensive would have excited them but it hasn't.

Yesterday evening I spoke at Ystradgynlais, a mining town of 16,000 inhabitants. The meeting was smaller & my impression was that a good many people at it were undecided in their minds – that sort of meeting is really more useful than an enthusiastic one. The audience were almost all miners – they seemed intelligent and hopeful.

I enclose a little leaflet which is distributed at my meetings. If you don't burn it at once, you are liable to imprisonment ...

Siân James
'Allies advancing'

Edward's marriage had an inauspicious beginning.

Rose was anything but a serene bride. A few hours before the wedding, she seemed to recover all her old spirit, feeling that her parents had taken advantage of her humiliating loss of nerve under arrest in order to get her safely off their hands, despising herself that she had allowed them to manipulate her into a marriage she wasn't ready for. She all but refused to go through with the ceremony, but once more she was not quite brave enough to act according to her conscience.

During their honeymoon in Devon, she confessed to Edward that she had married him largely out of weakness and fear, and was unable to accept his repeated assurances of sympathy or his insistence that marriage should not limit her opportunities in any way: she should continue to work for the Women's Movement in Oxford, where he, too, would throw himself into the struggle. He was unfailingly loving and undemanding, but couldn't help the occasional feeling that he had, perhaps, lost even more than she. Ten or eleven days passed bleakly by.

It was the imminence of war which brought them together.

Rose's cousin, Claire, had been studying in Europe for some months, and having missed their wedding, travelled to Devon to see them.

'We'll be at war in a few days,' she told them. 'The French are already mobilising and we can't let them fight alone, the Germans are breaking treaty after treaty. When I was in Berlin it was already obvious that nothing was going to stop them. I'll never forget the mood of the crowd in the Unter den Linden, cheering and singing whenever a company of infantry or a squadron of horse went by. They're a people so full of aggressive energy that they're ready to surge through Europe. And it's up to us to stop them. England must unite with France to defend the freedom of the little nations. To remain neutral would be treachery.'

Edward and Rose were fired by her patriotism. They read all the newspapers they had neglected and decided to cut short their honeymoon – they were to have spent a month in the West Country – in order to be back in London at the centre of things.

When they got off the train at Paddington, they realised that Claire's prediction had been proved right; the station was thronged with troops going to join their regiments, and the newspaper boys outside the station with their placards – 'War Official' – were being besieged by normally placid and sober citizens wrestling for copies of the evening paper. The King had already proclaimed that the Army Reserve should be called out on permanent service.

The next day, the Prime Minister, Mr Asquith, asked parliament for power to increase the number of men in the army by half a million and Edward immediately decided to apply for a commission instead of returning to Oxford.

London seemed transformed. There was wholesale panic-buying of food – even perishable goods – as though people expected an immediate invasion. German shops and businesses were boarded up, their owners gone. There were long queues of men standing for hours outside every recruiting office. Even the noises of London; the cries of street traffic, the hooting of horns, the screams of trains, seemed to have become more strident and aggressive.

Rose accompanied Edward as he went from one military garrison to another, waiting patiently and eagerly while he was interviewed, optimistic of the result even when he was despondent. At the end of the following week, when he succeeded in obtaining a commission in the Royal Artillery, she was immensely proud and happy. That afternoon, in the taxi-cab that took them back to her parents' home, she cried in his arms that she loved him.

A few days later, Rose managed to get work as a helper at the local hospital, and after passing a preliminary examination was accepted as a member of the Voluntary Aid Detachment.

She continued to live at home – the house her father had taken for her and Edward in Oxford had been re-let – and when he was free, Edward came from Woolwich to join her.

He looked older in his uniform, his hair was close-cropped and he had grown a thin moustache. They had much to talk about, the progress of the war engrossed them both; they were far happier than they had been on their honeymoon.

Life was hectic for each of them. As a full-time VAD, Rose had to get up at six-thirty every morning to get to the hospital by eight, and did not return until seven or seven-thirty in the evening.

Though her body was often exhausted, she felt happy and liberated again. Only three months after suffering her traumatic breakdown, feeling her life empty and wasted, she had been given a second chance. She wasn't going to be a drawing-room wife after all, she was a person in her own right, involved, as Mr Asquith had said in parliament, in the classless struggle to defend the civilisation of the world.

Her parents, naturally enough, were very anxious about her, resenting the fact that she seemed to be working as hard as any servant girl. However, she was now a married woman, so that their sense of responsibility was blunted. All in all, her father was rather proud of her, and even her mother talked about her at her tea parties, when the other women boasted about their soldier sons.

It was a warm, bright September that year. The British and French armies won victories on the Marne and the Aisne. 'Allies advancing,' announced the newspaper headlines triumphantly. 'Huge enemy losses.' Throughout the month, Edward was able to be with Rose several evenings a week and once or twice they managed to get a day off together. Rose hadn't begun to feel apprehensive on Edward's behalf; she was conscious only of the glory of his position as a leader of men.

At the beginning of October, Rose encountered wounded soldiers for the first time. They were classified as non-serious cases, and as she had no part in dressing their wounds, she soon got used to their weakness and pallor. It was the element of profound pessimism amongst them which disturbed and shocked her.

They called out to her and to the other nurses cheerfully enough, but left to themselves, they fell silent and morose, and when she had asked one of them about conditions at the Front, what it had been really like, he had flinched as though from a blow. 'It was hell,' he had said. 'Hell on earth. Don't ask about it.'

Robert Graves
'The Welch Regiment, at Cambrin'

I still have the roll of my first platoon of forty men. The figures given for their ages are misleading. On enlistment, all over-age men had put themselves in the late thirties, and all under-age men had called themselves eighteen. But once in France, the over-age men did not mind adding on a few genuine years. No less than fourteen in the roll give their age as forty or over, and these were not all. Fred Prosser, a painter in civil life, who admitted to forty-eight, was really fifty-six. David Davies, collier, who admitted to forty-two, and Thomas Clark, another collier who admitted to forty-five, were only one or two years junior to Prosser. James Burford, collier and fitter, was the oldest soldier of all. When I first spoke to him in the trenches, he said: 'Excuse me, sir, will you explain what this here arrangement is on the side of my rifle?' 'That's the safety-catch. Didn't you do a musketry-course at the depot?' 'No, sir, I was a re-enlisted man, and I spent only a fortnight there. The old Lee-Metford didn't have no safety catch.' I asked him when he had last fired a rifle. 'In Egypt, in 1882,' he said. 'Weren't you in the South African War?' 'I tried to re-enlist, but they told me I was too old, sir. I had been an old soldier in Egypt. My real age is sixty-three.' He spent all his summers as a tramp, and in the bad months of the year worked as a collier, choosing a new pit every season. I heard him and David Davies one night discussing the different seams of coal in Wales, and tracing them from county to county and pit to pit with technical comments.

The other half of the platoon contained the under-age section. I had five of these boys; William Bumford, collier, for instance, who gave his age as eighteen, was really only fifteen. He used to get into trouble for falling asleep on sentry duty, an offence punishable with death, but could not help it. I had seen him suddenly go to sleep, on his feet, while holding a sandbag open for another fellow to fill. So we got him a job as orderly to a chaplain for a while, and a few months later all men over fifty and all boys under eighteen got combed out. Bumford and Burford were both sent to the base; but neither escaped the war. Bumford grew old enough by 1917 to be sent back to the battalion, and was killed that summer; Burford died in a bombing accident at the basecamp. Or so I was told – the fate of hundreds of my comrades in France came to me merely as hearsay.

The troop-train consisted of forty-seven coaches, and took twenty-four hours to arrive at Béthune, the railhead, via St. Omer. We detrained at about 9pm, hungry, cold and dirty. Expecting a short journey, we had allowed our baggage to be locked in a van; and then played nap throughout the journey to keep our minds off the discomfort. I lost sixty francs, which was over two pounds at the existing rate of exchange. On the platform at Béthune, a little man in filthy khaki, wearing the Welsh capbadge, came up with a friendly touch of the cap most unlike a salute. He had orders to guide us to the battalion, at present in the Cambrin trenches, about ten kilometres away. Collecting the draft of forty men we had with us, we followed him through the unlit suburbs of the town – all intensely excited by the noise and flashes of the guns in the distance. None of the draft had been out before, except the sergeant in charge. They began singing. Instead of the usual music-hall songs they sang Welsh hymns, each man taking a part. The Welsh always sang when pretending not to be scared; it kept them steady. And they never sang out of tune.

We marched towards the flashes, and could soon see the flarelights curving across the distant trenches. The noise of the guns grew louder and louder. Presently we were among the batteries. From about two hundred yards behind us, on the left of the road, a salvo of four shells whizzed suddenly over our heads. This broke up 'Aberystwyth' in the middle of a verse, and sent us off our balance for a few seconds; the column of fours tangled up. The shells went hissing away eastward; we saw the red flash and heard the hollow bang where they landed in German territory. The men picked up their step again and began chaffing. A lance-corporal dictated a letter home: 'Dear auntie, this leaves me in the pink. We are at present wading in blood up to our necks. Send me fags and a life-belt. This war is a booger. Love and kisses.'

Private Frank Richards
(2nd Royal Welch Fusiliers)

'Christmas 1914'

The German Company-Commander asked ours if he would accept a couple of barrels of beer. They had plenty of it in the brewery. He accepted the offer with thanks and a couple of their men rolled the barrels over and we took them into our trench. The German officer sent one of his men back to the trench, who appeared shortly after carrying a tray with bottles and glasses on it. Officers of both sides clinked glasses and drank one another's health. Our Company-Commander had presented them with a plum pudding just before. The officers came to an understanding that the unofficial truce would end at midnight. At dusk we went back to our respective trenches.

Tony Curtis
From the City that Shone

The thing we dreamt of most was a bath:
so we crossed the wire and made for Gonnelieu
where, it was said, a tin bath lay abandoned
near the well of the convent school.
We kept to ruined shadows down the street,
towels and soap in our haversacks.

John had a canvas bucket and filled it from the well.
The bath held firm, the water cold and sweet.
I lorded it there in the weedy garden
amidst the ransacked books strewn all about,
broken glass wicked in the sun,
then towelled dry while
John tipped the water across the grass.

26

I drew fresh water for him and passed the soap.
'I always sing,' he said.
'Too risky.'
But he splashed and hummed
– *And who shall kiss her ruby lips*
When I am far away? –

I sat on the path, my hair drying,
my head thrown back to the clearing sky
where a Taube stuttered through clouds from the West.
In those moments before the guns started up
it seemed that summer was held in place.

John rose from the water
'Like a god,' he said,
his arms outstretched, then lobbed the soap
grenade-like at my head.
It squirted past me, diving in the slips.
We dressed
– each stuck a dog-rose in his tunic –
and turned back to our trenches.

Robert Graves
Letter to Siegfried Sassoon, 2nd May 1916

Erinfa, Harlech, N. Wales.

My dear Sassoon,

This is the first day that I have felt really strong enough to write you the letter you deserve, being now more or less recovered from the amazing lot of blood I lost last month.

Well, old thing, I'm really desolated at having deserted you and the battalion but I couldn't help it. My people forced me before a specialist who ordered an immediate operation which he said would only take three weeks, which would have meant that having got a three weeks' extension to my leave I would have gone straight back to the battalion. As it was, it proved much more serious and I am on a month's back leave after which bloody Litherland, I suppose. But I swear I'm not skrimming my shanks: though I can't pretend I like Fricourt better than this heavenly place I honestly would go back tonight if I could.

I can't do purple patches well, but Merioneth now is nothing but bright sun and misty mountains and hazy seas and sloe blossoms and wild cherry and grey rocks and young green grass. I am writing in my small, white-walled cottage of which I must have told you – the one that once belonged to a consumptive coachman, then to a drunken carpenter, then became a brothel, then a Sunday school and now serves as pleasaunce for me and my two sisters ...

There is a peculiar cuckoo in the woods just outside with a bad stammer. It says cu-cuckoo and sometimes even cu-cu-cuckoo. I must tell the *Spectator* about it ...

Siegfried Sassoon
The General

'Good-morning; good-morning!' the General said
When we met him last week on our way to the line.
Now the soldiers he smiled at are most of 'em dead,
And we're cursing his staff for incompetent swine.
'He's a cheery old card,' grunted Harry to Jack
As they slogged up to Arras with rifle and pack.

But he did for them both by his plan of attack.

Ivor Gurney
First Time In

After the dread tales and red yarns of the Line
Anything might have come to us; but the divine
Afterglow brought us up to a Welsh colony
Hiding in sandbag ditches, whispering consolatory
Soft foreign things. Then we were taken in
To low huts candle-lit, shaded close by slitten
Oilsheets, and there the boys gave us kind welcome,
So that we looked out as from the edge of home.
Sang us Welsh things, and changed all former notions
To human hopeful things. And the next day's guns
Nor any line-pangs ever quite could blot out
That strangely beautiful entry to war's rout;
Candles they gave us, precious and shared over-rations –
Ulysses found little more in his wanderings without doubt.

'David of the White Rock', the 'Slumber Song' so soft, and that
Beautiful tune to which roguish words by Welsh pit boys
Are sung – but never more beautiful than there under the
guns' noise.

Robert Graves
Sospan Fach [The Little Saucepan]

Four collier lads from Ebbw Vale
Took shelter from a shower of hail,
And there beneath a spreading tree
Attuned their mouths to harmony.

With smiling joy on every face
Two warbled tenor, two sang bass,
And while the leaves above them hissed with
Rough hail, they started 'Aberystwyth'.

Old Parry's hymn, triumphant, rich,
They changed through with even pitch,
Till at the end of their grand noise
I called: 'Give us the "Sospan" boys!'.

Who knows a tune so soft, so strong,
So pitiful as that 'Saucepan' song
For exiled hope, despaired desire
Of lost souls for their cottage fire?

Then low at first with gathering sound
Rose their four voices, smooth and round,
Till back went Time: once more I stood
With Fusiliers in Mametz Wood.

Fierce burned the sun, yet cheeks were pale,
For ice hail they had leaden hail;
In that fine forest, green and big,
There stayed unbroken not one twig.

They sang, they swore, they plunged in haste,
Stumbling and shouting through the waste;
The little 'Saucepan' flamed on high,
Emblem of hope and ease gone by.

Rough pit-boys from the coaly South,
They sang, even in the cannon's mouth;
Like Sunday's chapel, Monday's inn,
The death trap sounded with their din.

Wilfred Owen
Dulce et Decorum Est

Bent double, like old beggars under sacks,
Knock-kneed, coughing like hags, we cursed through sludge,
Till on the haunting flares we turned our backs
And towards our distant rest began to trudge.
Men marched asleep. Many had lost their boots
But limped on, blood-shod. All went lame; all blind;
Drunk with fatigue; deaf even to the hoots
Of tired, outstripped Five-Nines that dropped behind.

Gas! Gas! Quick, boys! – An ecstasy of fumbling,
Fitting the clumsy helmets just in time;
But someone still was yelling out and stumbling
And flound'ring like a man in fire or lime...
Dim, through the misty panes and thick green light,
As under a green sea, I saw him drowning.

In all my dreams, before my helpless sight,
He plunges at me, guttering, choking, drowning.

If in some smothering dreams you too could pace
Behind the wagon that we flung him in,
And watch the white eyes writhing in his face,
His hanging face, like a devil's sick of sin;
If you could hear, at every jolt, the blood
Come gargling from the froth-corrupted lungs,
Obscene as cancer, bitter as the cud
Of vile, incurable sores on innocent tongues, –
My friend, you would not tell with such high zest
To children ardent for some desperate glory,
The old Lie: *Dulce et decorum est
Pro patria mori.*

David Jones
'The Queen of the Woods'

And to Private Ball it came as if a rigid beam of great weight flailed about his calves, caught from behind by ballista-baulk let fly or aft-beam slewed to clout gunnel-walker
below below below.
   When golden vanities make about,
                    you've got no legs to stand on.
He thought it disproportionate in its violence considering the fragility of us.
   The warm fluid percolates between his toes and his left boot fills, as when you tread in a puddle – he crawled away in the opposite direction.

It's difficult with the weight of the rifle.
Leave it – under the oak.
Leave it for a salvage-bloke
let it lie bruised for a monument
dispense the authenticated fragments to the faithful.
It's the thunder-besom for us
it's the bright bough borne
it's the tensioned yew for a Genoese jammed arbalest and a scarlet square for a mounted *mareschal*, it's that county-mob back to back. Majuba mountain and Mons Cherubim and spreaded mats for Sydney Street East, and come to Bisley for a Silver Dish. It's R.S.M. O'Grady says, it's the soldier's best friend if you care for the working parts and let us be 'aving those springs released smartly in Company billets on wet forenoons and clickerty-click and one up the spout and you men must really cultivate the habit of treating this weapon with the very greatest care and there should be a healthy rivalry among you – it should be a matter of very proper pride and
   Marry it man! Marry it!
Cherish her, she's your very own.
   Coax it man coax it – it's delicately and ingeniously made – it's an instrument of precision – it costs us tax-payers money – I want you men to remember that.
   Fondle it like a granny – talk to it – consider it as you would a friend – and when you ground these arms she's not a rooky's gas-pipe for greenhorns to tarnish.
   You've known her hot and cold.
You would choose her from among many.
You know her by her bias, and by her exact error at 300, and by the

deep scar at the small, by the fair flaw in the grain, above the lower sling-swivel –
but leave it under the oak.

Slung so, it swings its full weight. With you going blindly on all paws, it slews its whole length, to hang at your bowed neck like the Mariner's white oblation.

You drag past the four bright stones at the turn of Wood Support.

It is not to be broken on the brown stone under the gracious tree.

It is not to be hidden under your failing body.

Slung so, it troubles your painful crawling like a fugitive's irons.
The trees are very high in the wan signal-beam, for whose slow gyration their wounded boughs seem as malignant limbs, manœuvring for advantage.

The trees of the wood beware each other
                         and under each a man sitting;
their seemly faces as carved in a sardonyx stone; as undiademed princes turn their gracious profiles in a hidden seal, so did these appear, under the changing light.

For that waning you would believe this flaxen head had for its broken pedestal these bent Silurian shoulders.

For the pale flares extinction, you don't know if under his close lids, his eye-balls watch you. You would say by the turn of steel at his wide brow he is not of our men where he leans with his open fist in Dai's bosom against the White Stone.

Hung so about, you make between these your close escape.

The secret princes between the leaning trees have diadems given them.

Life the leveller hugs her impudent equality – she may proceed at once to less discriminating zones.

The Queen of the Woods has cut bright boughs of various flowering.

These knew her influential eyes. Her awarding hands can pluck for each their fragile prize.

She speaks to them according to precedence. She knows what's due to this elect society. She can choose twelve gentle-men. She knows who is most lord between the high trees and on the open down.

Some she gives white berries
                    some she gives brown

Emil has a curious crown it's
        made of golden saxifrage.
Fatty wears sweet-briar,
he will reign with her for a thousand years.
For Balder she reaches high to fetch his.
Ulrich smiles for his myrtle wand.
That swine Lillywhite has daisies to his chain – you'd hardly credit it.
She plaits torques of equal splendour for Mr Jenkins and Billy
Crower.
Hansel with Gronwy share dog-violets for a palm, where they lie in
serious embrace beneath the twisted tripod.
Sion gets St. John's Wort – that's fair enough.
Dai Great-coat, she can't find him anywhere – she calls both high
and low, she had a very special one for him.
Among this July noblesse she is mindful of December wood –
when the trees of the forest beat against each other because of him.
She carries to Aneirin-in-the-nullah a rowan sprig, for the glory of
Guenedota. You couldn't hear what she said to him, because she was
careful for the Disciplines of the Wars.

At the gate of the wood you try a last adjustment, but slung so, it's an
impediment, it's of detriment to your hopes, you had best be rid of it
– the sagging webbing and all and what's left of your two fifty – but it
were wise to hold on to your mask.

You're clumsy in your feebleness, you implicate your tin-hat rim with
the slack sling of it.
Let it lie for the dews to rust it, or ought you to decently cover the
working parts.
Its dark barrel, where you leave it under the oak, reflects the solemn
star that rises urgently from Cliff Trench.
It's a beautiful doll for us
it's the Last Reputable Arm.
But leave it – under the oak
Leave it for a Cook's tourist to the Devastated Areas and crawl as far
as you can and wait for the bearers.

Mrs Willy Hartington has learned to draw sheets and so has Miss
Melpomené; and on the south lawns,
men walk in red white and blue
under the cedars
and by every green tree

and beside comfortable waters.
But why don't the bastards come –
Bearers! – stret-cher bear-errs!
or do they divide the spoils at the Aid-Post.

But how many men do you suppose could bear away a third of us:
drag just a little further – he yet may counter-attack.

Lie still under the oak
next to the Jerry
and Sergeant Jerry Coke.

The feet of the reserves going up tread level with your forehead;
and no word for you; they whisper one with another; pass on, inward;
these latest succours:
green Kimmerii to bear up the war.

Oeth and Anoeth's host they were
who in that night grew
younger men
younger striplings.

The geste says this and the man who was on the field … and who wrote
the book … the man who does not know this has not understood anything

R.S. Thomas
Remembering David Jones

Because you had been in the dark wood
and heard doom's nightingales sing,
men listened to you when you told
them how death is many but life
one. The shell's trumpet sounded
over the fallen, but there was no
resurrection. You learned your lettering
from bones, the propped capitals which described
how once they were human beings.

Men march because they are alive,
and their quest is the Grail, garrisoned
by the old furies so it is blood

34

wets their lips. Europe gave you
your words, but your hand practised
an earlier language, weaving time's branches
together to form the thicket the soldier
is caught in, who is love's sacrifice
to itself, with the virgin's smile poised
like a knife over it as over her first born.

Saunders Lewis
Letter to Margaret Gilcriest, 4th January 1917

My Dear Margaret,

We have just come out from an eight-day tour in the trenches.

I can't hope to describe to you the mixture of horror and grotesque humour of this line. Nothing at all of what I have seen before of trench warfare was at all like this. In the line we held we were in shell-holes waist-high in slime, without even the semblance of a trench; dead men were as common as the living. They had died in all kinds of positions, – numbers had merely drowned, – until your attitude towards them became one of mingled tenderness and sympathy and humorous acceptance. One joked with them and often joined them.

No regiment goes twice in this line to come out more than a quarter strong. More than any fire, exposure and exhaustion drain the battalion. And German and English here cease their fight to join hands against the conditions. I am splendidly fit physically, mentally I suffer also from exposure. It has rained and frozen all thinking out of me.

You are back in Holyhead. Your letter got drowned, and I know your address is Bryngoleu Avenue and there's an Irish name to the house, I cannot remember it. So I trust to this coming your way.

My leave has been drowned also; I expect by this time my father has gone south; and my aunt for the time remains at Wilton St. Ludwig, I'm glad to know, had a week there at Christmas.

No more news; make the best of your stay home. I should not be bitter to the Sharps, were I you. It calls for more pity.

Yours,
Saunders.

Edward Thomas
'Ronville'

March 11th Out at 8.30 to Ronville O.P. and studied the ground from Beaurains N. Larks singing over No Man's Land – trench mortars. We were bombarding their front line: they were shooting at Arras. R.F.A. [Royal Field Artillery] officer with me who was quite concerned till he spotted a certain familiar Hun sentry in front line. A clear, cloudy day, mild and breezy. 8th shell carrying into Arras. Later Ronville heavily shelled and we retired to dugout. At 6.15 all quiet and heard blackbirds chinking. Scene peaceful, desolate like Dunwich moors except sprinkling of white chalk on the rough brown ground. Lines broken and linesmen out from 2.30 to 7pm. A little raid in the night ...

12th ... then a beautiful moist clear limpid early morning till the Raid at 7 and the retaliation on Ronville at 7.30-8.45 with 77 cm. 25 to the minute. Then back through 6ins. of chalk mud in trenches along battered Ronville Street. Rooks in tall trees on N. side of Arras – they and their nests and the trees black against the soft clouded sky. W. wind and mild but no rain yet (11am). Letters, mess accounts, maps. Afternoon at maps and with Horton at battery. Evening of partridges calling and pip-squeaks coming over behind.

13th Blackbird trying to sing early in dull marsh. A dull cold day. One N.F. shoot at nightfall. I was in position all day. Letters from Eleanor, Mother and Ellis: wrote to Bronwen, Mother and Eleanor.

14th Ronville O.P. Looking out towards No Man's Land what I thought first was a piece of burnt paper or something turned out to be a bat shaken at last by shells from one of the last sheds in Ronville. A dull cold morning, with some shelling of Arras and St. Sauveur and just 3 for us. Talking to Birt and Randall about Glostershire and Wiltshire, particularly Painswick and Marlborough. A still evening – blackbirds singing far off – a spatter of our machine guns – the spit of one enemy bullet – a little rain – no wind – only far-off artillery.

15th Huns strafe I sector at 5.30. We reply and they retaliate on Arras and Ronville. Only tired 77s reach O.P. A sunny breezy morning. Tried to climb Arras chimney to observe, but funked. 4 shells nearly got me while I was going and coming. A rotten day. No letters for 5 days.

16th Larks and great tits. Ploughing field next to orchard in mist –

horses and man go right up to crest in view of Hun at Beaurains. Cold and dull. Letters to Helen and Janet. In the battery for the day. Fired 100 rounds from 12-1.30. Sun shining but misty still. Letter from Bronwen. The first thrush I have heard in France sang as I returned to Mess at 6pm. Parcel from Mother – my old Artist boots. Wrote to Hodson. A horrible night of bombardment; and the only time I slept I dreamt I was at home and couldn't stay to tea ...

17th ... Then a most glorious bright high clear morning. But even Horton, disturbed by 60-pounders behind his dugout, came in to breakfast saying: 'I am not going to stay in this __ army; on the day peace is declared I am out of it like a __ rabbit.' A beautiful day, sunny with pale cloudless sky and W. wind, but cold in O.P. Clear nightfall with curled, cinereous cloud and then a cloudless night with pale stains in sky over where Bosh is burning a village or something. Quiet till 3: then a Hun raid and our artillery over us to meet it: their shells into St. Sauveur, Ronville and Arras. Sound of fan in underground cave.

18th Beautiful clear cloudless morning and no firing between daybreak and 8. Drew another panorama at 7. Linnets and chaffinches sing in waste trenched ground with trees and water tanks between us and Arras. Magpies over No Man's Land in pairs. The old green (grey) track crossing No Man's Lane – once a country way to Arras. The water green and clear (like Silent Pool) of the Moat of the Citadel with skeletons of whole trees lying there. Afternoon washing and reading letters from Helen and Eleanor. I did 2 shoots. News came that we are in Beaurains and near Mercatel. Letters to Helen and Eleanor. The pigeons are about in the streets of this Faubourg more than ever and I could hear a lark till the Archies drowned it. Fired 600 rounds and got tired eyes and ears. Then early to bed and up at 4 to go to O.P. on

19th Nothing to do all day at Ronville but look at quiet No Man's Land and trenches with engineers beginning to straighten road up. Back to sleep at billet, but preferred to return to O.P. as I've to go to the front trench O.P. at 4 on the

20th Stiff deep mud all the way up and shelled as we started. Telegraph Hill as quiet as if only rabbits lived there. I took revolver and left this diary behind in case. For it is very exposed and only a few Cornwalls and M.G.C. [Machine Gun Corps] about. But Hun shelled chiefly over our heads into Beaurains all night – like starlings returning 20 or 30 a minute. Horrible flap of 5.9 a little along the trench.

Rain and mud and I've to stay till I am relieved tomorrow. Had not brought warm clothes or enough food and had no shelter, nor had telephonists. Shelled all night. But the M.G.C. boy gave me tea. I've no bed. I leant against wall of trench. I got up and looked over. I stamped up and down. I tried to see patrol out. Very light – the only sign of Hun on Telegraph Hill, though 2 appeared and were sniped at. A terribly long night and cold. Not relieved till 8. Telephonists out repairing line since 4 on the morning of the

21ˢᵗ At last 260 relieved us. Great pleasure to be going back to sleep and rest. No Man's Land like Goodwood Racecourse with engineers swarming over it and making a road between shellholes full of blood-stained water and beer bottles among barbed wire. Larks singing as they did when we went up in dark and were shelled. Now I hardly felt as if a shell could hurt, though several were thrown about near working parties. Found letters from Helen, Eleanor and Julian. Had lunch, went to bed at 2 intending to get up to tea, but slept till 6.30 on the [22ⁿᵈ].

Edward Thomas
Lights Out

I have come to the borders of sleep,
The unfathomable deep
Forest where all must lose
Their way, however straight,
Or winding, soon or late;
They cannot choose.

Many a road and track
That, since the dawn's first crack,
Up to the forest brink,
Deceived the travellers,
Suddenly now blurs,
And in they sink.

Here love ends,
Despair, ambition ends;
All pleasure and all trouble,
Although most sweet or bitter,
Here ends in sleep that is sweeter
Than tasks most noble.

There is not any book
Or face of dearest look
That I would not turn from now
To go into the unknown
I must enter, and leave, alone,
I know not how.

The tall forest towers;
Its cloudy foliage lowers
Ahead; shelf above shelf;
Its silence I hear and obey
That I may lose my way
And myself.

Edward Thomas
Letter to Merfyn Thomas, April 1917

I brought back a letter from you in the mail bags today and also a new battery for my torch. Thank you very much. Do you know I have been so careful that the first one is not exhausted yet. It must have been a very good one. It is most useful in crossing this dark street when crowded with lorries or columns of horses and limbers on all sorts of occasions.

I was so glad to hear from you and how much you were earning for Mother as well as yourself. At the same time I am more anxious for you to learn than to earn at present and I hope you will soon be moved to a new shop. You haven't found an OTC [Officers' Training Corps] yet, have you? I wish you could, though I hope you will not have to go further than that for a very long time! I don't think war would trouble you. I see lots of infantrymen no bigger or older than you. There was one machine gunner doing sentry over the parapet the other night when I was in the very front trench. He had to stand up there behind his gun watching for an hour. Then he was relieved and made some tea for me and himself and turned into his comic little shanty and slept till his next relief. He looked ever so much older as well as dirtier when morning came. He was a very nice bright Scotch boy. Well, I expect you could do just the same. His officer was the same age and very much like him so that I think he had to look unduly severe to show the distinction.

I wonder could you climb that chimney? There were iron rings all the way up and one I knew was loose, but I didn't know which. One bad feature was that you were always hanging *out* a bit, because the chimney tapered. It has been hit three times but only with small stuff.

Now I suppose it is likely to survive as the enemy is further off. The crossroads round it became known as Windy Corner because everybody got the wind up as he came near it. Thousands had to go that way and yet very few were injured and only about two killed. Isn't it wonderful how some men get hit and some don't. But it is the same with trees and houses, so that I don't see why it makes some people 'believe in God'. It is a good thing to believe. I think brave people all believe something and I daresay they are not so likely to be killed as those who don't believe and are not so brave.

You would have laughed to hear the machine gunners talking to one another and chaffing the infantrymen as they came along the trench tired and dirty.

The men all think we are fast-winning the war now. I wonder if we are: I hope so. Of course I am not a bit tired of it. I want to do six months anyhow, but I don't care how much so long as I come back again. It is going to be Spring soon. Are you glad? Are you often happy and usually contented, not often in despair? Try never to let despair at any rate make you idle or careless. But be as idle and careless as you can when you are happy and the chance comes. If you are troubled, remember that you can do what perhaps nobody else will be able to do for Mother, and Bronwen and Baba: only don't let that make you anxious either. All will come well if you keep honest and kind.

Upon my word, this sounds like a sermon and I do hate sermons, of which it is not true to say that it is more blessed to give than to receive, but it is more easy to give a sermon than to receive.

Do you have time to read now? I only read for 10 minutes in bed, Shakespeare's sonnets, with a pipe which I smoke about a quarter through and then put out the light and forget the flash of the guns across the street and the rattle of the windows, everything except the thud of a shell in the marsh behind, but that seems to have stopped now. Goodnight. Ever your loving Daddy.

Siegfried Sassoon
'Before Mametz'

In the evening we were relieved. The incoming battalion numbered more than double our own strength (we were less than 400) and they were unseasoned New Army troops. Our little trench under the trees was inundated by a jostling company of exclamatory Welshman. Kinjack would have called them a panicky rabble. They were mostly undersized men, and as I watched them arriving at the first stage of their battle experience I had a sense of their victimisation. A little platoon officer was settling his men down with a valiant show of self-assurance. For the sake of appearances, orders of some kind had to be given, though in reality there was nothing to do except sit down and hope it wouldn't rain. He spoke sharply to some of them, and I felt that they were like a lot of children. It was going to be a bad look-out for two such bewildered companies, huddled up in the Quadrangle, which had been over-garrisoned by our own comparatively small contingent. Visualising that forlorn crowd of khaki figures under the twilight of the trees, I can believe that I saw then, for the first time, how blindly war destroys its victims. The sun had shone down on my own reckless brandishings, and I understood the doomed condition of these half trained civilians who had been sent up to attack the Wood. As we moved out, Barton exclaimed, 'By God, Kangar, I'm sorry for those poor devils!' Dimly he pitied them, as well he might. Two days later the Welsh Division, of which they were a unit, was involved in massacre and confusion. Our own occupation of Quadrangle Trench was only a prelude to that pandemonium which converted the green thickets of Mametz Wood to a desolation of skeleton trees and blackening bodies.

Wyn Griffiths
'Mametz Wood'

Equipment, ammunition, rolls of barbed wire, tins of food, gas-helmets and rifles were lying about everywhere. There were more corpses than men, but there were worse sights than corpses. Limbs and mutilated trunks, here and there a detached head, forming splashes of red against the green leaves, and, as in advertisement of the horror of our way of life and death, and of our crucifixion of youth, one tree held in its branches a leg, with its torn flesh hanging down over a spray of leaf.

Each bursting shell reverberated in a roll of thunder echoing through the Wood, and the acid fumes lingered between the trees. The sun was shining strongly overhead, unseen by us, but felt in its effort to pierce through the curtain of leaves. After passing through that charnel house at the southern end, with its sickly air of corruption, the smell of fresh earth and of crushed bark grew into complete domination, as clean to the senses as the other was foul. So tenacious in these matters is memory that I can never encounter the smell of cut green timber without resurrecting the vision of the tree that flaunted a human limb. A message was now on its way to some quiet village in

Wales, to a grey farmhouse on the slope of a hill running down to Cardigan Bay, or to a miner's cottage in a south Wales valley, a word of death, incapable, in this late century of the Christian Era, of association with this manner of killing. That the sun could shine on this mad cruelty and on the quiet peace of an upland tarn near Snowdon, at what we call the same instant of Time, threw a doubt upon all meaning in words. Death was warped from a thing of sadness into a screaming horror, not content with stealing life from its shell, but trampling in lunatic fury upon the rifled cabinet we call a corpse.

There are times when fear drops below the threshold of the mind; never beyond recall, but far enough from the instant to become a background. Moments of great exaltation, of tremendous physical exertion, when activity can dominate over all rivals in the mind, the times of exhaustion that follow these great moments; these are, as I knew from the teachings of the months gone by, occasions of release from the governance of fear. As I hurried along the ride in this nightmare wood, stepping round the bodies clustered about the shell holes, here and there helping a wounded man to clamber over a fallen tree trunk, falling flat on my face when the whistle of an approaching shell grew into a shrieking 'YOU', aimed at my ear, to paralyse before it killed, then stumbling on again through a cloud of bitter smoke, I learned that there was another way of making fear a thing of small account.

It was life rather than death that faded away into the distance, as I grew into a state of not-thinking, not-feeling, not-seeing. I moved past trees, past other things; men passed by me, carrying other men, some crying, some cursing, some silent. They were all shadows, and I was no greater than they. Living or dead, all were unreal. Balanced uneasily on the knife-edge between utter oblivion and this temporary not-knowing, it seemed a little matter whether I were destined to go forward to death or to come back to life. Past and future were equidistant and unattainable, throwing no bridge of desire across the gap that separated me both from my remembered self and from all that I had hoped to grasp. I walked as on a mountain in a mist, seeing neither sky above nor valley beneath, lost to all sense of far or near, up or down, either in time or space. I saw no precipice, and so I feared none.

Thus it was that the passing seconds dealt a sequence of hammer-blows, at first so poignantly sharp that the mind recoiled in unbelief, but in their deadly repetition dulling the power of response and reaction into a blind acceptance, of this tragedy, and in the merciful end, pounding all sensibility into an atrophy that refused to link sight to thought. A swirl of mist within me had thrown a curtain to conceal the chasm of fear, and I walked on unheeding and unexpectant.

Gwyneth Lewis
The Telegraph Baby 1916

And now I remember the tall hussar
who gave me the halo of telegraph wire
which I wound round my body at the age of six.
Since then my hearing's been strangely acute,
for I watched as the workmen erected a line
of identical crosses all the way down
to the river that kept on discussing itself
out through the village, on to somewhere's sea ...
He was huge in his dolman and when he saw

my delight at the splitting and hewing of wood
he called me closer to his brilliant braid
then the world dipped and I could see the way
that men were cradled in the criss-cross tree,
hammering nonsense, till they left one man
like a Christ on the wire there, hanging alone
but listening to something that no one else heard.
My heart beat in dashes back down on the ground
and I knew that I'd learn how to understand

the metal's despatches. Now, since the war
I've crossed high passes to talk in Morse
to other transmitters, leading horses piled high
with the weight of talking, till I found my way
here to the trenches, to the news of troops,
disasters and weather, where now I'm stretched out,
nerves copper and all my circuits aware
they're transmitting a man on a wheel of barbed wire,
nothing but message, still tapping out fire.

Edward Thomas
'Beaurains'

[March] 30ᵗʰ Bright early, then rain. New zero line, planting pickets.
Arranging for material for new O.P. dugout – old one fell in yesterday.
Clear and bright and still from 6pm on. Air full of planes and sound of
whistles against Hun planes. Blackbirds singing and then chuckling as

they go to roost. Two shells falling near Agny Chateau scatter them. Letters from Helen and Mother and parcels from Mother and Eleanor. Too late to bed and had no sleep at all, for the firing, chiefly 60-pounders of our own. Shakespeare's plays for 10 minutes before sleep.

31ˢᵗ Up at 5 worn out and wretched. 5.9s flopping on Achicourt while I dressed. Up to Beaurains. There is a chalk-stone cellar with a dripping Bosh dug-out far under and by the last layer of stones is the lilac bush, rather short. Nearby a graveyard for the *tapferer franzos soldat* with crosses and Hun names. Blackbirds in the clear cold bright morning early in black Beaurains. Sparrows in the elder of the hedge I observe through – a cherry tree just this side of hedge makes projection in trench with its roots. Beautiful clear evening everything dark and soft round Neuville Vitasse, after the rainbow there and the last shower. Night in lilac-bush cellar of stone like Berryfield. Letter to Helen. Machine gun bullets snaking along – hissing like little wormy serpents.

April 1ˢᵗ among the ragged and craggy gables of Beaurains – a beautiful serene clear morning with larks at 5.15 and blackbirds at 6 till it snowed or rained at 8. All day sat writing letters to Helen, Father and Mother by the fire and censoring men's letters etc., an idle day – I could not sleep till I went to bed at 10. Letters from Helen, Baba and Deacon. A fine bright day with showers.

2ⁿᵈ Letter to H.K. Vernon. Another frosty clear windy morning. Some sun and I enjoyed filling sandbags for dug-out we are to have in battery for the battle. But snow later after we had fired 100 rounds blind. Snow half melting as it falls makes fearful slush. I up at battery alone till 9.30pm. Writing to Helen and Frost. Rubin and Smith sang duets from 'Bing Boys' till 11.

3ʳᵈ Snow just frozen – strong S.E. wind. Feet wet by 8.15am. Letters from Gordon and Freeman. The eve. Letters to Gordon, Freeman, Helen. A fine day later, filling sandbags. *Macbeth.*

4ᵗʰ Up at 4.30. Blackbirds sing at battery at 5.45 – shooting at 6.30. A cloudy fresh morning. But showery cold muddy and slippery later. 600 rounds. Nothing in return yet. Tired by 9.15pm. Moved to dug-out in position. Letter from Helen. Artillery makes air flap all night long.

5ᵗʰ A dull morning turns misty with rain. Some 4.2s coming over at 10. Air flapping all night as with great sails in strong gusty wind (with artillery) – thick misty windless air. Sods on f/c's dugout begin to be fledged with fine green feathers of yarrow – yarrow. Sun and wind drying the mud. Firing all day, practising barrage etc. Beautiful pale hazy moonlight and the sag and flap of air. Letters to Mother and Helen. *Hamlet.*

6th A lazy morning, being a half day: warm and breezy, with sun and cloud but turned wet. Billets shelled by 4.2: 60-pounders hit. In car with Hotton to Fosseux and Avesnes and met infantry with yellow patches behind marching soaked up to line – band and pipes at Wanquetin to greet them, playing 'They wind up the Watch on the Rhine' (as Horton calls it). After the shelling Hotton remarks: 'The Bosh is a damned good man, isn't he, a damned smart man, you must admit.' Roads worse than ever – no crust left on side roads. Letters from Helen, Mervyn, Mother, Eleanor.

7th Up at 6 to O.P. A cold bright day of continuous shelling N. Vitasse and Telegraph Hill. Infantry all over the place in open preparing Prussian Way with boards for wounded. Hardly any shells into Beaurains. Larks, partridges, hedge-sparrows, magpies by O.P. A great burst in red brick building in N. Vitasse stood up like a birch tree or a fountain. Back at 7.30 in peace. Then at 8.30 a continuous roar of artillery.

Edward Thomas
As the team's head-brass

As the team's head-brass flashed out on the turn
The lovers disappeared into the wood.
I sat among the boughs of the fallen elm
That strewed the angle of the fallow, and
Watched the plough narrowing a yellow square
Of charlock. Every time the horses turned
Instead of treading me down, the ploughman leaned
Upon the handles to say or ask a word,
About the weather, next about the war.
Scraping the share he faced towards the wood,
And screwed along the furrow till the brass flashed
Once more.
⠀⠀⠀⠀⠀⠀⠀⠀The blizzard felled the elm whose crest
I sat in, by a woodpecker's round hole,
The ploughman said. 'When will they take it away?'
'When the war's over.' So the talk began –
One minute and an interval of ten,
A minute more and the same interval.

'Have you been out?' 'No.' 'And don't want to, perhaps?'
'If I could only come back again, I should.
I could spare an arm. I shouldn't want to lose
A leg. If I should lose my head, why, so,
I should want nothing more ... Have many gone
From here?' 'Yes.' 'Many lost?' 'Yes, a good few.
Only two teams work on the farm this year.
One of my mates is dead. The second day
In France they killed him. It was back in March,
The very night of the blizzard, too. Now if
He had stayed here we should have moved the tree.'
'And I should not have sat here. Everything
Would have been different. For it would have been
Another world.' 'Ay, and a better, though
If we could see all all might seem good.' Then
The lovers came out of the wood again:
The horses started and for the last time
I watched the clods crumble and topple over
After the ploughshare and the stumbling team.

Corporal Ivor Watkins
(6th Battalion, Welch Regiment)
'Gas!'

At Houplines near Armentières, in March 1918, we were going up by
night as a covering party for an Australian tunnelling company, which
meant if Jerry come over we'd have got it in the neck before the
tunellers. We got into a house where there was a cellar, got some mat-
tresses and a brazier and made ourselves comfortable. There were
some 18-pounder batteries behind us and the Germans were going at
them. On the night of the 16th of March he started shelling those batteries with mustard-gas shells. Our gas guard must have got killed
because we had no warning. Gas is heavier than air and it must have
got down into the cellars because when we woke up in the morning,
we felt our eyes burning terribly and thought it was the smoke from
the brazier. We started rubbing our eyes but what we were doing was
rubbing the mustard gas into them. We soon realised with the smell,
which is akin to horseradish, what we had done. We all came up and
were rushed down to the casualty clearing station. Our eyes were
watering profusely. Nothing but water running from our eyes. They

were burning like hell. I could just see a mist in front of me, but I hadn't rubbed as hard as some of the others.

From the clearing station I was rushed to the 2nd Canadian Hospital. Within four days, I was at St. Luke's Hospital in Bradford, where they were clearing out the casualties as quickly as they could. They attached to me a sign 'Gas Shell. Very Severe.'

When I got to Bradford, I couldn't see. It was the most terrifying experience I have ever had. Was I going to be blind for life? What was I going to do? My trade, my employment gone. It hit me very, very hard. For the first month or so, I couldn't recognise anything, then there was a gradual haze. I had a Scottish army sister and I'll always remember the intonation, 'Taffy, I'll get your sight back, don't worry.' I was given goggles to wear to keep the glare out. I also had burns to the tender parts of my body which they treated with ointment. I had a steam kettle as well, to inhale. And then I started heavy smoking as I thought to clear my chest, but it was obviously just soothing the nerves. It was fashionable to smoke. We were given cigarettes in hospital. We were treated right royally. I recovered my sight. But so many didn't. I had my 20th birthday in that hospital.

Jack Jones
'The thick of it'

With the dawn back into the thick of it again. Same old game. First along the road a few miles, a road that we had to leave owing to it being shelled heavier the farther forward we went. Off the road on to cultivated, now trampled land. Open order. Moving forward, for the first time running targets in sight. Now we passed dead Germans as moving forward. The last-joined young officer is quite cool. 'Forward!' he was shouting; but he stopped where he was with a hole in the centre of his forehead. Clean and sweet his death was, and I collected his identity disc. 'Where's the sergeant of our platoon?' One of the chaps jerked a thumb backwards towards where the sergeant was lying ugly in death. 'You're in command of the platoon, Joney,' said the chap, who, as soon as we started to advance again, jumped and turned about with his hand to his backside.

'What's up with you?' I shouted.

'Shot in the bloody arse,' he shouted back.

'All the best.'

Some of us managed to reach the shelter of a wood, where for the first time I met and spoke to chaps of the South Wales Borderers who told me that they were all that were left of their regiment, an inaccurate statement, as was proved that night. I fell back with what was left of my platoon – bothering about cooker-carts and a drink of tea – to where I found Captain Berkeley walking up and down a narrow lane along both sides of which for about a hundred yards wounded were waiting to be taken back to where they could receive attention. I reported the death in action of the young officer, and handed his identity disc to Captain Berkeley, who took it, said: 'Wait here with those men of yours until ...'

He went off in search of the C.O., I think, only to find that he was killed. Also the adjutant, second in command – As far as I remember all but three or four were either killed or wounded.

Instead of the drink of tea we were dying for we had to start digging for our lives a trench in which to get down to fight in. We lost I don't know how many men when throwing up some barbed wire entanglements about ten yards in advance of the trench the other chaps were still digging. Berkeley, I heard, had been wounded. Not an officer left in the company; but Big Rees, now evidently in command of what's left of the regiment, is moving about as cool as a cucumber. His beard shows red in the light of a match with which he lights a fag. Great chap, Big Rees.

All of us manning the trench now. A German is seen sneaking forward to cut a passage through our barbed wire entanglement – BANG. 'Got him?' Who got him? What odds as long as we got him. He now hangs over the wire moaning '*Kamerad*'.

'Keep a sharp look-out on the right.' I pass the word to and fro, feeling whacked to the wide. Oh, for a drink of tea.

Dawn breaking, and hell is let loose again. German artillery smashing a way through for the infantry. The shell, *the* shell comes to burst and kill and wound. 'Bleeding, I'm bleeding, Joe.'

'Let's have a look at you, Joney.'

He clambers over the two dead men to get to me, not Joe Davies, but Joe Howells, who is a Merthyr chap like myself. He lives on the tramroad, I now remember, and likes his pint, and is a rough handful. Yet his is not rough with me now. Tender, loving. His face is covered with black hair. He binds first my head, nothing much the matter there, but it bleeds freely. Then the two fingers, one of which is almost severed. He robs one of the dead men of his field-dressing to finish bandaging me. Then he said: 'There you are, best I can do for you, Joney. Take a chance. All the best.' I left him in that bay of the trench, with a dead man each side him, facing the enemy.

On my way back to Ypres along a shell-swept road. Staggering along – oh, for a drink o' tea. Soldiers doubling forward along the hard road – into it. Glosters, I think. God help 'em – may God help us all. In the roadside ditches were those who had gone to Him. Other wounded reach hard road from more or less open country on both sides of hard road. Men using rifles as crutches, men limping, crawling, staggering – some are being carried as we carried young Evans the night he was calling 'Shoni hoy –'

We wounded are taking up too much of the road getting out of it, so we again have to make way for soldiers on the double going into it. 'What regiment's that?' What does it matter, anyway.

Ypres – queue-up for the doctor those of you still able to stand – oh, play the bloody game, Jerry. Haven't you done enough to us already? Must you send bloody shells after us now? Queue-up – all right, put him down there.

By ambulance to what I believe they said was a clearing-station. It had been a Seminary or something before it was a clearing-station. Oh, play the game, Jerry. Following us with bloody aeroplanes. On to a train. When it stops and I try to get out I fall down, down, down among the dead men, David John Thomas. Wake up in No. 4 General Hospital, Versailles. Ever been to Versailles? No, what's it like? Ask me another. When I got a bit better before I was taken worse again, I was out in a garden in which there were marquees where the wounded German prisoners were, I think. They carried me back to my bed, where I lay crying like a big kid. The Scottish matron said I was a nuisance, crying and stopping others to sleep at night. But the doctor who played with his silky black moustache as he looked down on me didn't say anything. Just wrote something on the sheet.

Carried out of that place again. Train, boat, train. Brighton.

Ever been to Brighton, chum? No, what's it like? There you've got me. You see, as soon as I was able to think properly, all I could think of was getting home. The hospital I was in had been a school, I think. If I'd have been content to stay there for a while no doubt I would have known now what Brighton is like; but before I was anything like fit, before I was marked 'up,' I was bothering the doctor to let me go home to Laura and the children, and to see our mam. 'My head's nearly all right again, and I can get my hand dressed in both Pontypool and Merthyr hospitals.' Must have got on the doctor's nerves, for he let me go. When? There you've got me, chum.

Anyway, what I do know is that in less than six months time after I had left Laura and the children, I was back with them again; I had sent a telegram to say I was coming. so she was waiting on the platform when my train steamed in, and she was searching each compartment for all she had in the world now, which was me. 'Jack.'

Hand in hand we hurried up the hill towards home. My right hand was in her left hand, and she held my hand tight. 'Jack.'

'Yes, dear. How are the children?'

'Fine – I left them with Mrs Wood. Jack?'

'Yes, dear.'

'Will – will you have to go back out there again?'

'Not if I can help it, dear –'

Then the children came running to meet me and I couldn't see them properly for crying.

Lady Margaret Davies
'Those mad British girls'

I'm rather afraid the position of barmaid suits me better ... alas I can never hope to become a leader ... my lot falls to the simple duty ... of paying the canteen bills ... we are those mad British girls, who have crossed the channel kindly intentioned no doubt but totally unaware of the fact, that the French nation is in the throes of a gigantic war, eager and anxious to play the role of fairy godmother to the inoffensive poilu who before their advent had no idea that he needed any necessary comforts [from] these eccentric philanthropists.

Lily Tobias
'The Task'

Once as she stood in the middle of the room, staring through the window at the broad-leaved sycamore, she recalled how she had rushed to Vincent here and asked him to marry her. The warmth of his hug enfolded her an instant, then faded away. How cold, how empty, the room – how much colder, more empty, the space in her heart. There was no Vincent in the world to calefy her. If she might strike a ray from his written words – ? She moved to a drawer and fetched the packet, sat down at a table, and pulled out the file of papers.

A medley of bits, soiled and crumpled. Laura had fastened them together with some attempt at order. But they were not easy to follow. One could only try to read them as they came – here and there a blue or white form, prison and army sheets, their margins filled irrelevantly; but mostly odd scraps torn and stained, webbed with faint pencil scrawl, some almost illegible through criss-crossing. Full paragraphs alternated with disjointed phrases, quotations, accounts of punishment in task and diet, dates, names, reports. A few of the jottings could not have been messages. They seemed like diary notes. How they were concealed was a mystery. One or two must have reached Laura in earlier days, for she had added them with dated comment. Others had been folded into a cover of envelope shape on which Vincent had written 'Keep for me.' But the soldier must have unfolded and mixed them with the rest, as Laura surmised and noted. The same thing had happened with the letter to Eunice, which was separated from the inscription of her name and address. Though more familiar with his writing than Laura could be, Eunice found classification more difficult. But that, after all, did not matter much. She read each scrap that her finger turned. The reports to Laura had the fraternal intimacy that the wife might once have resented, with disdain if not with suspicion; if she winced now it was for other reasons. Two sentences recurred throughout – 'Keep in touch with my wife' – 'Don't tell my wife.' They received a ghastly illumination from the rest of the text.

★ ★ ★

... Found an inch of pencil today, no matter how. Priceless jewel. Wonder if I shall ever catch the post. Most likely catch P.D.

... Worse than Mil. detention. Frightful combination – being cut off, shut in, caged, put away in a box 11 by 7 – with the constant surveillance of spyhole. Knowing one can't move, sit, stand, breathe, without an eye looking on – perhaps a sudden shout, an order *not* to do what you are doing, or to do what you are not ... Oh God, what a worm, what an insect one feels.

... It was funny at exercise that first day. The savage-looking hulk in front with a fierce beard I took to be a murderer at least. He was the gentle Quaker H. But the meek little man behind was an old hand. He whispered to me – 'I'm here for trying to do a man in. What'r you here for?' – 'For *not* trying to do a man in' – Pause, then whisper again – 'Gawdstrewth!'

... If I only knew about E. otherwise calm, confident, never clearer in my mind, never more certain. My soul is free. All the free souls who have been in prison before me ... great task given us to do. Not only now. After it's over – the slaughter, hate, chaos, wreckage – new world to come. Work for reason, justice, brotherhood. Ideals must come to earthy. Practical schemes. Wish I could communicate with F. and A. Can F. visit me? Three allowed. But only want one first. Six weeks yet. E. will come. I'll see, I'll hear her. God bless my d. God to keep me to the mark ...

... Conquer it. Strength. My mind's my own. Another month – 672 hrs. – 40,320 min. before I can write home – before I can get letter. Eternity, where is thy sting? ...

... I wish I knew about my wife. Please keep in touch with her – if away, write as often as you can. She must be making a very slow con-valescence at Mold. I'm eagerly awaiting news ...

... So they sacked you for refusing to Trafalgar. Good girl. I heard just *before* I got out. How? Things travel round the exercise yard. B – you remember him? was behind me (He's still there). In front was a C.O. from Cardiff. When I passed the news, he said (ventriloquially, of course) Traffic-vulgar. Laura, forgive him – it was the best he could do.

... Cheerio. Keep out of gaol if you can. If you can't – well – bring in your 'lustre and perfume'. Remember Cowper? *You'll* never be 'a weed'. ...

... No, I don't want to go back. At least there's the human touch in camps. Harv. was unlucky. You've done marvels for him – good thing you got hold of Furnall. – The men here are decent. Some of them listen, which isn't good for the army, but mighty good for the world. Of course they say the conchies are mugs. But one said, 'We're bigger ones, if you arsks me!' Expect to be read out today. Here are the names ...

... She didn't come. Why? Why doesn't she write? Aunt C. says all's well. My d. can't mean to be cruel. How can I go on if she – no, I won't think it. If L. could talk to her – no, I can't let L. on to this. Not fair to my d. She'll come next time. She'll come. She'll come. I'll will her. No, she'll will herself ...

Sorry my last letter home was two weeks late. Hope my wife wasn't too anxious. Naturally I couldn't explain! No letters, no visits – it was pretty hellish. Punishment, of course. For passing bread to another chap. He's always hungry, poor devil. I'm not. At least not now. Once I found an insect in my dinner, and it put me right off. Anyway, the stuff gives one indigestion ... It's a rotten system. No wonder crimi-nals are made in prison. Some of us must look deep into this when we come out for good. ... This time my window is of opaque glass, so even when I reached it by stretching my bones, I couldn't see out.

Beastly disappointing. Silly, but it 'got me. P.D. again for sulks. A likely cure. Don't tell my wife ...

E. can't be forgetting me. She can't, already. Already? It's a year – ten million years. I forget a lot myself. Why I'm here. War, peace, work to be done. Not really, though. One frets about little things. Nonsense. It all comes back. As to forgetting E. – what a joke. As much as if *she* could ...

Hospital again. A relief to know flu' is cause of depression. Awful nights, sleepless. Worrying about E. Why doesn't she write, is she well? Feeling all is lost. Haunted by facts of war learned in camp. World seems full of irredeemable horror. Will the ghastly business ever end? My effort – efforts of comrades – puny – futile. Who cares? Why am I shut away from the world – from my love – Eunice, Eunice, I want you, I want to shout your name. Am I getting dotty?

... Thank God for physical ills. I could bless the pain in my chest. Doctor's been. Blunt, but fairly decent. Says there's nothing wrong but a cold, touch of flu'. Says I'm sound – of course I am. Cough's nothing. Mustn't tell E. Think out cheerful letter. Perhaps she'll come.

Refused the scheme. It's a trap. Must be. Poor Aunt C. She can't know. But if E. – if it made her change ... Five have gone. Good chaps, straight, never give in. Why not? I'd have E. back. I could go home. See her, no bars. Have her to myself. Oh God, I must, I will. I wrote God. Who is He? Where? Still small voice. Conscience. Am I a C.O.? Aren't the five who went? Nothing to do with *me*. Don't go by others. Is it right for me? If it's only for E. – only – only my life, my love –

> But there is yet a liberty, unsung
> By poets, and by senators unpraised,
> Which monarchs cannot grant, nor all the powers
> Of earth and hell confederate take away:
> A liberty, which persecution, fraud,
> Oppression, prisons, have no power to bind;
> Which whoso tastes, can be enslaved no more.

Good thing I memorised Cowper. Never thought *The Task* would help me to sleep.

Notes for next Court-martial.

I still believe war to be wrong, a savage and utterly futile method of settling disputes. I still believe it my duty to humanity to refuse participation in the present war. All I know of the conditions prove the soundness of my belief. There seems to me no sort of justification for the continuance of slaughter and destruction, when the negotiations for peace which must eventually take place might as well begin today, and save millions of men from injury and death ...

I have been asked to accept 'alternative service', whatever that may mean. Some C.O.'s have accepted it. They have never had any objection to doing national work under a civil authority. They believe they have successfully resisted militarism, and see no difference between civil work outside and *inside* a prison. Everyone must judge for himself. To me "alternative service" seems a kind of industrial conscription. And as I am opposed to every form of conscription, as to every form of war, I cannot agree to undertake it ...

I believe in the freedom of personality. Military discipline crushes this freedom, paralyses the will and judgment of the individual, and enslaves him to a cruel and contemptible system ...

... So here I am, waiting for the usual farce. But there are all sorts of rumours. Last week seven C.O.'s went out from here to France. It isn't supposed to be done now, is it? Thought the Fellowship had got it stopped. That lot were frog-marched to the station, while the band played the Dead March. I haven't got all the names, but I'll write down as many as I know on the back of this ...

I hear that King and Snowden have kicked up ructions in the House about B– and H–. Good work. All the same, I don't think too much fuss ought to be made about hardships. There's the inevitable comparison with the sufferings in the trenches. It's the spirit of persecution that's so revolting ... Loss of liberty, loss of human dignity ... Not always the big things, but the little things, bring degradation, paralysis of the higher faculties. The stage when one can't think – when one's mind gets numb ...

Physical ill-treatment can be serious, of course, for the weaker chaps. This is the roughest place I've been at. They think nothing of using handcuffs and ropes, kicking the bound, chaining one to walls with hands upraised. Yesterday I refused to do pack drill. They stripped me and turned on the hose – with sewage water. Worst of it was standing for an hour, drenched, in a bitter wind. It's pretty bleak up here. I can't get rid of my cold. Don't tell my wife of this. I wonder if you have seen her lately ...

If only they'd get on with the C.M. But they say they mean to break me first. What fools ... Two more C.O.'s came in today. Their names are –

Things are easier now. The officers have stopped roughing us. The men won't do it. Not bad fellows. They don't get much better treatment themselves. There's a particular brute here. ...

I hear we are to be sent to France. The idea is that we shall be given the chance of disobeying orders at the front, where of course we are liable to be shot. I'm not sure that wouldn't be the best thing. But I don't really pine to be a martyr. And strange as it may seem, I'm not sure that I'm quite sick of my life. So I think something ought to be done to checkmate these military fellows. Or do the Big Civilians want it as well? Has Asquith gone blotto? Parliament doesn't seem to mean much nowadays. I've heard of Ponsonby's magnificent speech. Do you ever meet Furnall? He ought to know about things ...

My guard's just told me – marching orders any minute. I'll write again when I can. I've some scraps I want you to take care of. I hope to see you yet. But if not you'll know I've served my turn. You'll keep in touch with my wife, won't you? Do all you can for her. Yours in the hope of a saner world,

V.F.

Wilfred Bowden
'To encourage the others'

About the end of January 1918, we mustered for a battalion parade which was very unusual and we all wondered as to the purpose. The colonel handed over to the adjutant who came to the front equipped with a sheaf of papers which he read aloud. The burden of his speech was as follows:

'Private ... of the so-and-so regiment on the ... date is accused of cowardice in the face of the enemy. Was tried by General Court Martial on ... date and sentenced to death. Sentence duly carried out on the ... date.'

This was repeated for a considerable time, perhaps fifty or sixty cases, all with the same end, until the assembled battalion, very restive, emitted loud groans and noises of great disapproval which the authorities were unable to subdue. It reached a crescendo almost and whether the end of the list was reached or that the obvious resentment of the troops caused them to desist, I do not know. In retrospect and in the happening that followed it would appear that the High Command knew of an impending attack from the Germans, hence the reminder of the consequences inherent in the way that war, the acme of man's foolishness, has to be conducted. I had still a disturbing memory of the incident at Rouen rifle range two days after my arrival on French soil.

David Gwenallt Jones
Dartmoor

Once again looking between iron bars,
Hearing doors, double-locked, clang through the gaol,
And the strangely inept mutter of prisoners
As they sow, and reap, and lift the flail –
We see how August downs the heavy sun
Like blood of murder, in each ditch and mere;
How criminal, warped fogs are by November sown
Like a prison for the prison on the moor.

And the fiends and hobgoblins come crying at night,
In the rough marsh their chilly conventicle try;
From some valley or dip, ghost screams and sprite,
The guilt of ages that has failed to die;
And Tywi's blue thread, like old beatitudes, drawn
Winding through husbandry of hay and corn.

Kate Roberts
'A great shock'

It was a great shock to Jane and Ifan Gruffydd that Twm was in France. The possibility of someone like Twm having to go into action had never occurred to them. They had always thought the war would be over before that.

From that time, a dark cloud hung over their lives, and they felt as if they were just waiting for it to break. Somehow they thought it would never clear. Their greatest trial was waiting for the post and expecting a letter. After receiving one, they would be happy for a few days; then their hearts would begin to ache again.

The mother baked cakes and sent a parcel to France twice a week. That was the only thing she did into which she put all her energy. She disapproved when she saw her husband putting cigarettes into the parcel, and he also so much against them. The neighbours did the same.

'Since you are sending a parcel, put these cigarettes in for Twm,' they would say. They said this, until their own sons went to the war.

There was no work to be had now in Moel Arian. The young and middle-aged had gone either into the army or into ammunition factories, or else to work in the docks in Liverpool and other places. Now and again Ifan would go to unload ships in Holyhead, and then he would come back to work a bit on the farm. Whenever he worked on the docks, he was able to return home for the Sunday. It was a blessing that they had Eric now.

Those people who were at home began to ask themselves and others what was the meaning of it all. They had seen bad times very often. They had endured wrongs and injustices in the quarries; the tyranny of masters and owners, the oppression of favouritism and corruption. They had seen their friends and sons killed alongside them at work, but they had never experienced their children being taken away from them to be killed in war. Trying to find some explanation for it all, they discussed it from every angle in the Sunday School, for there was no quarry hut now in which they could talk things over.

They did not believe at all now that the war was being fought to save the smaller nations, or that it was a war to end all wars; neither did they believe that one nation was to blame more than another. They came to realise that, in every country, there were people who regarded war as a good thing, and were taking advantage of their sons to promote their own interests. These were 'the Ruling Class', the same who oppressed them in the quarry, who sucked their blood and turned it into gold for themselves. Deep down, they believed by this time that some people were making money out of the war just as they had made money out of the bodies of the men in the quarries, and these were the people who wished to prolong the war. But they knew that if their sons refused to go, these people would be sure to come for them and take them by force.

The great problem for them in Sunday School was why God did not intervene, if God existed. Why did he always allow the poor to suffer? Just as there were great changes taking place in the world outside, so their views began to change. Their faith in preachers and politicians was shaken. Preachers, who a short time before had been like little gods to them, were now condemned because they were in favour of the war. Some people stayed away from chapel for months because a preacher had spoken of the justice of the war. Similarly other preachers were idolised because they had declaimed against the injustice of it all. The people were unanimous in this; and the names of some famous politicians stank in their nostrils.

But the war continued. Many more of the boys came home in uniform, and the news of the deaths of some began to filter through.

In Tre Ffrwd, the same anxiety oppressed Owen. The same things went through his mind. He deplored the empty foolish talk that went on everywhere, and that from people generally considered intelligent.

In that small town, there were people who spoke of the glory of war and the bravery of the boys, and they believed the newspapers word for word. It is true they worked hard to send comforts to the troops and to give them a welcome when they came home on leave, and so on, but their silly, empty talk and their cliché-ridden opinions, endlessly repeated, were enough to drive a person wild. Their sons would come home from the camps, and if they were officers, they would turn up their noses at people like Owen who dared to walk the streets in civilian clothes. Owen thought it was all very well for these boys, boys from the grammar school, who had been brought up in luxury and had never known what it was to go without anything; if they were suffering hardship now, it was for the first time. As for his own people, they had endured hardships all their lives, and as if that had not been enough, suddenly the war came like an invisible hand to crush them into the ground. He would like to go up to these erect, well-bred officers and tell them so. But what for? How were they, in the midst of their plenty, with their rich lowland pastures, to know or care about a little place like Moel Arian, with its thin crust of soil too poor to support such cattle as theirs? What could they know of the struggle to survive, wrenching a hard living from peat and clay? But sometimes that kind of land did produce some brains.

Some of the mistresses in the school began to reproach him for not enlisting. He sometimes felt like telling them that his call-up had been temporarily postponed because of his health, but he felt too ashamed. The only thing that would make him join was a feeling of loyalty to those of his friends and relatives who had already enlisted. He felt like this: if they were suffering, he should be with them, not because he agreed with the war, but because he sympathised with them. This came to trouble him more and more as letters arrived from Twm; not that his brother was complaining. The absence of complaints, when he knew there was so much to complain about, was what made him think that he should go and suffer with Twm. But then he would think of them at home. He well knew what they were feeling now, and what they would feel if he were to enlist. But the next moment he felt a responsibility to be with Twm.

At school there was a young teacher named Ann Elis – a girl from Merionethshire. Owen had not spoken more than an occasional 'Good morning' to her. She was strangely quiet, and some days would look very sad.

One day a telegram arrived for her to say that her young man had been killed in the trenches. When she returned to school a few days later, she seemed like one who had been grieving for months. Owen would have liked to go to her and tell her how sorry he was, but she now passed by him, and everybody else, without saying a word.

Within a month a telegram came for Owen asking him to come home, and nobody had to tell him what was the reason.

That morning, at the beginning of July, 1916, Jane Gruffydd was expecting a letter from Twm. She had not received one for six days. She was worried, but not too much because once before there had been a delay and then two letters arrived together. These days she could manage to do nothing but milk the cows and see Eric off to school before the postman came, and sometimes he would be late. He was late today, or he had already gone past. Yet she remained in her chair instead of going about her work. No, there was his whistle by the yard gate, and she ran out excitedly. But it was not a letter from Twm, nor was it from any of the other children. It was a long envelope with an official stamp on it. 'Drat it,' she said to herself, 'another old form with questions to answer. They must think we own a thousand acre farm.'

But when she opened it, she saw that it was not one of the usual forms. These were sheets of paper, written in English. She saw Twm's name, and his army number, and there was another sheet of thick white paper with only a few words on it in English.

She ran with the letter to the shop.

'Some old letter in English has come here, Richard Hughes. Will you tell me what it is? Something to do with Twm, anyhow.'

The shopkeeper read it, and held it in his hand for a while.

'Sit down, Jane Gruffydd,' he said gently.

'What is it?' she said. 'Has anything happened?'

'Yes, I'm afraid so,' he replied.

'Is he alive?'

'No, I'm afraid not.'

He called from the shop to the kitchen, 'Ann, please bring a glass of water.'

Ann came through and held her arm, 'Come through into the kitchen, Jane Gruffydd.'

Later, she was taken back to Ffridd Felen.

Ifan was working for a few days at the hay harvest on a nearby farm, where the harvesting started earlier than at home.

When he saw a man crossing the field towards him, he knew why he was being called home.

All the children came home before nightfall. The neighbours came; they did the housework. They showed every kindness. And that night, after shutting the door behind the last of them, the children and their parents drew round the fire, for they felt that that was the way to be now that the first gap had been made in the family circle.

As Jane Gruffydd put her head down on the pillow and tried to close her eyes against the hurt, tens of sad thoughts came into her head. Amongst them was one further thought; she would not dread the sound of the postman again.

Jonah Jones
'His "little war"'

It is no wonder that that generation of men marched so willingly to the Kaiser's war. They were so innocent. It was an adventure, and for the working class there had been little enough of that. Charles, Fred, Norman and Stanley were off at once, Norman under age. Charles was killed, leaving a widow who then disappeared, leaving a granddaughter to add to John's household of daughters. Stanley survived unscathed but Norman sustained a bad head wound at Vimy Ridge in 1917.

After the strict Congregationalist upbringing, Norman must have suffered appalling temptations once he left home. The leaving itself would be traumatic in a family whose normal orbit of travel would not extend beyond what could be attained by a pony and trap or a bicycle. A train journey of any distance was still largely a bourgeois exercise. Holidays were no more than a few days off at home, at Easter to plant the potatoes, in August to have a day at South Shields. The Great War changed all that.

Norman, like most of his generation, was flung at once into the disciplines and temptations of the Army. According to that Letts Diary of 1916 he was Pte Norman Jones (7809), 6th Batt. East Yorks Regt., Mustapha Base Camp, Alexandria, Egypt. His home address is, dutifully, still Primrose House. He was a small, neat man, 5 feet 7 inches in height, eleven stone two pounds in weight, size boots 6. Under the entry 'No. of bank book' and 'Size of gloves' he gives no answer. Neither item had so far graced his life.

On New Year's Day, 1916, despite the Egyptian address, he is on the Island of Lemnos in the Aegean, and the first entry, written very neatly, begins: 'Started the New Year in a soldiering fashion. Washed out of camp. We got drownded [sic] out in the early hours.' The Gallipoli episode is safely behind them and until the next move, they are safe.

January 2nd continues piously enough: 'Church in Morning, fine time, 23rd Psalm and Lesson God, Same, Yesterday, Today and For ever. Very Stricking Sermon.' As an addendum he notes 'Sent letters Home and Mabel.'

January 5th reads: 'Cemetery Picquet. Searching the Greeks.' He was quite prepared to enjoy the natural delights of an Aegean island: 'Had a bath in a small stream on Lemnos Island. Sent letter to Mabel.'

January 11th indicates a call to arms. He notes iron rations, then: 'Left Mudros 7.30 am Embarked and sailed 11 am Landed Imbros 5.15 pm' As for weather, the Greek Islands are not all they are cracked up to be: 'Very wet weather. No more parades.' He was not to know he was providing the title of Ford Madox Ford's immortal trilogy. Under January 30th, after reveille at 4 am on a 'cold and wintry morning, could not embark *Lighter* through sea been rough. Slept ready yoked.' (He was always a good sleeper in any conditions.) 'Sent letter to Mabel.'

Next day things improve. 'Reveille 2.30 am Left 6.30. Embarked *Ermine* at Imbros for Mudros. Transhipped into *Briton*. Slept under table. On Boat guard, got hammocks out. Enjoyed ourselves all day on deck on landing at Alexandria. [February 3rd] Slept on Deck all night. Sport at night.' He is back at base. Cavafy, we may recall, is writing some of his best verse about now, but of that he would not have been aware.

February 4th: 'Disembarked *Briton*. Landed at City Beach Camp. Rough night.' Alex providing temptation: 'Down in Alex with Vincent. Buying silks.' For Mabel perhaps? Although later he was to fall, at this stage the old nonconformist piety still prevails. Most of March and April, if sparse on military interest, does record a certain evangelical mood, not uncommon in the First World War, when the preachers got into the camps and conducted their meetings. They were very much part of Empire, searching for souls among our far-flung subjects, but ever ready too, to keep our lads up to scratch. 'P.M. Brown converted' Norman records. 'Corporal Lilly converted', and so on. Heads were rolling for the evangelists. One imagines the Missions in Alex working overtime, with such an influx of raw material. For death stalked the ranks. The Dardanelles and Flanders were no cushy billet.

Home looms large in the diary, of course. Mabel continues faithfully. Letters to and fro are frequent. Norman bathes regularly in the Suez Canal, once recording difficulties. He was like that, prepared to take risks, to try certain long distances, and to cut corners. Amid all this canal bathing and night duty on signals, a little disillusion seems to set in. 'Nothing doing.' I remember him as easily bored if there was no action about. But on 16th April they strike camp and by the afternoon they have marched to another bivouac, then on the next day to Ismailia, about midway down the canal.

Oddly enough, I covered much of the same ground myself in the

Second World War. I bathed in the Canal with my young wife (just demobilised from the ATS), and in the Great Bitter Lake. We contrived to get lost, deliberately, as only the Army can lose one, so that we should not be separated. It worked, and we weren't. We crossed the Mediterranean like Norman on a troop ship, and altogether the 'Med' voyage was much the same – the last throes of Empire and of our route to the Glorious East and the Jewel in the Crown.

Norman's Eastern Mediterranean tour of duty ends in June 1916 when he embarked at Alex and sailed via Malta for Marseilles. He and his comrades were being mustered for the subsequent slaughter on the Somme. The brief entries thereafter tell the story of a typical British Tommy in that fateful year. 'Left Ambriends [Amiens?] for Somme district.' 'Marched up to Martinsart. Up in the line.' He is in and out of the line, the entries are scribbled in. September 26th reads ominously: 'Over the top.' Then: 'Bringing in the wounded' – 'Mending the wire at night in the rain.'

These brief scribbled diary entries continue into the New Year of 1917, mixed up in the same diary of 1916. There was neither time nor opportunity to buy another Letts Diary. Then they cease abruptly. He was badly wounded in the head at Vimy Ridge and the rest is silence as far as the diary entries go. He was returned to Blighty, in a coma.

Besides these brief records of military duty in the worst of wars, Norman's diaries also record a certain loss of innocence. Brought up strict Congregationalist, it was in the Army that he learned both to smoke and to drink. I do not know who Mabel was, but all references to her cease also. He becomes utterly independent of home by the end of the war. He has been through too much to be constrained by Congregational faith, and though the traditional piety (or was it simply respectability?) remained with him throughout life, he is no longer, so to speak, card-carrying. Yet he was keen that his children should have the same benefits of piety and respect (we were, I now realise, very well brought-up), but it is left to Grandfather to provide the paternal rules, to see that we attend Sunday School and learn our verses for the Anniversary. Norman ended the war a drinking man, and feeling all the intermittent remorse of a 'back-slider'. On occasion the drinking got quite heavy and I remember the bitterness and despair as he mumbled in his cups: 'Ah, I'm a back-slider, a back-slider.' The late twenties and thirties had little to offer a man returned from what he came to call his 'little war'.

Wilfred Owen
Strange Meeting

It seemed that out of battle I escaped
Down some profound dull tunnel, long since scooped
Through granites which titanic wars had groined.

Yet also there encumbered sleepers groaned,
Too fast in thought or death to be bestirred.
Then, as I probed them, one sprang up, and stared
With piteous recognition in fixed eyes,
Lifting distressful hands, as if to bless.
And by his smile, I knew that sullen hall, –
By his dead smile I knew we stood in Hell.

With a thousand pains that vision's face was grained;
Yet no blood reached there from the upper ground,
And no guns thumped, or down the flues made moan.
'Strange friend,' I said, 'here is no cause to mourn.'
'None,' said that other, 'save the undone years,
The hopelessness. Whatever hope is yours,
Was my life also; I went hunting wild
After the wildest beauty in the world,
Which lies not calm in eyes, or braided hair,
But mocks the steady running of the hour,
And if it grieves, grieves richlier than here.
For by my glee might many men have laughed,
And of my weeping something had been left,
Which must die now. I mean the truth untold,
The pity of war, the pity war distilled.
Now men will go content with what we spoiled,
Or, discontent, boil bloody, and be spilled.
They will be swift with swiftness of the tigress.
None will break ranks, though nations trek from progress.
Courage was mine, and I had mystery,
Wisdom was mine, and I had mastery:
To miss the march of this retreating world
Into vain citadels that are not walled.
Then, when much blood had clogged their chariot-wheels,
I would go up and wash them from sweet wells,
Even with truths that lie too deep for taint.

I would have poured my spirit without stint
But not through wounds; not on the cess of war.
Foreheads of men have bled where no wounds were.

'I am the enemy you killed, my friend.
I knew you in this dark: for so you frowned
Yesterday through me as you jabbed and killed.
I parried; but my hands were loath and cold.
Let us sleep now ...'

The Thirties

R.S. Thomas
'The war to end all wars!'

The war to end all wars! After 'the hostilities were over', the return to cross-channel. So many hours at sea, so many more on shore. The salt waters were spat into from Welsh mouths. Dreams were laid at the roots of a boy's curls. The seahorses were ridden by dark riders. Watching steamers was more exciting than watching trains, though sometimes the harbour was a forest of masts, where ships of sail sought shelter from the storm.

★ ★ ★ ★ ★

There was this sea,
                    and the children
sat by it and said
nothing. A ship passed,
                    and they thought of it,
each to himself, of how it was fine
there or irksome
                              or of little account.
The sun shone and the sailors
                    were faces at the air's
window. They were going
home: one to his wife's lips,
or his wife's tongue;
                    one to remember
this was not what he had seen
                    from the ship's bridge.
                              The whirling propeller
beat out the time, but nobody
danced. And three people looked
over a slow surface at three people
looking at them from a far shore.

Emyr Humphreys
'Roll of Honour'

The walls of Llanrhos County School, said Michael, are eloquent with its short history. This is Mr Longwind James, first Chairman of the Governors, senior deacon at Moriah, a prominent tradesman, chairman of the Chamber of Commerce, town and county councillor, died 1917 (in bed). May the dust on the picture frame rest in peace. This still and silent group still displays the original pupils of the school, solemn unsmiling boys and girls of another century, in old clothes with young faces. The first headmaster sits in the middle, wearing a mortar-board and gown, a high, stiff collar and a drooping black moustache. This is a photograph taken at the opening ceremony; Lady M – key in hand, half turns to face the cameras, her smile lost in the shade of her immense wide hat. Her skirt brushes the steps leading to the front door. Aldermen, clergymen, unknown officials and their wives are also captured in the same frame. And here in faded sepia are the pupils of the school who were killed during the war of 1914-18, boys in uniform, with sad surprised faces.

In the Assembly Hall there is a Roll of Honour, said Albie, a black wooden image, stretching like a totem pole from the ceiling to the floor. Upon it there are names inscribed in gilt lettering, thus – JOHN ED. JONES, Burton School, U.C.N.W., 1899. This is the first name, at the top of the list; the last, almost on the floor, is FLORENCE HAYES, Cohen Exhibition, Liver. University, 1927; and after her honourable pupils such as myself must pass without mention.

On either side of the dais at the end of the Assembly Hall are two large portraits; on the left, O.M. Edwards; on the right, Sir Herbert Lewis. The ruling headmaster stands between them, still liable to the law of change. We grow under his feet.

Gwyn Thomas
Letter to Nana Thomas, Christmas 1940

From somewhere about 1932 I stopped living ... I saw society decay. I got to know practically every distressed area in Britain. As a social servant I got on speaking terms with a million out of Britain's two million pre-war unemployed. And the few millimetres of my mind and heart that had not been Bolshevised by the Rhondda and the inherent decency of my being turned scarlet ... I became so calloused by the spectacle of misery liberally administered and patiently, enduringly borne I became something of a John the Baptist. I sensed that a terrible vengeance would come upon the agents and the victims of such inhumanity. But not even J the Bap could have foretold a vengeance quite as horrible as the one that the joint Imperialisms of Germany and Britain are now pouring nightly and daily from the skies of Europe. Men asked for this by their refusal to be decent. In odd corners, in the unemployed clubs of our great land, I preached the gospel of dignity and brotherliness. But the corners were too odd and too dark and my voice and all the voices like mine were as whispers compared with the roar of the tool-makers and the lie-makers who were forging the new instruments of force and injustice.

Dylan Thomas
I dreamed my genesis

I dreamed my genesis in sweat of sleep, breaking
Through the rotating shell, strong
As motor muscle on the drill, driving
Through vision and the girdered nerve.

From limbs that had the measure of the worm, shuffled
Off from the creasing flesh, filed
Through all the irons in the grass, metal
Of suns in the man-melting night.

Heir to the scalding veins that hold love's drop, costly
A creature in my bones I
Rounded my globe of heritage, journey
In bottom gear through night-geared man.

I dreamed my genesis and died again, shrapnel
Rammed in the marching heart, hole
In the stitched wound and clotted wind, muzzled
Death on the mouth that ate the gas.

Sharp in my second death I marked the hills, harvest
Of hemlock and the blades, rust
My blood upon the tempered dead, forcing
My second struggling from the grass.

And power was contagious in my birth, second
Rise of the skeleton and
Rerobing of the naked ghost. Manhood
Spat up from the resuffered pain.

I dreamed my genesis in sweat of death, fallen
Twice in the feeding sea, grown
Stale of Adam's brine until, vision
Of new man strength, I seek the sun.

Richard Hughes
'The Nazi Labour Camp'

On their way to Ulm the English party met with such welcoming loving-kindness at every wayside stop (as well as that all-pervading odour of sunburn-cream) that Jeremy found himself sorely puzzled why: for surely this couldn't be normal – it isn't in human nature to love the whole human race. Suppose it some day went in reverse ... When a barmaid even ran from an inn to give Joan a rose, while three of her customers left their beer to dispute the honour of changing a wheel, he decided the symptoms were downright pathological, marking a very queer kind indeed of euphoric state these people must all be in.

But they presently made a detour. A turning-off to the left was sign-posted ARBEITDIENST. 'It must lead to one of their Labour Camps,' said Ludo.

'They don't have women: I wonder whether they'd let me in?' said Joan.

'We can only try.' Then they overtook a bunch of glistening torsos shouldering shovels who told them to go right ahead and ask for the Camp Commandant; and one of them jumped on the running-board to show them the way.

When they got to the huts the Camp Commandant (he was rather a scoutmaster type) raised no objection to Joan, and seemed only too happy to have them talk to his lads. 'It's their rest-time now.' A hint of the showman crept into his voice: 'Reveille is half-past-five and they work six hours a day. We feed them and clothe them and pay them twenty-five pfennigs. They're all volunteers – except that the students have made their own rule that no one can sit his degree till he's done six months like this on the Labour Front. They come from all walks of life, for we've utterly finished with Class in the Nazi State – and Gott *sei Dank*!'

'How many camps like this have you got?'

'Twelve hundred. That's nearly a quarter-million of lads all told, kept busy draining marshes and making roads instead of propping up lamp-posts. They're all of them young and unmarried, and taking them out of the labour-market has helped a lot with providing jobs at regular wages for older, family men. In the eighteen months since we came to power unemployment has halved – six million workless has dropped to three.'

'I wish we had something like this in England!' said Joan, her mind on all those desolate dole queues: 'I simply can't think why we don't. It seems such a simple solution.'

But meanwhile Jeremy did a rapid sum in his head. 'All the same, that can't be only because of your twelve hundred camps: the Industrialists must have helped. What about heavy industry in the Ruhr – about Krupp for instance?'

'They are splendid: they all do their bit. Krupp alone has provided three thousand new jobs in the last few weeks: he's an ardent Nazi now.'

Krupp, the Armament King ... 'And all making safety-razor blades, I suppose!' thought Jeremy, rather surprised at getting such vital information quite so easily (spying seemed money for jam!).

'Ask the Commandant if he's ever met Hitler in person,' said Joan, whose German was somewhat shaky.

The Commandant turned towards her: 'Yes, I indeed have talked with my Führer face-to-face,' he answered slowly in English, then lapsed again into German: 'For only five minutes; and yet he is so transparent I feel I have known him the whole of my life.'

'Then tell us about him,' said Joan.

'I shall tell you exactly about him. He's ... Well, to begin with he's what a Christian would call a "saint" – there's no other word for the manifest supernatural power working through him; and yet he's as simple and unassuming to meet as you and me. And gentle: all children love him at sight. But he has one fault: so pure and honest himself, he's a little gullible – easily hoodwinked by self-seeking rascals hanging on to his coat-tails. But then he's a man so loyal to all his friends that he won't hear a word against one of them – more's the pity, in certain cases ... ' He sighed. 'But now you must talk to my lads.'

He shouted a word of command and they all came tumbling out of their bunks, their tins of sunburn-cream in their hands. What struck Jeremy most about them – apart from their blooming health – was how almost everything made them laugh, as if something irrepressibly joyous was bubbling up inside them: more like schoolboys than men in their early twenties. Even their 'Heil Hitlers' sounded like somebody passing on a wonderful piece of news; and Jeremy commented on it.

'That's just what it is!' said the Commandant: 'What Hitler has done for us all is to wake us out of the nightmare we've lived in for sixteen years. He has started us Germans hoping again, when we'd almost forgotten how to hope.'

With a glance to make sure that Ludo was out of earshot, 'For *you* – but I don't see very much hope for your Jews,' said Jeremy bluntly: 'Why do you hate them so?'

For the fiftieth part of a second a curious flicker had crossed the Commandant's clear blue eyes. 'Lads – Go back to your bunks!' he cried, and the audience vanished. Then he went on: 'We don't *hate* the Jews, not as individual persons: you mustn't think that. All we ask is justice. In England you've never known what it means to live under a Jewish hegemony: one per cent of the population with more than fifty per cent of all the important jobs – you can't call that fair! But once they're reduced to the one per cent of important posts they deserve ...'

'All the same you set about combing them out pretty brutally,' Jeremy ventured: 'Your Storm Troops beating them up and looting their shops.'

'Ah, that was the early days – enthusiastic Youth kicking over the traces. It's been put a stop to now.' Then he laid a hand on Jeremy's shoulder: 'However your English, French and American Jews don't help us to love ours much by boycotting German goods, and trying to cripple Germany's export trade: you should tell them they're doing their brethren here a very bad turn indeed.'

But even one percent of the creamy jobs ... 'I don't believe a word of it,' Jeremy thought: 'And this time, neither does he.'

On the way to Augsburg Anthony sat so silent that Jeremy asked him what was wrong. 'Why can't we have an American Hitler?' Anthony burst out at last: 'We sure do need him.' He paused. 'But I reckon there aren't two born in a thousand years.'

★ ★ ★ ★ ★

Augsburg they found a blazing sunset of red with its Nazi flags, which vied with the natural sunset behind its steepling gables: banners hung out to welcome some World War Veterans' group. But the party seemed to be over, with veterans filing out of the Rathaus and wandering off in twos and threes. Jeremy couldn't see very much 'hope' in the eyes of these middle-aged men who had fought one war already; and beer seemed only to make them sadder.

In Munich, Jeremy went by himself to look at the famous 'Brown House', the Nazi headquarters. Some buildings next door had just been torn down, and whatever was being done to the site was securely hidden by ten-foot palings; but Jeremy found a knot-hole to peep through. 'There's somebody here who doesn't set very much store by the Ten Year Rule,' he thought: for those massive concrete domes could be nothing else than underground air-raid shelters.

After Munich, Ludo still had business to do in Leipzig, and then Berlin. But June was running out, and so was Jeremy's leave: so he left the others at Nuremberg, travelling west by train. As he sat in his second-class carriage he pondered what kind of report to write. He had seen enough of the public mood to know that the Nazis had certainly come to stay; but what else could he put? Talk about 'pathological friendliness' wouldn't make very much sense to the D.N.I.! Increased production at Krupp's would be more his line ...

Just then, through the open window, he heard a distant burst of firing. 'Ah, Saturday rifle-practice' he thought: 'I must put that in.' But he wasn't quite right. What he really had heard, that peaceful last day of June, was the sound of a firing-squad in some lonely place; and it wasn't the only one.

Tony Curtis
The Portrait of Hans Theo Richter and his Wife Gisela, Dresden, 1933

This is the perfect moment of love –
Her arm around his neck,
Holding a rose.

Her wisps of yellow hair
The light turns gold.
Her face is the moon to his earth.

Otto's studio wall glows
With the warm wheat glow
Of the loving couple.

This is after the dark etchings,
The blown faces. This is after Bapaume –
The sickly greens, the fallen browns.

She is a tree, her neck a swan's curved to him.
His hands enclose her left hand
Like folded wings.

This is before the fire-storm,
Before the black wind,
The city turned to broken teeth.

It is she who holds the rose to him,
Theo's eyes which lower in contentment
To the surgeon's smock he wears for painting.

This is the perfect moment,
The painted moment
She will not survive.

This is before the hair that flames,
The face that chars. This is before
Her long arms blacken like winter boughs.

This is the harvest of their love,
It is summer in the soul,
The moment they have made together.

From Otto's window the sounds of the day –
The baker's boy calling, a neighbour's wireless
Playing marches and then a speech.

Dannie Abse
'July 1934'

It was July 1934 and a heat-wave when the mercury jumped to eighty-three degrees in the shade, when fires started on the English heaths; and in the forest, terrible jaws of flame consumed the turf and the shrieking trees with their jagged yellow fangs. Even as Keith and I sun-bathed at Barry Island, all day long elsewhere there was the great crashing of dead branches, and columns of black smoke sat in the windless blue-hot skies. Yes, that July began with the torture of burnt trees in halcyon English woods; Captain Roehm shot dead in Germany, Dr Dollfuss shot dead in Austria, and a man called Hitler screaming: 'I beat down the revolution before it had time to spring up. I gave the order to burn out the tumours. He who lifts his hand for a blow against the State must know that death is his punishment.' In the Reichstag, they sang the Horst Wessel song with tears staining their eyes. In England, the amazing July of drought. In San Francisco, a general strike that paralysed that city and there were bullets in the streets and men, ordinary men, with curious grey flesh dead in the stricken gutters. The noise fell over the world: 'Stormy Weather', 'Lazybones', 'Miss Otis Regrets', and Mussolini strutting through the Piazza Esedra, Oswald Mosley posing on a lonely platform in London behind an immense red, white and blue Union Jack. 'We the English' – shouted Mosley – 'we the English are being throttled and strangled by the greasy fingers of alien financiers.' And he was talking about Dad and Mam, Wilfred and Leo, me and Uncle Isodore.

Jack Jones
Letter to the Miners' Lodge, Cross Hands,

March 1938

... The events of last week and the crisis in the Cabinet confirms to the full the correctness of my decision to go to Spain. It is clear the National Government is prepared to surrender to the Fascist Powers, to give endorsement to the Nazi aggression in Austria and to give support to the Italian-German invasion of Spain ...

The world is at the crossroads, and the battle is being fought in Spain. I am convinced if the working-class forces of this country permit the present policy of Fascism to continue in Spain it will seal the fate of the workers of this and every other country for many decades.

I accept the policy being pursued by the National Council of Labour, and the steps being taken by the E.C. of the S.W.M.F. [South Wales Miners Federation] to do all possible to bring about the defeat of the National Government, and change the policy of this country towards foreign affairs and particularly Spain.

It is absolutely correct to fight for the ending of the Non-Intervention farce in Spain, that the Spanish Government be granted full rights to purchase arms, that we do all possible to help the Spanish Democratic people with food and milk, but I am more convinced that we should help Democratic Spain with men to strengthen the International Brigade ...

Brailsford has stated in last Sunday's *Reynolds' News* that the future of European democracy is being fought out in Spain and that the fight is not going to be won for Democracy on condensed milk. I can go further and translate his statement to mean that more men are wanted for the International Brigade.

... May I draw to a close with a personal note. I am thankful for the experiences I have gained in Cross Hands, for the help and courtesy I have received in general. It will be encouragement in my new activities ...

My decision to go to Spain is in accord with all ideals and ideas I hold. It is my proud claim to be one of the oldest members of the South Wales Communist Party, being one of its foundation members, and in going to Spain, I believe I am carrying out a fundamental tradition of the Party to serve the Working Class ...

With Warmest Greetings and Salud,
Jack Jones.

Dannie Abse
'Jimmy Ford'

Near the door at the back of the bare Hall I could see Mr Thomas standing disconsolately, trilby hat in his hand. His parched wrinkled face was tilted towards the naked electric bulb as if he expected some austere angel to descend from the cracked ceiling and embrace him. But then all the audience appeared strangely moved as they intently listened to the chairman who spoke from the raised platform. You could have heard a pin drop. When somebody coughed it seemed a horrible intrusion, a vulgar familiarity. For my part I felt a righteous pride that, up there on the platform, sat my brother Leo, obviously a person of some importance. Mrs Ford, Jimmy Ford's mother, held her handkerchief tightly in her skeleton hand. There was a murmur of assent when the chairman sat down. He drew his chair nearer to the wooden table and poured out, from the stone jug, a glass of cold water, wiping his perspiring forehead with the back of his hand. But it was not warm in the October Hall. One of the other men, not my brother Leo, rose to speak, fingering his bright red tie.

'We are gathered here,' he said, 'on one platform, myself a communist, Ted Pattison an anarchist, and a socialist' – here he indicated my brother Leo – 'to pay tribute to a valiant comrade, Jimmy Ford, who now lies dead in Spain. Jimmy, as we all knew him, understood well the historic significance of ...'

On the floor lay a trampled pamphlet – orange, white and black – which showed a good-looking young man in a torn tunic. The face was just familiar to me despite the bandage around his head and his ageless smile. Beneath the indistinct photograph was written simply, *Memorial Meeting for Jimmy Ford*. The speaker told the audience of Jimmy's courage, of Jimmy's sense of realism, his selflessness; but I could only remember Mr Ford's tired mechanical voice, his tall stooping figure, his eyes vacantly puzzled and how, when he came round to play chess with Leo, he had the habit of twisting a lock of sandy hair about his index finger. Or how mother would always make him sardines on toast for which he seemed to have a special addiction ...

We sat there in the bare October Hall in the days of blackshirts, Potato Jones, Unemployment and Tommy Farr. Mrs Mary Ford walked in, just as the speaker was thumping the table, making the water shake in the glass as he shouted, 'THERE CAN BE NO VICTORY WITHOUT SACRIFICE', and she joined her mother-in-law quickly. The speaker seeing her, forgot momentarily his rhetoric, hesitated, and his voice seemed spent. All the audience eyed her pinched, translucent face, her frail shoulders draped in black. Mr Thomas who had come to sit behind me said, 'He was just a kid.' And then, 'It's a hell of a world.'

Because I felt embarrassed I hummed to myself:

> Roll along, Cardiff City, roll along,
> To the top of the League where you belong;
> With a bit of luck
> You'll win the F.A. Cup.
> Roll along, Cardiff City, roll along.

At Brunete, the International Brigade had marched through the dark; nobody dared speak at all, but the night air hummed with the murmur of marching thousands. Lorries, lights damped out, extinguished, rumbled over the cart-grooved roads. Madrid seemed a long way now: the drinks, the earnest conversations, the ambulance, and the sandbags, and a Spanish poet reciting, 'Singing I defend myself and I defend my people when the barbarians of crime imprint on my people their hooves of powder and desolation.' Now there was darkness and anonymity. Before dawn trickled its grey oil into the Spanish skies the various units had taken up their positions. In the dawn light Jimmy Ford looked at his silhouetted comrades for comfort. The man on his right was from Manchester – that's all he knew about him. Yesterday each had mingled through the lines looking for someone from his home town. And when they found a compatriot from a town away, or a street away, they would talk avidly, their location of birth giving them some kinship. Names of streets, pubs, dance halls were swopped as if they were names of exotic treasures. To be born in Cardiff and to meet a man from Newport was not to be solitary. But now everybody stood unspeakably alone. Waiting there, Jimmy tried to recall home, Cardiff and Mary – and what this war in Spain meant. Nothing would stay in his mind. He fingered the creased and greased peseta notes in his pocket, and there, beyond the tobacco fields, a white roofless farmhouse caught his attention. It was obviously deserted. Singing I defend myself, but nobody sang. He hardly heard the noise, though he saw the yellow and red tongues of flame spitting from the artillery guns. Soon after, the enemy began a counterbombardment and he could smell the acrid smoke and odour of cordite. The shells were unaccountably landing on the San Theresa cemetery, this side of the tobacco fields. Tombs, stone angels, memorials, crosses, were hurled into the air. Nobody said anything. It took a long time for the dust to settle. Together they marched forward despite the incessant whining hail of shrapnel that ricocheted off the stony surface of the road. Involuntarily, Jimmy with his free hand pulled out the peseta notes from his pocket. It was the only thing he could give away, but though he spoke no words came and the youth from Manchester marched on oblivious of Jimmy's fate. The Fifteenth Brigade, ragtime idealists, advanced; but Jimmy Ford lay horizontal, akimbo, on the dusty road near the tobacco fields, the vision of a white deserted farmhouse leaking out of his surprised eyes. An hour later the small wind blew some peseta notes across the blind quiet grasses skirting the empty road.

And the meeting fell silent in that dry, cold Hall as Leo concluded his speech; Mary Ford couldn't stop sobbing and her mother-in-law sat bolt upright, staring in front of her, slowly nodding her head back and fore, back and fore, incapable of consoling her son's wife. Uncomfortably the audience sat there, angry and resolved, as Leo sat down. They sat there in straight wooden chairs touched with divine pity, divine anger because of a boy unjustly dead on some road in Spain. Yet, if they had spoken, they would have used worn-out phrases, words that were but currency of second-hand emotion.

The chairman sipped some water from his glass. 'Perhaps Mrs Ford would like to say a few words,' he said. Slowly, painfully, Jim Ford's mother rose to her feet. There could be no victory without sac- rifice, somebody had said. They waited for her to say something, prayed with all their hearts that she should find the right words. She stood there, dumb. And the audience became more angry, more resolved, watching her stand there inarticulate. Mary Ford stopped sobbing, looked up at her mother-in-law's face moulded as hard as stone. Finally Mrs Ford said quietly: 'I brought Jimmy into the world. You have all been most kind. Thank you.' Then she sat down again and the chairman, clearly moved, recited:

> They shall not grow old, as we that are left grow old:
> Age shall not weary them, nor the years condemn.
> At the going down of the sun, and in the morning,
> We shall remember them.

Suddenly there was a disturbance. Mr Thomas. walked out, knocking a chair down. People looked round to see what happened. Mr Thomas walked through the door marked EXIT. The meeting fumbled to a close and a box was passed from hand to hand, into which folk stuffed sixpences, shillings, florins. A washed-out looking woman stood at the end of my row shaking a box half-filled with coins. They didn't expect me to put anything in because I was just a boy. Anyway, I had no silver to give. The chairman was saying: 'Comrades, give generously. Give all you can. Jimmy Ford gave generously ... He gave his life.'

Eventually everybody in the Hall stood up to sing 'The Internationale'.

> Arise ye starvelings from your slumbers,
> Arise ye criminals of want.

Sadly, the male and female voices resounded in the mean Hall. I noticed Mary Ford was singing too. The portly chairman loudest of all. Now and then you could hear his voice racing a syllable in front of the rest.

> Then, Comrades, come rally,
> And the last Fight let us face.
> The Internationale
> Unites the Human Race.

Afterwards, gradually, they moved towards the door marked EXIT. It seemed all so sad, brave and tired: the voices singing and the door marked Exit, Exit; the woman shaking her box of coins; another lady selling the *Left Review* at the back of the Hall. Leo began talking earnestly to Ted Pattison on the platform, and nearby, the communist, Alan Fellows, spoke to a group of sympathisers gathered around Mary Ford and her mother-in-law. I sat patiently waiting for Leo. Now everybody had left except those assembled on the platform. Distinctly I heard Jimmy Ford's mother saying, 'It's all very well, Mr Fellows, but you're not dead in Spain.' Mary pulled at her arm but her mother-in-law's voice rasped louder, 'You can say that easily, Mr Fellows, but you're not dead and your mother is not mourning for you.' The portly chairman interceded: 'That's not fair, Mrs Ford. Alan is doing a fine job, he's ...' I couldn't hear the rest of his remarks and old Mrs Ford never replied.

Leo and Ted Pattison didn't seem to hear the argument, they just continued talking avidly. Ted Pattison was nodding his head and waving his arms. At last Leo shook hands with everybody, and stepped off the platform, and together we walked through the door marked Exit.

Outside we strolled under the X-rayed trees of October. Leo didn't speak at all and I almost had to run to keep up with him. All the time I was thinking: Mr Thomas was crying. Mr Thomas was crying but he wasn't drunk. I wondered if Keith had ever seen his Dad weeping. Mr Thomas was crying. Mr Thomas was crying like a baby, but he wasn't drunk. Drunk people often cry. Wilfred said so. But Mr Thomas was as sober as his black suit. Fancy Mr Thomas crying. Leo didn't cry. He looked sad but he didn't cry. Leo made the speech but he didn't cry. Mr Thomas listened to his speech. Mr Thomas cried. I saw it. Tears were streaming down his face and he walked through the door marked Exit. If I was bigger perhaps I could go to Spain. It was worth fighting for. Maybe if I got killed they'd have a memorial meeting for me. It was very sad all these young men dying. One week Leo would show me a short story by Ralph Fox in *Left Review*. The next week there would be his obituary. There'd been an article by Christopher Caudwell, then a week later his obituary also. One week a poem by John Cornford, the next another obituary, and so on and so on. Nobody seemed to care except a few like Leo and some of his friends. Even Keith wasn't angry about it until he read Comford's 'Huesca'. Why didn't the Government do something? The Germans and Italians murdered them and some old fogey would talk talk talk in Parliament.

Leo and I take a short cut home through Waterloo Gardens. We walk over the gravel pathway, paved with the brown, the rust-gold, the anaemic green of the fallen leaves. They crackle beneath our feet and Leo recites:

> A handsome young airman lay dying,
> And as on the aerodrome he lay,
> To the mechanics who round him came sighing
> These last dying words he did say:
> 'Take the cylinders out of my kidneys,
> The connecting-rod out of my brain,
> Take the camshaft from out of my backbone
> And assemble the engine again.'

'Poor Jimmy Ford,' I said. Leo looked away. 'Non-intervention,' he laughed bitterly, 'non-intervention.' 'Mrs Ford was so upset,' I said. Near the summer-house, yellow chrysanthemums scattered the sentenced air like abbreviations of colour. 'If you feel so strongly about Spain,' I said, 'why don't you go there?' Leo gazed down at me from his twenty-one-year-old eyes, as if he had been struck a blow. Scrawled across the wooden summer-house, in white chalk, was 'SIDNEY LOVES

SHIRLEY'. Underneath it in bigger letters someone had written: 'WHOEVER THINKS THAT IS CUCKOO'. 'Why don't you fight for Spain?' I repeated, though I had no wish to ask the question again.

The other side of the summer-house we see Mr Thomas. He sits on a park bench withdrawn into himself. From a little brown bag he pulls out slices of bread which he breaks into crumbs before throwing the food on to the gravel pathway. As we pass him the sparrows, that excitedly scurry about his feet, fly off, whirr into the air timidly. He looks up with disenchanted sadness, raises his proper trilby hat. 'Good evening,' he says. 'Good evening,' Leo replies. We walk on in silence across the autumn park, knowing the sparrows already have returned to peck at the crumbs on the pathway, and that Mr Thomas has somehow come to the point of his destiny, there, where the evening gathers, as the darkness comes out from the trees, and the waterfall of the nearby brook crashes down into the imperturbable and absurd night.

R.S. Thomas
Guernica
Pablo Picasso

The day before
   it was calm.
In the days after
   a new masterpiece
was born of imagination's wandering
   of the smashed city.
What but genius can re-assemble
   the bones' jigsaw?
The bull has triumphed
   at last; the tossed
humans descend up-
   side down, never
to arrive. The whole is love
   in reverse. The painter
has been down at the root
   of the scream and surfaced
again to prepare the affections
   for the atrocity of its flowers.

Raymond Williams
'Spain, February 1937'

'Bert!'

'Aye?'

'Did you hear that?'

Bert Lewis pushed himself closer to where Sandy Ross was lying, in the shelter of a gorse bush on the lip of the hollow they had found for a listening-post. They had been sent out after dark, a hundred yards down from the company trench. They were to try to pick up sounds of movement from the enemy infantry. During the day these had overrun and half-destroyed the three companies holding the inter-mediate ridge, on the long slope down to the Jarama.

Through the first hours there had been so much noise from their own lines – occasional bursts of machine-gun fire but mainly the long chip-ping of pick and shovel as the volunteers tried to dig deeper into the hard, dry white earth – that listening for anything else had seemed pointless. Now most of that had died down, and the night was quiet. It was very cold, with frost forming; the stars were brilliant overhead. Sitting off watch, Bert had been nodding into sleep when Sandy had roused him.

'What did it sound like?' he whispered, lying on Sandy's shoulder and pressing his mouth to his ear.

'It was voices.'

'Our lot?'

'No. It wasn't English or Spanish.'

'Moors, then?'

'Aye.'

Bert rolled away and cocked his rifle. They both listened intently. They heard voices again. Sandy whispered that they were further away. Then there was a snatch of song, in a high voice, followed by a shout and then silence again.

Bert stared across the bushy ground to the white farmhouse on the ridge where yesterday's worst fighting had been. There was a light there suddenly, standing out clearly in the dimness of starlight. He was lifting his rifle to fire at it when there was a burst of machine-gun fire from behind him. The light went out. He pulled his rifle back. It would have been wrong, he now knew, to fire himself, giving away their exposed position.

He stared again into the barely visible land. He was less than twenty-four hours into his first battle but it already felt as if there had never been any other kind of life. Since the real fighting had started, at midday yesterday, everything else had dropped away. There was only this strange dry land, among the gorse and weeds below the olive trees, and the interminable noise of the firing. He had seen more dead and wounded, in those few hours, than anyone could expect in a hundred ordinary lifetimes. The effect, after the first shocks, was to shift the mind into an unknown dimension: one in which an extreme physical alertness was strangely compounded with an overbearingly heavy fatigue and numbness. These quiet minutes of listening were like a door back into memory of a life in which people still moved and talked in what they took for normality; a life in which excitement and crisis could happen but still connected to some base from which people knew themselves and each other. That was far from this other dimension, noisy and bloody and isolated, which could only ever be known by those who, without expectation or warning, had so strangely entered it.

The door back still opened, slowly. Lying beside Sandy, staring across at the ridge where thousands of Moors must still be encamped, he was tempted to slam it shut. For it was now inconceivable that he would ever get back there, and while this was so the memories were only an encumbrance. Still they pushed through, somehow, of their own accord. Yet there was nothing beyond the top-floor office above the fruit barrows in Covent Garden, where he had signed up, without conditions. After that the memories came quickly. The Channel ferry and the train to Paris; the free taxi ride to the big trade-union hall; then the crowds, the banners and the wine as the Red Train left for the south.

'There again, Bert.'

'Aye, but no nearer.'

He had got drinking with Sandy and a group of other Scots on the long train journey south. Many, like himself, had been on the dole, but Sandy, a Communist branch secretary, had left a good job in the ship-yards. They had stayed together in the buses after the border crossing, and in the kitting-out at Albacete: the thin cotton corduroy uniforms, the khaki peaked caps, the groundsheet capes, the old French tin helmets, the heavy leather belts and ammunition cases; no rifles. Trucked into Madrigueras for training, they had been put in the same company: parading and drilling and political lectures in the almost permanent drizzle; still with no rifles. The only interesting day had been when he and Sandy had tried to talk to the old men in the village, poorer than anybody they had come across on Clydeside or in the Welsh valleys. They had been shown their livelihood: the little bulbs of meadow saffron that they planted and harvested for the shreds of spice: a field of flowers for a bowl of stamens.

There was heavy firing suddenly, away to the north, and repeated gun flashes. It was beyond the road and out of their sector. Bert settled again.

For the poor of the world – but there was poor and poor again, right down to this scratching in the dry earth. These enemy Moors on the ridge above them: they had been like bundles of old brown rags through all the fighting yesterday. They wore blankets with holes for their heads to push through. They were small and swarthy. In the attack they ran weaving and ducking, like dirty paper scraps in a wind. It was not just the rich of the world and the poor lifting their rifles against them. It was now these other poor, signed up for a bit of bread in a colonial army and fighting here like devils: for their lives, for their livelihood.

There was the crump of a shell beyond, to their left. That sector had been quiet since the battle yesterday. The rifles had been issued at last, and there were eight heavy machine-guns for their company. They had all piled into the train of open trucks, for the night-time journey to the south of Madrid. Then it had been unloading and the heavy march towards the front, the new-issue boots getting their first long go and protesting. The assembly point, where they had tried to sleep. That boy with the big binoculars, which he had kept hidden till they were at the front: offering Bert a look at some bird he had spotted. Up again, half asleep, and the climb to the plateau. Most of the men had left their inessential stuff to collect on the way back when the battle was over. Taking their going back for granted, as anyone might who had not yet been in battle.

'What d'you make it, Bert?'

'Nearly two.'

'It's stand-to at three. In case the buggers come up before dawn.'

'Give it till quarter-to, we'll get back.'

Bert crouched, thinking carefully. It can all be drawn on paper: positions and enemy positions; lines of advance, fields of fire. In the sun, all morning, following the paper plan, it had been an ordinary working world, like back in the colliery, only on strange ground. Seventy-two men in the machine-gun company, cutting that hundred-yard trench in the hard dry soil, behind the little stone wall. Cutting it with bayonet points and tin helmets for shovels: someone had forgotten to bring up the digging tools. It was work most of the men could manage: eight out of ten of them were hard working-class lads. They had dug machine-gun pits and then began sighting and calculating. That boy with the binoculars again, singing out distances in his posh English voice: a little dark, plump chap; shiny hair, very red cheeks, you could take him for a Spaniard. It was the kind of war you heard about: like lines and arrows on paper.

Sandy grunted and pushed himself up, stamping his feet and

beating his arms.

'I'd rather get bloody shot than freeze to death.'

'Aye.'

Bert had wrapped one blanket round his legs and another over his shoulders and head. The cold struck only when he tried to unbend. Everything was quiet in front of them but as they stood they could both hear what seemed a low buzz of sound, away down to their right. They listened intently, but could not pick out any definite sounds.

'If I didn't know better,' Bert whispered, 'I'd say there was hundreds of men in that dip down there.'

'But not moving or doing anything.'

'No, I've heard it at night on the mountain back home. If there's sheep, all quiet, you pick up something that they're there.'

'Shall we try a few rounds? See what happens?'

'Better not,' Bert whispered. 'If they're there at first light they're just made for us.'

They squatted again. Now that the idea was in their minds, what they were hearing seemed clearer with every moment. Yet there was still nothing certain: only that sense of the presence of many hundreds of men in the darkness. They were probably curled and sleeping among the bushes in their bits of blankets.

Bert closed his eyes. The thought of those sleeping men, and of who they must be, had forced back the worst hours of yesterday. The company had been at ease in the long trench, looking out in the sun at the three forward companies on the intermediate ridge, and beyond them to the high cliffs of the river gorge, on which the plan of the battle had been centred. The boy with the binoculars, having finished his measurements, had been sitting near Bert. He was pointing out Madrid in the distance – a hazy frontage of high buildings that could as well have been one of the cliffs in the Jarama gorge.

'So you can see it makes sense that we're here,' the boy had said. 'Standing guard at the heart of the Republic.'

A couple of the others had smiled when he said that. In his parson's voice he sounded like the endless booming talk of the political commissar's lectures. Bert had not smiled. He could hear the same words in his own mind, as familiar inhabitants, still deeply and closely connected. The words were at a great distance from the stumpy bayonets trying to cut a trench in the white earth, and from the fatigue and muddle of all their movements so far. But that was the distance they had set out to close: from the rhetoric to the practice; from the party to the army. It was the language he had used himself, on that day at the barn, above Danycapel.

'Can I borrow your glasses and see Madrid?'

'Of course,' the boy had said. 'I'm sorry, I should have offered.'

He had then come so eagerly to sit beside Bert. The binoculars had been terrific, bringing up buildings as the sunlight caught them.

'Lovely glasses,' Bert had said, handing them carefully back.

'Yes, my mother bought them specially. They're German.'

'German? Well, they're not the only things the Germans have sent to Spain.'

'That's right. But we must use what we've got.'

He had looked so sad and embarrassed that Bert stared, trying to make him out.

'Did your Mam not want you to come, then?' he asked.

'Why do you say that?'

'I don't mean it hard, boy. I just wondered.'

He had looked then into Bert's face. His dark eyes were rounded.

'Of course she didn't want it. She thought I was rejecting her. Rejecting the kind of life she'd been making.'

'Well, that's it, isn't it?'

The boy had put the strap of the binoculars back over his head, disturbing his stained khaki cap.

'She was more right than she knew. I *was* rejecting everything. That was all it was, when I decided to come. But what I've found, since I've been here ...'

Bert waited.

'What I've found is what *comrade* means. I would never have believed it. It's here on the ground, a real movement, not of strangers but of comrades.'

It was just as he finished speaking, and with a shattering suddenness, that the barrage had opened on the ridge and the forward companies. The artillery shells and mortars were concentrated on the ridge, and the company was safe, lying back. In the sudden weight of it they had all ducked for cover. After a minute the boy had got up to run back to his post.

'What's your name, lad?' Bert had called after him.

'Paul,' he had said quickly. 'Paul Howe.'

The barrage had intensified. The whole ridge below them, where the rifle companies were lying with hardly any cover, was already shrouded with rising dust and smoke. A great weight of explosives was continuing to pour down on it. From time to time their own men could be seen running for some cover, but under the hail of bursting shells there was none, really. Many men had run for the white farmhouse but it was easy to see, from above, that this was the ranging target for the barrage.

Bert had imagined shelling, from stories about the Great War. But this was so heavy and so prolonged that the knowledge from the stories was simply wiped out, and there was only this hellish and unbearable noise. Soon they could see wounded men being helped back from the ridge behind their line. But most of them were still there, under the endless explosions. There was a brief cheer when they saw a few planes from their own side, two bombers and three of the little Chato biplane fighters, flying beyond the ridge to the river and trying to silence the guns. They were Russian planes going in against the weight of the German Condor Legion, which they had been told had most of the Fascists' heavy weapons. The little fighters broke away and began machine-gunning the ground. The bombers swung back, in a wide arc. The heavy barrage continued, unaffected.

It had lasted for three hours. It could as easily have been for ever, imposing itself as normality. The streams of wounded coming back had got wider. There were reports of many killed. Then, in the strange silence after the artillery had stopped, there was the unforgettable sight of the infantry attack. Many hundreds, perhaps thousands, of the Moorish infantry, weaving and darting for cover up the steep slope, firing and then disappearing behind bushes and dips in the ground. They looked like bundles of rags swarming up the slope, more and more of them, getting nearer all the time. There was very little the machine-gun company could do, since their own men were between them and the enemy. There was rifle fire from the survivors on the ridge: a surprising amount of it, after the weight of the barrage. Then suddenly, over the crest of the ridge above the now ruined white farm-house, the enemy infantry were running in great numbers, and there was a high screaming. There could now at last be machine-gun support but the battle for the ridge had been lost. There was confusion every-where but by late afternoon the survivors had made their desperate way back. Different stories, complaints and anger were everywhere. The most common story was that a hundred and twenty-five had got back, out of the four hundred who had been there. It was on this heavy loss and confusion that darkness had closed their first day of battle.

'Bert!'

'Aye?'

'Time to get back.'

'Aye, I suppose.'

It was still dark. The stars were bright and high. They crouched and made their way up towards the edge of the plateau and the company's trench.

'Halt!' came a loud command.

'It's Bert and Sandy,' Bert shouted.

'Come: on slowly, then.'

'He thinks we're Fascists,' Sandy said.

They passed the sentry: old Neil, a man of forty, an Irish republican, who had fought in the Irish rising. They found their commander and reported. They explained that they were certain there were hundreds of the enemy, in the low ground down to the right. Young Paul Howe was with the commander.

'Sir, I got that distance yesterday, there's an old dry streambed,' he said excitedly.

The rest of the company were stirring, along the trench. Men were sent back to bring up the machine-guns, which had been pulled back from the forward position overnight. Bert and Sandy got some bitter coffee. The guns were brought up and set into position. The stars were paler now. There was a loose grey light in the sky. They crouched and waited, looking out.

Dawn came suddenly. They could then hardly believe what they saw. In the low ground on their side of the ridge, and stretching back to the little road, there were many hundreds of enemy soldiers. As they watched more and more seemed to get up from the ground but they were not thinking of attack; they were rousing from sleep and being formed into sections. These could not be the Moors who had captured the ridge yesterday, though about half of them were Moors, in their cloak blankets; the others were Spanish Fascists of some sort. They seemed not to know that they were being looked at down gun-sights, from the edge of the plateau above them.

The whispered order passed along the trench: alignments for a box of fire, moving steadily in towards the centre. Then the machine-guns opened up. The bullets scythed into the half-awake, stumbling groups of men. There was a frantic diving for cover but hundreds were hit. Some return fire came, but for the most part the machine-guns poured bullets into an exposed and passive encampment. Bert, as a rifleman guarding the observer for one of the guns, fired until his own barrel was too hot to touch. The water for cooling the machine-guns was nearly boiling. Still the firing went on and now the survivors below were running, frantically, away towards the road, many hit and falling as they ran. As the last of them got beyond range there was a cheer along the trench. The sun was already hot above them.

Bert crawled back from his forward position. Men were standing from the trench, behind the low stone wall, stretching and pissing. Moving along, Bert met Paul. He was drenched with sweat.

'A bit of revenge for yesterday,' Paul said.

'Aye.'

Sandy came over to them, buttoning his thin corduroy trousers.

'They were there, then, Bert.'

'Aye.'

'Poor sods, waking up to that lot.'

'Aye, I suppose.'

'They were Fascists,' Paul said.

'Aye,' Sandy said. 'Little doubt about that.'

Bert was trying to wind down, after the intensity of the firing. He sat on the low wall, doing his best to clean his rifle with an old purple handkerchief. Paul and Sandy were looking down to the road, where the enemy had disappeared.

Bert heard the mortar shell as if from a distance: a low whistling and whirring sound. He flung himself behind the wall and then the explosion came at once. He saw the white dust rising. He waited and then slowly lifted on to his elbows. Sandy and Paul were lying sprawled, half out of the trench. Sandy was rolling on his back and holding his hands to his stomach. Paul was lying very still.

As Bert moved towards them other mortar shells landed, along the line of the trench. He flung himself face downwards. Always, it seemed, the first move was to protect the face.

'They've got our range!' somebody shouted.

Bert lifted himself.

'Stretcher bearers!' he shouted.

He could not hear through the explosions whether anybody answered. He crawled to look at Paul, who was nearest. He had been hit on the scalp and in the throat and had died instantly. His out-stretched hand still grasped the leather strap of the binoculars. Bert moved towards Sandy. Sandy seemed to feel the movement and reached out and grasped Bert's hand. The hand that he had taken from his stomach was thick with blood, and his whole body there was soaked. Bert held his hand tightly.

'Hang on, boy, I'll get help!'

He shouted again for stretcher bearers.

Sandy forced his head up a little. He looked at Bert and smiled.

'Poor sods,' he said, in a surprisingly normal voice.

'Aye.'

There was a cry along the trench: 'On guard!' On either side, along the trench and the wall, men were getting into firing positions again. One of the machine-guns started firing and the others followed it. Bert looked down where they were firing. There were, so far as he could see, no enemy at all in sight. He looked back down at Sandy. In those few seconds he had gone. His mouth had fallen open and was filled with blood. He had been wearing an upper denture and this had been pushed out, covered with blood, over his lower lip.

Bert released his hand. He wiped his palm and fingers on a weed like a dock that was growing under the wall. The firing stopped.

'On guard!' the shout came again.

Bert took the binoculars from Paul's hand and focused them along the lower ground to the road. It was still empty, as far as he could see, but then suddenly he saw a movement, no more than the edge of a blanket beside a bush, and it was gone as soon as he saw it. He focused more closely on that ground. It was as if it changed as he stared at it. What had seemed an unbroken slope had a long dip within it, running uphill, and now that he was alerted to it he could see many small signs of movement along it. Only the binoculars made this possible. He glanced back at Paul, lying dead.

He went along the trench to report what he had seen. It was evidently a stealthy advance to the edge of the plateau on their right. It seemed not to threaten them directly. But orders were given to swing the fire of the guns along that dip. It was all they could do.

Bert went back to where Sandy and Paul were lying. He touched their eyelids to close them. Then he lifted the binoculars and resumed his watch. The sun was hot now, and there was a heavy smell in the trench.

'There they are!' he shouted, pointing excitedly. A section of Moors was running from the road towards the cover of the dip. Two guns fired immediately, but most of the section had reached cover.

Now all along the line the survivors were standing to. A few of the wounded had been got back but the dead had to be left. There was a long period of quiet, as if the battle had moved away from them. There was still heavy shelling and rifle fire in the distance, and two tanks with infantry moved beyond the road and were lost to sight. It began to look as if they would hold the line without challenge.

There was then shouting behind them. Bert swung round and saw two enemy soldiers, not Moors, on his own side of the wall and the trench. At the same moment grenades were thrown into the trench, from behind but also from the slope below them. As he kneeled, lifting his rifle, Bert saw the Moors rising from the bushes within ten or fifteen yards of them. They were shouting now, and running fiercely for the trench. He fired without stopping to aim. Others were firing but there was confusion along the trench because the enemy were also behind them, shooting down from the higher ground.

It was all over very quickly. Bert had his rifle knocked from his hands with a blow on his shoulder from behind. The Moors were shouting excitedly and pushing their prisoners along the trench at rifle point. The other enemy soldiers, Spaniards, were at the machine-guns and swinging them round. In no time, as it seemed, they were firing them back towards the Republican lines.

Bert stood numb with shock and shame. It was still impossible to believe that they could have been caught like that. As he stood he was hit with a rifle butt in his back, and stumbled forward. A detachment of Moors was lining up the prisoners who could walk. They were a few over twenty, of the nearly eighty who had been in the company. They could not understand the shouted words of their captors but whenever they hesitated they were hit and pushed forward. They were being handled so fiercely that Bert thought it probable they were simply being taken to be shot.

One very small guard, with an almost square brown face, his black hair standing up from his scalp and his moustache curved from his mouth to join a narrow beard along the line of his chin, slipped quickly ahead of Bert and turned on the wall to stand level with him. He shouted and spat into Bert's face. Bert thought the shout sounded like 'Infidel'.

A Spanish officer was directing what had been the company's machine-guns. He paused and looked at the line of prisoners and shouted an order: Bert could not understand him but made out the words for 'Russians' and 'Communists'. Then he was prodded forward again, and the line of prisoners was forced to run down the slope, along the track where yesterday they had watched their comrades from the left forward company retreating. They ran a long way down, forced by their more agile guards, and were getting in among trees again before Bert realised that he was still wearing Paul's binoculars. His rifle had been taken from him but the binoculars were still around his neck. They had been bumping his chest as he was forced to run but he only now became fully aware of them. Looking for the guard, and half-turning to try to conceal his movement, he slipped the binoculars from his neck and thrust them inside his uniform tunic and vest. The casing was sharp and cold against the sweating skin.

He had not been noticed. In among the trees, the line of prisoners was halted. They were ordered to sit with their hands over their heads. The guards began talking to each other. They were not looking at the prisoners.

'Now so long,' Bert said to himself under his breath, and closed his eyes.

Dannie Abse
'Freud, Marx and Sid Hamm'

I was fortunate during those early Cardiff years for, at home, I was exposed to the adult dialogue of the thirties – to the dialogue between Sigmund Freud and Karl Marx, as it was interpreted and argued by my two elder brothers, by Wilfred who would become a psychiatrist and by Leo the future MP for Pontypool. Leo, already, was quite a persuasive orator, and used to stand on a soapbox in Llandaff Fields. I heard him quote: 'It is given to man to live but once and he should live not to be seared by the shame of a cowardly and trivial past, but so live that dying he might say, "All my life and all my strength have been given to the finest cause in the world, the enlightenment and liberation of mankind".' I was moved perhaps for the first time by words, by the order of words – not by poetry, though, but by rhetoric.

Outside, in the streets of Cardiff, there were yellow, bouncing tramcars, and occasionally a hearse would pass by pulled by six coal-black horses. The newspaper headlines were about Mussolini and Abyssinia, later about Hitler and 'Last Territorial Claims'. Always J.C. Clay was taking wickets for Glamorgan and Cardiff City lost at home. BLUEBIRDS FLATTER TO DECEIVE headlined the back page, and somewhere in the middle pages of the *South Wales Echo*, Beverley Baxter irrevocably wrote about 'The Red Sea of Bolshevism'. It was colour, colour all the way, and one of my non-doctor uncles had more than a drop to drink. 'Leo will be Prime Minister one day,' he said to my father. 'Wilfred's got an 'ead on 'im.' He looked at me then. 'Never mind, you've got a diabolical right foot. *Diabolical.*' And he shouted, 'Up the City.'

Stimulated by my brothers' conversations and arguments I began to write essays in a little blue exercise book. I wrote these essays in order to clarify my own attitudes. They were 'On Fascism', 'On Socialism', 'On Jazz', and so on. I showed them to Wilfred who seriously encouraged me to write more. Wilfred was infallibly kind. But there was still no poetry in the little, blue exercise book. Just one line of Keats: 'No hungry generations tread thee down'. For that I thought was the greatest line ever written – not that I had read many lines. In this reference to a nightingale, and its inference about his brother's and his own pulmonary tuberculosis, the poet had captured my youthful social conscience. After all, I knew of the miners who coughed, the TB that was rife in the Valleys, the processions of the unemployed. That line was the embodiment of the sad, bitter soul. 'No hungry generations tread thee down.' It contained my father playing *Humoresque*, my mother wailing Longfellow, quotations of Lenin, and even the lyric my sister sang in the bathroom: 'Ten cents a dance, that's what they pay me, Lord how they weigh me down' and the old pipes in the house knocked and shook because of an air bubble.

But it was my youthful engagement with the tragedy of Spain that oddly led me to 'modern poetry'. That war seemed to me, as it did to many others much older, to be a straightforward case of white v. black. The *News Chronicle* used to come into the house with its bitter accounts of the fighting in Spain and its attacks on the Government non-intervention policy. Besides, I lived in the same house as Leo and was moved by his declamatory and righteous protestations. Also, I went to a Catholic school where I was taught by Christian brothers. I was the only boy in the school who was against Franco. There is nothing like being in a minority of one, especially at fourteen years of age, to be wholly and fiercely committed to a cause – especially if that cause is a losing one. 'Do you know what the Reds would do if they came here?' said one of the brothers in his black grieving gown. 'Why, boy, they'd burn me down and the school wid me,' and when my fist clenched I think he mistakenly assumed I was giving a surreptitious Communist salute. 'Green and gold, green and gold, / Strong be your heart and bold.'

So I find it strange to read a poem by Donald Davie, a poet and critic of my own generation, who, remembering the Thirties, writes:

> The Anschluss, Guernica – all the names
> At which those poets thrilled, or were afraid,
> For me mean schools and schoolmasters and games;
> And in the process someone is betrayed.

For me Guernica meant Cornford dead, Lorca dead, Caudwell dead, Fox dead, heroes dead, dead, dead. It meant a long fight in the back lane with the school's hooker because he saw Franco as a knight on a white horse, a protector of nuns. It meant particularly a book of poems that came out two years later.

Yes, it was 1940, when I was still a schoolboy, that I came across a book of verse in a yellow jacket, edited by Stephen Spender and John Lehmann, called *Poems for Spain*. Some of the work in that volume was of the public platform variety where what was said was more important than how it was said. The poems of Miguel Hernandez, particularly, seemed urgent. They were articulate and terrible cries for help. Hernandez was a young Spanish peasant poet who fought against Franco, who in his poems begged the democratic nations to intercede against Franco, who later was imprisoned by Franco and who, in 1942, died in one of Franco's dark jails.

I read Hernandez with rapt assent and growing anger. Here was a voice that could arouse a reader's indignation and, perhaps, *move him to action*. Here was a persuasive, pleading, prophetic and admonitory voice and one which, in some unspecified future, I hoped to emulate:

> Singing I defend myself
> and I defend my people when the barbarians of crime
> imprint on my people their hooves
> of powder and desolation.
>
> The lament pouring through valleys and balconies
> deluges the stones and works in the stones,
> and there is no room for so much death
> and there is no word for so many coffins ...
>
> Blood, blood through the trees and the soil
> blood in the waters and on the walls,
> and a fear that Spain will collapse
> from the weight of the blood which soaks through her meshes
> right to the bread which is eaten ...

Hernandez wrote such poems during the worst of the Spanish Civil War – when Spain was being turned into 'a vast cemetery, red and bombarded'. One of Leo's friends, Sid Hamm, had been killed out there fighting for the International Brigade. I knew Sid Hamm. He used to come to our house and he was old enough for me to call him Mr Hamm, and I was young enough to be teased by him and to be given a shilling – and now Sid Hamm was dead. I remember the memorial meeting for Sid Hamm at a dolorous little hall in Cardiff, misnamed Sunshine Hall. A platform, one hundred wooden chairs, some women in black, the chairman reciting with a Welsh fervour, 'They shall not grow old, as we that are left grow old,' and then sipping water as a few people coughed. A man near me, a grown man crying, crying for Sid Hamm and the Spanish Republic. A pamphlet, orange, white, and black, poorly printed, with Sid Hamm's face over a caption: THERE CAN BE NO VICTORY WITHOUT SACRIFICE.

Leo regularly brought home a magazine into the house called *Left Review*. It would contain a short story by Ralph Fox – in a later issue there would be Fox's obituary. It would contain an article by Christopher Caudwell – in a later issue there would be Caudwell's obituary. One week, a poem by John Cornford, and then, later, inevitably, in another edition of *Left Review*, Cornford's obituary. I had never seen photographs of Fox or Caudwell or Cornford. But I imagined them to look very much like Sid Hamm. Sid Hamm, killed at Brunete, and apparently very few people caring.

I found a most beautiful love poem in the yellow-jacketed *Poems for*

Spain. It was called 'Huesca' and it was by John Cornford. Not yet twenty-one, Cornford had been killed at the battle of Huesca while fighting for the International Brigade. How poignant his melancholy premonition of his own death; how terrible those lines of his, the last lines he ever wrote:

> Heart of the heartless world,
> Dear heart, the thought of you,
> Is the pain at my side,
> The shadow that chills my view.
>
> The wind rises in the evening,
> Reminds that autumn is near.
> I am afraid to lose you,
> I am afraid of my fear.
>
> On the last mile to Huesca,
> The last fence for our pride,
> Think so kindly, dear, that I
> Sense you at my side.
>
> And if bad luck should lay my strength
> Into the shallow grave,
> Remember all the good you can;
> Don't forget my love.

'Huesca' was the first poem that I ever voluntarily memorised. I can recite it still, and it moves me still, its piquant directness, its sad music, its silence between the quatrains, the time and the place and the young man who wrote it, and the woman he wrote to, whom I can imagine reading that love poem addressed to her, reading it after he was dead, reading it in privacy, in a room, in a house, somewhere in England.

To be sure, my schoolboy political awareness of 1940 derived from Leo's altogether more informed and enduring engagement. Ever since I can remember, he had spoken persuasively about class injustice, about unemployment in the Welsh valleys, about the Fascists in Italy, the Nazis in Germany and so on. Even before I was ten years old Leo had told me, as I listened, big-eyed, the truth about imperialistic Cowboys and oppressed Red Indians. So while my friends were firing Tom Mix guns, bang bang bang you're dead, from bosky paths in the local park, Waterloo Gardens, I crouched behind the summer house ready to ambush them with my Ugh and my imaginary bows and arrows. When I was a small boy, Leo not only taught me an alphabet that began:

> A stands for Armaments the Capitalists' pride
> B stands for Bolshie the thorn in their side

but also took me along to hear orators like Arthur Horner, the miners' leader. True, I could not understand what Arthur Horner was saying exactly but I sat privileged in the front row and stared, fascinated, at his false teeth that were much too loose for him and which perpetually threatened to slip out of his mouth as he pointed one index finger up to heaven and the other towards Barry Island. It had all the excitement of watching a trapeze artist who threatened Death and Destruction to all Fascist Hyenas and Cowboys.

Goronwy Rees
'A winter in Berlin'

I spent the winter of 1934 in Berlin. It was then, in intellectual circles, an unfashionable thing to do, because Hitler had already been in power for a year, and in that short time had totally destroyed the culture which had made Berlin as irresistibly attractive to enlightened young men, particularly English ones, as Rome is to Catholics or Mecca to Muslims. It had been a place of pilgrimage, with its own particular Holy Places, on the Alexanderplatz, in Wedding, on the Kurfürstendamm, but now the shrines were desecrated and abandoned, their high priests and their congregations scattered to the four winds, hunted, persecuted and traduced. The more fortunate of them sat in cafés, editorial offices, publishing houses, in Paris or Prague, or took ship to England or America; in their own country, they took refuge in attics and cellars or in remote hiding places in the provinces, and by their hundreds and thousands were hunted down and herded into prisons and concentration camps. It was the greatest intellectual diaspora since the fall of the Temple in Jerusalem.

In Berlin one felt as if the Germany of Weimar had never existed, or, as in some transformation scene in a pantomime, had totally disappeared overnight. A friend of mine, Werner von Trott, to whom I had been introduced by his brother Adam, walking with me on the sandy shores of the Wannsee kicked his foot into their thin soil and said contemptuously: '*Das ist ja Preuseen – auf den Sand gebaut*' ('That is Prussia – built upon sand'). And indeed, in that winter of 1934, it was as if the whole structure of life had crumbled away in the capital of Prussia, and of Germany, and under the shock of disaster Berlin had become again what it had been before and would one day become again; a city of phantoms.

It had been the vulgar and ostentatious capital of the Hohenzollerns, and had seen their empire and their dynasty disappear without a trace in the ignominy of military defeat. It had been the capital of republican and democratic Germany and had seen that regime also collapse equally ignominiously under the assault of Hitler and his Storm Troops. And one day, many years later, I was to see the city almost totally destroyed by the fires which descended upon it from heaven as upon the cities of the plain. Of this, in 1934, I had no premonition, but already it seemed to me that Berlin was essentially a city in which everything was provisional and ephemeral, desperately balanced between disasters past and disasters yet to come; in 1934, it was still too early to say which would prove to be the worst.

In the meantime the city waited, in the new-found silence and order of streets which only a year before had reverberated with the clash of arms and threats of civil war. Yet even to those who welcomed the restoration of order there was something sinister in the silence of the streets, as if by straining one's ears one might hear the cries and screams of those who were being hunted to death like rats in a cellar. One entire section of the population, the Jews, which had made a particularly brilliant contribution to the life of Berlin, had been officially pronounced unclean, outside the law, extruded like excrement from the body politic, and lay defenceless at the mercy of anyone who chose to take advantage of its helplessness.

Not that such horrors pressed themselves upon the attention of even inquisitive observers. The total *Gleichschaltung* of the press and the radio had deprived the city of its eyes and ears, and its only source of information was rumour and gossip, or what the Nazis called *Greuelpropaganda*, atrocity mongering, which was itself a crime deserving the death sentence, or worse. Prudent men did not listen to it, for fear of being contaminated by it. Political differences were being settled, on terms that allowed of no mercy; at such times a good citizen is well advised to turn a deaf ear to screams in the night, and then it was all the more tempting to do so because of the peace and order, as of a mortuary, which ruled the streets. *Solitudinem faciunt pacem appellant.*

It was a peace which was welcome to many, perhaps even a majority of Germans, their powers of resistance drained and exhausted by the long terrible years of the depression and the violence of the political struggles which had torn to pieces the body of the Republic. If, in a quiet street at night, where one could once again walk in comfort and security, one were unlucky enough to meet a lorry load of Storm Troopers, revolvers and *Gummiknuppeln* at the ready, engaged on a *razzia* against some suspected enemy of the regime, or some Jew whose mere existence was an offence against German blood, it was best, whatever one's feeling, to hurry home and lock one's door, and hope or pretend that this was some isolated incident which should be left to be forgotten in the darkness and obscurity of the night.

The suppression of all organs of opposition had deprived the vast majority of Germans of any means of making an objective assessment of what was happening to themselves or to their country. No one who has never experienced it can quite understand the sense of helplessness and apathy which affects a people which is denied access to any source of information except that which is officially approved. And since, in politics as in other matters, people cannot live without believing something, they almost by default and often unconsciously begin to accept the official version of their situation, which, in Berlin at that time, was that of a Germany which had suddenly recovered its vitality and virility, and thereby had come to rediscover the old Prussian virtues of *Treue, Pflicht, Gehorsamkeit* (Loyalty, Duty and Obedience).

For myself, things were rather different. I was not, after all, a German and the old Prussian virtues had very little appeal to me. But what was more important, I had access to the foreign press and could read the admirable, though gruesome, accounts of the Nazi terror by Frederick Voigt which were that winter appearing in the *Manchester Guardian*. Better still, perhaps, I could talk to some of the foreign correspondents who congregated every evening at their *Stammtisch* in the Taverne café, and hear by word of mouth the monstrosities they were aware of, even though, in most cases, their editors did not encourage them to report them. It was from the correspondents chiefly that one could discover what was happening in Berlin, and in particular the fate of men and women who for years had played a distinguished part in the cultural and political life of Germany and had now suddenly sunk into oblivion. For the most part it was a repetitive story, of exile, arrest, imprisonment, torture, murder; they had been swallowed up in an abyss too terrible to contemplate and I sometimes felt that, if one were to keep one's sanity, it was better not to think too much about such things.

Among those who listened with me to the talk at the Taverne were a few young Germans who, like me, found it the best way of learning what was happening to their country. They were not, as one might have expected, liberal or left-wing opponents of the regime; they were young men of conservative, even reactionary principles, and from the best military families, to whom Prussian virtues still meant something different from National Socialism, and perhaps their strongest feeling was a sense of shame, not unmixed with snobbery, that such a man as Hitler should exercise unlimited power over them; but they were also very brave and gay young men whose natural instincts were to enjoy life, and I found it very easy to make friends with them. How could I guess that one day, ten years later, on a battlefield in Normandy, I would pick up an English newspaper and find their names, von der Schulenberg, von Hase, von Prittwitz, inscribed, *honoris causa*, on the list of those who had been executed for their part in the attempted assassination of Hitler? Such things were still far from our minds; bad as things were that winter, no one had any idea of how much worse they would become later.

For as yet it was still possible to hope, though not in the way of those who believed that murder and torture were juvenile excesses of a young and vigorous regime which, recognising its errors, would quickly return to the paths of legality and respectability. The hope of those who opposed the regime was that the situation in Germany was still so precarious and uncertain that Hitler might find his position intolerable and become once again what he had so recently been, an obscure Bavarian politician, in no way qualified to govern a great and civilised country. In the last twenty years in Germany there had been so many changes and reversals of fortune, so many plots and counter-plots, so many threats of revolution and counter-revolution, and in the last months before the *Machtubernahme* the air had been so charged with uncertainty and speculation, with intrigue and counter-intrigue, that Germans had become used to thinking that anything might happen at any moment; in politics, the exception had become the rule.

When General von Blomberg had been hastily summoned to Berlin from the Disarmament Conference in Geneva, to become Minister of Defence in Hitler's newly formed government, he had been met at the station by two emissaries with conflicting orders. One, Major Ott, came from General von Schleicher and summoned him to the Kriegsministerium in the Bendlerstrasse; the other, Oskar von Hindenburg, ordered him to the Presidential Palace. Von Blomberg obeyed the latter, and had thus assured Hitler of the support of the Reichswehr; but what would have happened if he had gone to the Bendlerstrasse?

When the fate of nations hangs upon such hazards a prudent man assumes that luck, chance, fortune, providence may undo what they have already done. In 1934 there were many Germans who, on prudential grounds alone, hesitated to commit themselves finally to Hitler, whose regime still had the marks of illegitimacy and instability. As for the imprudent who were willing to accept the appalling risk of active opposition to Hitler (and there were still some of them), it seemed impossible to believe that the German working class, in which they had for so many years placed their hope and their trust, had capitulated so completely and ignominiously. After all, might not the Communists be right in claiming that Hitler's triumph was the last convulsive effort of a capitalist system on the point of collapse, and that somewhere, even now, in secret, under-ground, in Moscow, in Berlin perhaps, the forces were organising which would undertake the revolutionary seizure of power for which Hitler had prepared the way. Others had less visionary, if no less deluded, reasons for indecision or for hope. Was not Hindenburg still alive? It was notori-ous that he detested Hitler, whom he regarded with ill-concealed contempt. Was not Papen, whom Hindenburg loved, still Vice-Chancellor and had he not set himself the task of bringing Hitler to heel and, ultimately, disposing of him? Papen had got rid of Brüning, he had got rid of Schleicher, he had even, as in some dashing cavalry charge, got rid of the government of Prussia; was Hitler the man to withstand his subtleties and intrigues and treacheries? And even in his own ranks Hitler had his enemies. In that winter of 1934 the Storm Troops were dissatis-fied, sullen, mutinous. They had not yet received the rewards they had earned by their sacrifices in fighting the Communists in the streets of Berlin. They might enjoy the freedom to revenge themselves on their enemies, but blood alone was not enough for men who looked for, and had fought for, something more solid than revenge, in the shape of jobs, appointments, salaries, recognised positions in society and the state. Was not Dr Goebbels grumbling that the Party had not put Hitler into power to satisfy the greed and ambition of the *Märzhasen*, the March Hares who in the previous year had rushed to join the party once its victory had been assured? It was said that Röhm had threatened to resign; and from Breslau came rumours that Heines, the convicted murderer and homo-sexual now elevated to be Gauleiter of Silesia, was on the point of open revolt. Gregor Strasser was calling for a second revolution in which the Party would finally settle all its accounts with its enemies, left, right, and centre, and in particular with the timorous bourgeoisie which was now trying to rob it of the spoils of victory.

History is written when the consequences of men's actions are known, so that everything seems determined by what went before; but it is made by men who cannot foresee the results of what they do and can only guess at what they may be. In Berlin, in 1934, there was plenty of room for guessing, even though many of the guesses were wide of the mark. For Hitler, though Reich Chancellor, had not yet established that total domi-nation over the German people which he was to achieve later, nor was he surrounded by that aura of victory which his spectacular triumphs were to bestow on him in years to come. Even a dictator, and even a Hitler, cannot destroy an entire culture and replace it with another in a space of nine months. Such things take time, even when they have brute force and unrestrained violence behind them; and as yet indeed Hitler did not even have a monopoly of force, for alongside the Party and the Storm Troops stood the Reichswehr, a military and political power in its own right, still relatively immune to the blandishments of National Socialism, and capable, if it so wished, of blowing Hitler and his entire regime to bits.

So gossip, rumour, speculation multiplied wherever men might meet without fear of Party fanatics and informers. For in that winter of 1934 there still remained two great imponderables and incalculables. No one knew what Hitler was thinking, and no one knew what the Reichswehr was thinking, and so long as this remained so, no one could foretell the future. So the city waited, like an animal which feigns sleep yet is still alert to any sign of approaching change or danger. And as it waited it held its breath, because the only thing that seemed certain was that so precarious a situation could only provide a transition – but to what? Everywhere one heard the same phrases. *Das kann doch nicht mehr länger dauern* (Things can't go on like this much longer). *Entweder oder* (One thing or another). For some people the alternative provided a hope when all hope seemed to be lost; for others, an added determination to carry Hitler's seizure of power to its logical conclusion.

And so Berlin waited. It was very cold. Flakes of snow fell slowly, heavily, congealing on the frozen waters of the Spree, and Schinkel's monuments of the dead past looked more than ever austere, aloof, withdrawn. Hungry Storm Troopers, still awaiting their awards, aimlessly tramped the streets. In the icy air there was a feeling strangely compounded of expectancy and fear. It was the air of a city waiting to see the Janus head of the future, without knowing which face of it would be revealed.

Dannie Abse
'The night of broken glass'

A cold wind blew through the streets of Europe. Wilfred and Leo were discussing the events in Germany. It was November 1938.

In every part of the Reich, synagogues were set on fire or dynamited. Jewish homes were smashed and ransacked. Individual Jews were arrested, hounded or baited by bands of Nazis who toured the streets of Berlin smashing up all Jewish shops. Large crowds joined in the wholesale looting; nor would the police interfere. Fire brigades remained silent except to protect neighbouring Aryan houses from the infection of flames. Youths broke into the remaining synagogues to use them as urinals. This in Berlin, Munich, Vienna, Nuremberg, Stettin, Frankfurt-on-Main.

'It can't happen here,' said Wilfred.

This in Cologne, Lubeck, Leipzig, Breslau, Stuttgart.

'It's unlikely to happen here,' said Leo.

This in Hanover, Hamburg, Constance, Reichenberg.

'Supposing it did?' asked Wilfred.

This in Germany.

'No. It wouldn't happen here,' said Leo.

In Frankfurt and Munich all male Jews arrested between the ages of eighteen and sixty were sent to concentration camps at Oranienburg near Berlin, Dachau near Munich.

'Mosley has no support,' said Wilfred.

'If Grynszpan hadn't gone to the German Embassy it would have taken place anyway,' said Leo.

'Who is Grynszpan?' I asked.

'They killed Grynszpan's parents,' Wilfred continued. 'Wouldn't you have done the same in his place?'

'I don't know,' said Leo.

'Who is Grynszpan?' I repeated.

'Read the paper,' commanded Leo.

I picked up the paper and read: 'Decrees have taken away the last possibility of economic existence from the German Jews ... They cannot obtain the barest necessities of life ... Not food, not shelter ... Few visas can be given to those Jews who are besieging the foreign consulates ... Flight across the frontiers ... Refugees turned back, by neighbouring countries ... Work of Jewish relief organisations brought, to a complete standstill by the arrest of the responsible officials and thousands already dependent on them left penniless ... Jews afraid to return home ... Jews hiding in the woods ... in the fields ... Fate of those arrested unknown ... Infirm Jews and the Jewish aged turned out of the hospitals and old people's homes ...'

'There's nothing in the paper about Grynszpan,' I said.

My brothers looked at each other.

'Who is Grynszpan?' I asked imploringly.

'Not a person,' said Leo, 'but a condition of history.'

'I'll try and explain to you,' said Wilfred.

L'addition,' called the youth. Outside, November crept like a cold dark implacable tide through the streets of Paris. Though it was but the middle of the afternoon the lights of the restaurant had been switched on – it hung there in a frozen cascade of stiff electricity over the table Grynszpan occupied. '*L'addition, s'il vous plaît,*' repeated Grynszpan.

Georges, the waiter, walked over to the table fascinated, wondering whether, after he had presented the large bill, this customer, whose dress suggested the worst of poverty, would be able to pay. Grynszpan couldn't understand enough French, so, finally, the waiter wrote down the figures on the paper cloth that covered the table. The youth counted out the money, examining each note, assessing its value, and the eyes of Georges and Grynszpan, when this ceremony was over, met momentarily like an accident. There was something in the dark emotionless eyes of this pale youth that erased the habitual smile from the waiter's mouth. He. helped the boy into his shabby frayed overcoat. '*Merci*,' said the youth.

The waiter noticed the lifeless cold set lips of the boy and then Grynszpan had gone out into the November street. Georges watched him through the plate-glass window, remembering how this customer had taken such an eternal time to devour his meal. It was as if the youth had tried to taste every crumb of meat, every single molecule of fat, carbohydrate, protein, like a man at the beginning of a long farewell, like a man partaking of food for the last time.

'*Garçon!*' shouted somebody and Georges, shrugging his shoulders, shuffled off to another table.

Eventually a taxi stopped for Grynszpan. '*Au consulat allemand*,' he commanded. The cab-driver looked at him doubtfully, but Grynszpan pulled some money out of his pocket and the driver, suddenly all smiles, gesticulating, talking loudly, beckoned him into the taxi.

It was simple to lie back there on the leather seat watching Paris pass by, pass by. This was how life was for the fortunate, good meals, the best wine, transport by taxi. The cab-driver glanced curiously at the face of the boy through the cracked mirror above the steering-wheel. It was a long mask-like face, drained of blood, a face too old for the voice that had issued out of it, for the head and body to which it was attached. And then a bicycle careered crazily in front of the taxi, and the cab-driver pressed angrily on his horn, which in turn prompted like some involuntary reflex the surrounding traffic to hoot and to toot in unfailing sympathy. Here was the language of Paris traffic, the dead vocabulary of a city.

Grynszpan's right hand strayed into his overcoat pocket. The object there lay as a threat, cold and reassuring in his hand. He felt no fear now, only hate; no grief – that had gone with his tears – only hate for the murderers of his parents. And yet, now, murder seemed such an easy, such a little thing.

'*Vous êtes allemand?*' asked the driver.

'*Non.*' Grynszpan paused. '*Je suis polonais.*' Then added in a voice hard as a laugh, '*Je suis juif.*'

The taxi-driver said no more. He understood. Later that night he would tell his wife casually that he took a young Jew to the German Embassy. 'Polish, you know.'

Outside the German Embassy, a beggar braced himself, put on his face to meet the face that would alight from this taxi. He moulded his features into a resemblance of abject agony. He tried to make his face look like that of Jesus on the Cross – and then he would stretch out his clawlike hand for the pieces of silver. The beggar watched Grynszpan come out of the taxi with rage. He had been cheated. Yet, seeing the youth pay the cab-driver generously and the driver salute, he felt a certain pride. For here was one dressed like himself, one who evidently had hungered, had known humiliation, had known the body-louse. The shoddy figure of Grynszpan somehow renewed his faith. Today the youth had alighted from a taxi, well tomorrow perhaps, he himself ... Well, one never knew: the world was a miracle. When Grynszpan emptied his pockets, giving away all his money, the beggar accepted it without a look of gratitude, without even surprise; but took it as if it were his rightful inheritance.

Once the youth had passed through the doors of the German Embassy he stood there shocked by the silent dignity of the place. And the thick, grey-coloured luxurious carpet beneath his feet intimidated him. The carpet more than anything, even more than the knot of officials who inquiringly looked at Grynszpan from the other side of the foyer. The carpet made him conscious of his own appearance, his own inadequacy. He noticed how, when he walked over to the desk, it was as if he walked on cotton wool. The carpet was so thick that it disturbed his balance organs: he walked over like a drunkard, but with no noise. They stared at him dispassionately. 'State your business,' the taller man said. Grynszpan's left hand lay as dead on the shining desk. Somebody near the stairs had a fit of coughing and the officials looked across annoyed, seeming to suggest that to cough here was a singular discourtesy. The shorter man meantime examined the pale small hand that lay on the blotting-paper, noting like a detective the millimetre of dirt rimmed under each fingernail.

'I want to see the German Ambassador,' Grynszpan said, and he felt the blood flush his face. He cursed himself. There was no need to blush. And his voice had sounded so meek as if he only wanted to see the German Ambassador in order to ask permission to see his bride-to-be. The short official had the habit of frequently half-closing his eyes: the lids would flicker for a moment and the pupils disappear upwards out of sight.

'How old are you?' asked the taller man.

'Seventeen,' he replied.

'What do you want to see him about?'

A door opened somewhere and Grynszpan could hear a typewriter clicking. Then a harsh voice shouting something in German. Feet shuffled and the door closed.

'It's private,' the boy said.

Supposing they wouldn't admit him to the Ambassador. Should he make a dash for it: run up the stairs?

'Go away and write a letter,' said the short official. The lids flickered, the pupils went upwards showing the whites of the eyes and the little twisted blood-vessels.

'It's urgent,' stated Grynszpan, looking steadily at the shorter man's eyes. He heard his own voice coming back queerly. 'It's urgent, it's urgent, it's urgent.' Not like his voice at all. Perhaps it was because his mouth was so dry.

The taller official became afraid – the boy looked so pale – from another world almost: the clothes rotting on him as if they had been buried underground for a long time. Another man, too short for his weight, ambled over to the desk and whispered to the other two. Grynszpan gazed downwards and noticed that one of his own shoe-laces was undone. How terrible the carpet was. If there was no carpet he could have made a run for the stairs, his voice could have been stronger. There was something about its luxuriousness, its thickness, that he could not understand. He hated it, as much anyway as he could hate a thing.

'What's that?' asked the taller official, startled. Again the third man whispered something: it was obscene the way he leant over to speak into the ear of the official. The whisper grew large, inflated itself, burst on the thick carpet where the two words 'Jew boy' fluttered dying, emotionless. Grynszpan noticed the hairs that sprouted out of the taller official's ear. Now six eyes looked at him, coldly. It was then Herr Ernst von Rath strode from the street, through the glass doors, into the foyer of the Embassy. He had just been accosted by a particularly impertinent beggar. He walked in angrily. Grynszpan realised it was someone important by the way the others looked up. The doorman had clicked his heels.

'Throw the Jew out,' shouted the tall official.

When the youth pulled a gun out of his overcoat pocket, everybody stopped thinking. They all appeared like figures in a photograph, caught in one pose eternally. They waited there listening for something. Von Rath stood precisely still staring at the gun stupidly. The short official's pupils shot under his upper lids as if he didn't want to see anything. And Grynszpan aimed at von Rath's face. As a child, Grynszpan, in street corner fights, had never been able to punch his opponent in the face: he had always directed his blows to the body. Grynszpan absurdly remembered this now as he pointed the revolver at von Rath's mouth that had fallen open in stupid surprise. It was strange; and then the gun went off and Herr von Rath, the Third Secretary of the German Embassy in Paris, sank to the deaf carpet, holding his stomach with both hands. And Grynszpan smiled.

They were all yelling at him now, kicking him and punching him. '*Jude*,' they were shouting. '*Jude, Jude*.' The short official was twisting his wrist trying to break his arm, but the boy hardly felt it. 'Mama, Dada,' he. said under his breath, 'Jews of Germany ... I did what I could.'

He heard a crack and he knew they had broken his arm, but there was no pain, only the delight of seeing, near the hunched body of Herr von Rath, a bright spot of blood like ordure staining the light, grey, luxurious carpet of the German Embassy.

Richard Hughes
'Hitler's coup'

It surprised Franz when at last they arrived at Röttningen to find Dr. Reinhold there. The eminent jurist was a busy man and seldom came to his brother's house; but now Franz heard his unmistakable throbbing voice as soon as they entered the hall.

It seemed to come through the open library door where Dr. Ulrich had just appeared to greet them: '*Two* shots!' the exciting voice thrilled in tones rich with pathos: 'Straight through the ceiling! *Phut-phut!* Surely a remarkable way of catching the chairman's eye at a meeting ... and indeed he caught *every* eye, balancing there erect on a little beer-table – all those grandees in full fig, and him in a dirty mackintosh with his black tails showing under its skirts – like a waiter on the way home. In one hand a big turnip-watch, and a smoking pistol in the other ...'

A subdued buzz of appreciation was audible from the library. In the meanwhile Franz had been trying to murmur his parents' excuses, but Dr. Ulrich seemed in a towering hurry and wouldn't stop to listen to them – he would scarcely let the Lorienburg party get their furs off before he shepherded them in front of him into the already crowded library and pushed them into chairs. 'S-s-s-sh!' he admonished them excitedly: 'Reinhold was there, he saw everything! He left Munich before dawn and has just got here by way of Augsburg. They're all in it – Ludendorff, Kahr, Lossow, Seisser, Poehner ...'

'You muddle everything, Uli! It's all that Hitler!' said Reinhold plaintively, 'I keep telling you!'

'... and Otto Hitler too,' Dr. Ulrich added hurriedly: 'One of Ludendorff's lot,' he explained.

'*Adolf* ...' his brother corrected him. 'But not "*and* Adolf Hitler *too*"! As I'm trying to explain – only you will keep running in and out – little second-fiddle Hitler entirely stole the show! Ludendorff, today? Kahr?' he continued with ironical disdain, and snapped his fingers: '*Pfui!* – For months those two have both been stringing this Hitler along, each trying to use that empty brain and hypnotic tongue for his own ends: now Hitler has turned the tables!'

'It must all have been richly comic,' someone remarked comfortably.

'But on the contrary!' Dr. Reinhold was palpably shocked. 'How can I have conveyed to you any such idea? – No, it was deeply impressive! – *Macabre*, if you like: a *mis-en-scene* by Hieronymus Bosch: but in no way comic!'

Once more everybody settled down to listen. 'The hall was packed – by exclusive invitation only, for a pronouncement of Great Importance. Everybody who was anybody was there including our entire Bavarian cabinet – and Hitler too of course, he'd somehow been invited ...'

'*When was this, and where?*' Franz whispered to Ulrich, aside.

'*Last night. Munich.*'

'*But WHERE?*'

'*S-s-s-sh! The Bürgerbräukeller: Kahr had engaged their biggest hall.*'

'We all knew what we'd been summoned for, of course – more or less. It would be monarchy, or secession – or perhaps both ... federation with Austria, even. But Kahr seemed in no hurry to come to brass-tacks. He droned on and *on*. That tiny square head of his – for anthropometrically he's a veritable text-book Alpine, that old boy, and his little head sank lower and lower on the expanse of his chest till I truly thought it would end up in his lap! Nothing about him looked alive except those two little brown eyes of his: from time to time they'd leave his notes and take just one peep at us – like mice from the mouths of their holes! *Eight-fifteen – eight-twenty* – on and on – *eight-twenty-five* – still endlessly saying nothing – *eight-twenty-eight, twenty-nine,* and then – you should have seen Kahr's look of outrage at the interruption – that inexplicable *Phut! Phut!*'

Reinhold paused dramatically, palpably waiting till someone asked him, 'What happened then?'

'Silence, at first – a moment of utter silence! But the watch in Hitler's hand was fully as significant as his pistol. On the very stroke of eight-thirty – at the very moment he first pulled the trigger – the door burst open and in tumbled young Hermann Goering with a machine-gun squad! Steel helmets seemed to appear instantly out of nowhere: at every door, every window, all over the hall itself And then Pandemonium broke loose! Shrieks and shouts, crashing furniture and smashing beer-jugs ... punctuated by that short sharp ululation peculiar to women in expensive furs ...

'Hitler jumped off his table and began pushing to the front, revolver still in hand. Two of Goering's strong-arm boys half-lifted him onto the platform, and Kahr was shoved aside. So there he stood, facing us ... You know those piercing, psychotic, popping eyes of his? You know that long, comparatively legless body? ("Incidentally you're *another* Alpine, dear boy," I thought: "You're certainly no Nordic ...") But oh the adoring gaze those brawny pinhead gladiators of his kept turning on him from under their tin skull-cups, those ant-soldiers of his (and there seemed to be legions of them, let me tell you, there last night)!

'Now in a moment it was so quiet again you could hear Hitler panting – like a dog circling a bitch! He was profoundly excited. Indeed whenever he faces a crowd it seems to arouse him to a veritable orgasm – he doesn't woo a crowd, he rapes it. Suddenly he began to screech: "On to Berlin! The national revolution has begun – *I* announce it! The Hakenkreuz is marching! The Army is marching! The Police are marching! *Everybody* is marching!"' Dr Reinhold's voice rasped harsher and harsher: '"This hall is occupied! Munich is occupied! Germany is occupied! *Everywhere is occupied!*"' In his mimicry Dr Reinhold glared round the room with quivering nostrils, as if daring anyone to move in his seat. Then he continued: '"The Bavarian government is deposed! The Berlin government is deposed! God Almighty is deposed – hail to the new Holy Trinity Hitler-Ludendorff-Poehner! Hoch!"'

'Poehner?' said someone incredulously: 'That ... long, stuttering policeman?'

'Once – Gaoler of Stadelheim! – Now, Bavaria's new prime minister!' said Reinhold with ceremony: 'Hoch!'

'And Ludendorff ... so Ludendorff is behind it all,' said someone else.

'Ye-es – in the sense that the tail is "behind" the dog,' said Reinhold: 'Commander-in-chief of a thrice-glorious (non-existent) National Army – *Hoch!* It's Lossow who's to be minister of war. I tell you, when Ludendorff at last came on the scene he was in a smoking rage: it was perfectly obvious Hitler had bounced him – he'd known nothing about the coup until they got him there. He *spoke* honeyed words, but he *looked* like a prima donna who's just been tripped into the wings.'

'And Egon Hitler himself?'

'"*Adolf*," please ... our modest Austrian Alpine? He asks so little for himself! Only ...' Reinhold stood exaggeratedly at attention – 'Only to be Supreme Dictator of the Whole German Reich – Hoch! Hoch! HOCH!'

Someone in Reinhold's audience made a more farmyard noise.

'My friend – but you ought to have been there!' said Reinhold, fixing him with his eyes: 'I couldn't understand it ... frankly, I can't understand it now so perhaps you clever people will explain it to me? Hitler retires to confer in private with Kahr & Co. – at the pistol-point I've little doubt, for Kahr and Lossow were flabbergasted and palpably under arrest – while young Hermann Goering in all his tinkling medals – all gongs and glamour – is left to keep *us* amused! Back comes Hitler: he has shed his trench-coat now and there his godhead stands revealed – our Titan! Our New Prometheus! – in a slop-shop tail-coat nearly reaching to his ankles, *das arme Kellnerlein!* But then Hitler begins to *speak* again: "November criminals" and "Glorious Fatherland" and "Victory or Death" and all that gup. Then Ludendorff speaks: "On to Berlin – there's no turning back now ..." "That's spiked Kahr's separatist, royalist guns pretty thoroughly," I thought: "and just in the nick of time! Prince Rupprecht is right out of it from now on – he's missed his cue ..." But no! For then the notoriously anti-royalist Hitler chokes out some intentionally only half-audible laudatory reference to "His Majesty": whereon Kahr bursts into tears and falls into Hitler's arms, babbling about "Kaiser Rupprecht"! Ludendorff can't have heard what Hitler said or Kahr said either – fortunately, for he'd certainly have burst asunder ... but as it is, everyone shakes hands all round ... then State-Commissioner Baron von Kahr speaks, then Commanding-General von Lossow, then Chief-of-Police Colonel von Seisser – all licking the Austrian ex-corporal's boots! All pledging him their support! Not that I'd trust one of them a yard if I were Hitler ... any more than I'd trust Hitler's new-found reverence for royalty if I were Rupprecht.

'So much for the stage and the professionals: in the audience we're all jumping on our seats and cheering ourselves silly. "Reinhold Steuckel, you level-headed eminent jurist!" I kept telling myself. "This isn't politics, it's Opera. Everyone's playing a part – but everyone!"'

'Grand Opera – or Opera-bouffe?' asked someone behind the speaker.

Reinhold turned right round in his chair and looked at his interrogator very seriously: 'Ah, that's the question! And it's early days really to know the answer,' he added slowly. 'But I *think* it's what I hinted earlier: something not quite human. – Wagner you say? You're thinking of that early, immature thing of his, Rienzi? Perhaps. Yes, the score is recognisably at least *school* of Wagner ... ah, but those ant-soldiers – all those sinister, animated insects and those rabbits and weasels on their hind legs ... and above all, Hitler ... Yes, it was Wagner, but Wagner staged *by Hieronymus Bosch!*'

He said all this with such compelling earnestness, enunciating those last words in so sibilant a whisper, that a chill hush fell on the whole room. Dr Reinhold had not gained that courtroom reputation of his for nothing.

Christopher Meredith
My mother missed the beautiful and the doomed

My mother missed the beautiful and doomed
by a few years.
Where Waugh, hot for some pious ormolu,
dreamed Brideshead
she swept carpets, cleaned grates.

Sepia expects a tear
but none comes. She holds
the yellowed postcard of the House
at arm's length, beyond her two dead children,
two atom bombs ago.

'It was like that film. You know. *Rebecca.*'
She smokes.
Echo of casual elegance in the wrist, the gesture,
masks slow scorching of the fuse.
The drag of air
accelerates a hundred small ignitions.
'The drive and all. They had a maze.'
Ash hardens into brightness
small flames eat the paper
worming back along tobacco galleries.
She frowns and jewels, salvers, gleam the harder.
'Her Ladyship 'ould doll up to the nines
come dinner, like a filmstar.'

The mind drags air through fifty years of fading
burns off the filmdream, comes to other stuff,
makes it glow again.

Through half open doors
down perspectives of the glassy rooms
she hears them.
Iw. Mmn. Yiss. Tongues all twangs and daggers.
The Foreign Secretary stands in the hall
his collar of vermiculated astrakhan
flawed with sparkling rain.
She kneels by the scuttle with
an egg of coal in either hand.
His chauffeur in double breasted rig
loiters, one glove removed, ruffles her hair,
sets her neat white cap awry.
'Little Cinderella' he says.

She frowns to brighten memory's fuse,
looks down the maze of galleries where
her people cut the coal.
The hand had rained a blow or a flirtation,
the words half flattered her
and kept her down.

She glances sideways at the tight black boot,
the echo of the bentarmed cross.
Krupp's bombs rain now on undefended children
glimmer through smoking Barcelona.

Unwilled complicity can hurt so much.
She clutches at the deaths of millions.

'A skivvy all my life' she says
and strikes another match.

Glyn Jones
'Autobiography'

... Overshadowing the agony of south Wales was the fear of war. I could not see how war was ever to be reconciled with Christian belief, and I felt convinced pacifism was implicit in Christianity. And how, I asked myself, was the desperate plight of those around me to be improved by war, which was more likely to impoverish them further and even destroy them and their community? I was quite wrong. About a twelvemonth before war broke out I remember sitting by the fire in a large bus garage at the derelict top end of one of the valleys, chatting to a group of unemployed miners. They were cheerful. As we talked one of them got up, went to the work-bench under the window and returned with half a pint of engine oil which he poured on the fire. The flames went up bright and yellow, illuminating the gloomy barn-like garage with their brilliance. This was a celebration. The men, after years of unemployment, had been promised jobs within a matter of days. One, a miner who hadn't worked for fifteen years, was the next day to start in an arms factory.

Pacifism was no new creed to me, thought up during the thirties. As a schoolboy I knew that Merthyr conscientious objectors to the First World War, of whom there were several, were being ill-treated and imprisoned and were suffering social ostracism; but I never at home, although my own father was serving in France at the time, heard any word of disparagement or condemnation or contempt for the stand of these men; rather the reverse, admiration for their courage and tenacity in the face of so much mass scorn, derision and ill-treatment. Merthyr in fact had a strong pacifist tradition, a combination of the pacifism of Welsh nonconformity and of left-wing politics. Here the old ILP with its influential anti-war element had flourished. One of Merthyr's members of Parliament had been the near-pacifist Keir Hardie, and an earlier one was Henry Richard, the Apostle of Peace. Some of the nonconformist ministers of the town had preached pacifism from their pulpits with great courage even when the First World War was in progress. The Cardiff pacifists in the thirties, Quakers, Peace Pledge signatories, members of *Urdd y Deyrnas* and the Fellowship of Reconciliation, had a propaganda stall in the busy Cardiff market, and it was in attendance here during the thirties that I spent my agonised Saturday mornings.

Tony Curtis
The Death of Richard Beattie-Seaman in the Belgian Grand Prix, 1939

Trapped in the wreckage by his broken arm
he watched the flames flower from the front end.
So much pain – *Holy Jesus, let them get to me –*
so much pain he heard his screams like music
when he closed his eyes – the school organ at Rugby
Matins with light slanting down
hot and heady from the summer's high windows.
Pain – his trousers welded by flame to his legs.
His left hand tore off the clouded goggles –
rain falling like light into the heavy trees,
the track polished like a blade.
They would get to him, they were all coming
running across the grass, he knew.

The fumes of a tuned Mercedes smelt like
boot polish and tear gas – coughing, his screams rising
high out of the cockpit – high
away back to *'38 Die Nurburgring.*
He flew in with Clara
banking and turning the Wessex through a slow circle
over the scene – sunlight flashing off the line of cars,
people waving, hoardings and loudspeakers, swastikas
and the flags of nations lifted in the wind he stirred.
She held his arm tightly, her eyes were closed.
He felt strong like the stretched wing of a bird,
the course mapped out below him.
That day Lang and Von Brauchitsch and Caracciola
all dropped out and he did it – won
in the fourth Merecedes before a crowd of half a million
– the champagne cup, the wreath around his neck,
An Englishman the toast of Germany
The camera caught him giving a Hitlergruss.
Waving arms, shouts and faces, a mosaic
laid up to this moment – La Source – tight – the hairpin
the trees – tight – La Source – keeping up the pace
Belgium – La Source hairpin too tight.

With the fire dying, the pain dying
the voices blurred beneath the cool licks of rain.
To be laid under the cool sheets of rain.
A quiet with, just perceptible, engines roaring
as at the start of a great race.

Dylan Thomas
The hand that signed the paper

The hand that signed the paper felled a city;
Five sovereign fingers taxed the breath,
Doubled the globe of dead and halved a country;
These five kings did a king to death.

The mighty hand leads to a sloping shoulder,
The finger joints are cramped with chalk;
A goose's quill has put an end to murder
That put an end to talk.

The hand that signed the treaty bred a fever,
And famine grew, and locusts came;
Great is the hand that holds dominion over
Man by a scribbled name.

The five kings count the dead but do not soften
The crusted wound nor stroke the brow;
A hand rules pity as a hand rules heaven;
Hands have no tears to flow.

The Second World War

Raymond Garlick
'Looming and sombre'

We heard Mr Chamberlain broadcast his brief factual announcement, on September 3rd, that 'this country is now at war with Germany' (or some such flat, formal wording) in the upstairs sitting-room of my aunt and uncle's premises in Degannwy, with its spectacular panorama of Mynydd Conwy opposite, the wide river estuary, the open sea looking towards Anglesey. It was a view whose changing moods I was to come to know very well, but never to cease to wonder at: coming into the room was like being ushered into a gallery seat in a cinema showing a wide-screen film. On this autumn morning, as we listened to the Prime Minister, I recall vividly that the huge reflection of the mountain in the millpool-still water was looming and sombre.

Gwyn Jones
Editorial in *The Welsh Review* (October 1939)

As I write these words the peoples of half Europe are at war: by the time they are read the state of things will be no better and may well be frighteningly worse. This is not because those peoples hated each other or because they wanted war. The hate may come – it probably will – but meantime we must seek other reasons why we are to eat our bellyful from the grisly dish. And unless we are content to be borne along unthinkingly with prejudice and noise, this is a matter that demands all our honesty.

In trying to work out our own position, we shall do neither ourselves nor our cause good service by shutting our eyes to any of the truth. I believe honest conviction will be no weaker stay in the testing-time ahead than the thoughtless bawling of catchwords. The immediate cause of this war was Hitler's aggression – there can be no doubt of that. It is clear enough now, and will become increasingly clear in the dry light of history, that not only is the German Chancellor a treaty-breaker, a liar, a brutal persecutor, but that he has come to share the madness of would-be dominators of the world. By his speeches, his writings, and his actions he has set himself beyond the pale of decency, and revealed till now even the dullest understand that the conceptions of right, faith, honour, tolerance, humanity are at all times the objects of his derision and loathing. With that said, we may turn to assess our own share in the responsibility of conjuring him from the ignorance and insignificance in which he was nurtured and in which he might well have continued. I do not think we need blame ourselves unduly for the Treaty of Versailles. It was not a very good treaty, but it was certainly not a very bad one, and many of its so-called mistakes have become apparent only since 1931, and then only by the manufacture of grievances. It is due to later blunders that it has served the Nazis so well that they might well circulate copies inscribed in gold among the public libraries in Germany. It was *after* Versailles that Great Britain, France, and America acted with such incredible shortsightedness. America refused to be a good citizen of the world and for domestic reasons withdrew from the League of Nations; Great Britain had not strength of purpose enough to deflect France from her bitterly anti-German policy nor 'realism' enough to go wholeheartedly along with her. The result was that period of internal strain and disorder in Germany which ensured the emergence of an iron dictatorship. There are certain lessons history has taught over and over again, and this is one of them; but the politicians of France and this country either knew no history (which is unlikely) or lacked the intelligence and integrity which allowed them to draw any practical lesson from it. With dictators and militarists coming up like a crop of weeds, they had not sense enough to know the consequences of the inevitable turn of events in a country long used to severe military discipline and temporarily the prey of lawlessness and brutal faction. We are hearing very frequently these last weeks that every country gets the government it deserves. For a long time past the saying would be the sorriest compliment to ourselves.

As frequently we hear that the German people has created its own Frankenstein. This is too modest a statement, for we were part manufacturers of the monster, and by an irony that would have delighted the Greek tragedians are now set the task of destroying him. Yet, when we have shouldered our share of the blame and frankly admitted our faults of omission and commission, what are we to say of a great people, sharing our common heritage and contributing not a little to that heritage – what can we say that it allows itself to be so abjectly enslaved? A people that allows Heine's name to be forgotten by its children, but can stomach Streicher – surely the foulest creature of our age! That rejects the bearers of its culture, killing, beating, imprisoning, forcing them to flee, but admires Himmler and Goebbels. That can look on at pogroms, endure the Gestapo and the concentration camps, and acquiesce in the ravings of its jackbooted louts. What can we say? Many Germans were my friends; I share the common debt of mankind to German thinkers, writers, musicians, scientists, artists of all kinds; as a student I felt little short of reverence for the stupendous labours of German scholars in fields I was but timidly exploring; nowadays in half my work I am daily grateful for their diligence and sincerity. And are these they who allowed without one word the prostitution of a nation's scholarship, who lecture from the same platforms as perverters of their truth, who solemnly support by their silence such fantastic theories of race and history as they themselves supplied the evidence to refute, who – worst of all – were as dumb at the breaking of Ossietzky as at the deification of an illiterate Führer? Not altogether. Some have suffered, some are suffering now, many have fled their country. There must be sick hearts in Germany these last six years. And in their position many of us, I fear, would have played a part no more heroic.

Yet the wonder remains. It is true that we have no quarrel with the German people – for my part I know I have none – yet they have allowed themselves to become the weapon of a quarrel against us. They have permitted their masters to begin a second great war. One thing we in this country know: that no government, or whatever political colour, could have led our peoples into a war of aggression. We would *not* have gone. There could be no stronger proof that our way of government is better than that of the totalitarian states. For the Germans *have* gone to a war of naked aggression. And I fear the result of the Polish success upon their obedient spirit. We must be free from malice but we must also be free from self-delusion. The responsibility of the German people is far, far heavier than ours.

★ ★ ★ ★ ★

There are many today who are able to say they spoke more wisely than our rulers. It is a futile satisfaction – if it be satisfaction at all. Yet I sympathise with, because I share, their resentment at the course of events. They have consistently advocated a course that would have avoided war had it been adopted early enough, and now find themselves in the grip of inescapable chop-logicians. Those who shouted for disarmament when disarmament was still possible were called fools by the very individuals who have since pointed to a world in arms as justification of their policy. Those who throughout the thirties forecast the inevitable catastrophe that would crown British diplomacy get no credit for their prescience – astonishingly, it is the blunderers who are praised first for their blunders and secondly for their belated conversion. Apologetics can hardly go further than 'We had to do the foolish thing to see whether it would work before we used our senses.' But for the peculiar criss-cross of purposes discernible in Nationalist government during the last five years in particular, we should be justified in doubting whether the sense was there to fall back on.

★ ★ ★ ★ ★

But this is to look on the past, when our concern should be with the present and future. Whatever the share of blame, we are at war with Germany. God knows I have hated and hate war with all the strength of my being, and warmongers with such passion that I regret I have no belief in a hell in which they might burn for all eternity. Indeed, this is not a subject I can trust myself to write on – and I pass it by. At the moment there are three prospects before us. The first, that we may in short time find an honourable peace, I regard as next to an impossibility. I do not think Hitler capable of an honourable peace. I do not think he would honour any obligation or bate one step of his insensate way, whatever he were offered. Either Hitler must be got rid of or there must be such international guarantees of restraint as he dare not transgress – and I see no hope of the latter. We are all too selfish. There remains, at the time of writing, the choice of victory for Great Britain or for Germany. The issue may be widened by allies of either side, but the principle remains the same. A victory for the democracies might mean either of two things. If the war continues long enough, if all the hellish inventiveness of armourers and scientists is unloosed over the heads of soldiers and civilians alike, it may well breed a vicious hatred that will lead to a peace as ill-managed as the last, a peace that is but a short truce for the rearing of new citizen armies from the children whose present ignorance is the most blessed thing left to them. On the other hand, we may use that victory to make a new Europe. No one can tell. But if Germany wins the day, we need look no further than the expressed views of Nazi writers to know what use will be made of success. I think it certain Germany will *not* win, but a consideration of the contingency should help us establish our position.

We are dealing now not only with the military mind, but with the Nazi mind too. It is not a pleasant combination.

There never has been the time when tyranny could stomach rival? and the Nazis would see to it that Great Britain and France are brought to ruin. From this would come, I imagine, two main results. The first would be the annihilation of liberal thought in both countries. We too should have a controlled press and radio. We too should see holocausts of the written works of our finest spirits, and listen to the hooting of hooligans in all our forums. We should inevitably pass under dictatorships, which with the encouragement of Hitlerism would blot out every form of opposition to their views and resort to the totalitarian weapons of the rubber truncheon and the concentration camp. He greatly errs who thinks we have no such willing tools in our midst. If we have civil war, it will be of that hopelessly weighted kind that led to the extinction

120

of the incipient democracy of Spain. The second result would be the growth of an insane militarism under the new dictatorships, the organisation of the state on a permanent war footing, as happened in Germany, and the certainty of further European wars waged not even for such tarnished ideals as we still hold, but for the personal ambition of the scourges of mankind. Let our minorities judge what awaits *them*. The prospect needs no elaboration. And it is clear that the collapse of democracy in Great Britain and France must mean its collapse throughout Europe, and probably throughout the world. What then of the small nations 'determined to preserve their independence at all costs?' We should enter an Iron Age of pain and bloodshed, of regimented thought and thoughtlessness, the thin flame of human worth guttering in a night of all save scientific ignorance. Those ideals towards which, hesitantly, and with many burnings of our fingers, we have been reaching for hundreds of years, would be stifled for generations, ourselves but the wreckage of a reign of insanity.

★ ★ ★ ★ ★

'The coldest of all cold monsters is the State.' So said Nietzsche – who also said that democratised Europe would be but the breeding ground of tyrants destined to rule a herd of mindless animals. There are many to approve the prophecy and point to its fulfillment, but I am not of them. The strongholds of democracy are democratic still. The dictators have arisen where there was no democracy or but its emptiest forms. It is not in the democracies that you hear the imbecile equation 'Hitler is Germany, and Germany is Hitler'; not in the democracies that you find the six-feet high exhortations to mindlessness: 'Work, Obey, Fight!' or whatever the precise nonsense is that disfigures sun-bright southern walls. The democracies have their faults, and tremendous faults they are, but they have not sunk within measurable distance of these impious absurdities. It is our shortcoming that we have not realised to the full our own principles and done all in our power to prevent our citizens from ever becoming that yeastless mass of uninformed, thoughtless, will-less, gullible material over which Nietzsche saw that the 'strong man' would exercise a dangerous and fascinating influence. It is our mission at this moment to keep guard over the best features of our civilisation, and to prevent this rottenness of citizenship from spreading. It will be our duty (I think our privilege) later to re-establish in Germany the self-respect of its people, now utterly overborne by a foul government. And our best brains should be grappling now with the problem of the peace as with those of the war. For in a way, our determination to clear the rising scum of Nazidom from the top of the pot is but to put ourselves in a position to do good. It is, to change our metaphor, but washing filth from a wound: the wound will remain for treatment. And unless the wound is healed, what hope for Europe?

★ ★ ★ ★ ★

I must keep a few lines for the *Welsh Review,* though they come in by way of postscript. Our readers will notice considerable change from our announcement in the September issue of this month's contents, but I am glad to say there is a good prospect of contributions in the near future from those writers who through no fault of their own, had to disappoint us; I have received many inquiries and several expressions of solicitude. It would be useless to pretend that we shall not feel something of a squeeze, but an atmosphere of crisis, as our friends know, is not entirely new to us. We are going ahead, and for no reason more than that the *Welsh Review* stands for just those values of creativeness, tolerance, goodwill and understanding that we are fighting this war to maintain. Civilisation and Culture are not, if we judge aright, abstractions, but rather aggregates of which all efforts to regulate man's inner and outer life are part. Our monthly appearance does not rival in importance the foundation of an empire; on the other hand it is more than the birth of a sparrow. We shall maintain it as long and as strongly as we can.

John Davies
Riders, Walkers

Damp, cold, dust? They were for the pack.
For one man in 1939, arriving on horseback
with his company, air conditioning was installed.
Swept slate caverns at Manod became halls
when Charles I, painted by Van Dyck, was stored
out of bombing range with London's hoard.
He looks grand still, unsurprised to be around.
The quarrymen, alas, stay underground.
But in the National Interest, common sense
says things of value must take precedence.
Think of the painting that you value
most. Walkers give way to riders. Which are you?

They had their place in the picture, cold, damp,
for Mary E. Thompson at this time. Cramped
by ill-health, she leant ambition's ladder up as far
as the Brussels Academy but surfaced in Bethesda.
From a split block, a small cloud of dust
escapes; a pencil can feel rock's upthrust.
She walked, climbed, and for almost twenty
years the galleries she toured were quarried,
sheet after sheet, as pale drawn workday
faces against stone in all the colours of grey
defied mass. In time, she could tell them who,
when they asked, pointing, '*Pwy di'r un acw?*'

So here is Alun Jones, blacksmith, concentrating
down a studious nose. Will Proudley cutting slate.
Here is the art of shaded surfaces, its value
that record sparked revelation. Not high art, true,
but true not low. Part of the story
half-buried still, it redefines nobility –
like the slate bust of Gwilym Hiraethog, icon
of nonconformity detached from the salon
at Penrhyn Castle (and carved by?), firebrand
snuffed by the country of the bland.
In a cluttered glass case: the fate
of art, shown to an antechamber, in an unfree state.

David Lloyd George
Letter to Frances Stevenson, 4th October 1940

Criccieth
Friday
7am

My sweet & courageous girl
　　What a bad time you have passed through since I left you at
Bron-y-de. MacDougall, who is an old Highland soldier has told me
all about it. I am glad you arranged for his wife and two children to
sleep in the maids' shelter. I hear Mrs Skelton is very grateful for the
use of my shelter & says it is like Heaven after her experience in the
Ridge cellar. As Gwilym & Dick & Tom may be there this weekend

it will be difficult to arrange matters. Last week they disdained the shelter & pigged it in the old dining room. The women might all go to the shelter & leave the men in the dining room.

I have had my experience here. They have been bombing various parts of Caernarvonshire for a week. This morning at six we all woke up with the sound of a bomb followed by machine gunning & we then heard the various snarls of aeroplanes hovering around for one hour during which time 7 bombs were dropped in the direction of Pwellheli. We all got up & huddled under the stairs. I have had no news so far as to what has happened. MacDougall will tell you all about it. I had already given instructions for the erection of an air shelter that will accommodate the whole household. But that must take three weeks & these planes are humming over us every night on their way to Liverpool. They have now taken to dropping bombs on their way back.

I have been hesitating as to whether I shall come up for Tuesdays meeting. If there were an open discussion I think I might – & would. But to run the gauntlet of the incessant bombardment in & around London merely for the privilege of hearing a speech from Winston explaining his Dakar fiasco & a speech I can read at leisure the following morning or hear at 6 o'clock the same evening is more than I care to do. All the discussion will be in secret session with a handful of ministers listening with one ear cocked up to the ceiling for the raid warning. The time has not yet come for criticism or alternative suggestions. Look at these last changes in the Cabinet. It is less of a War Cabinet than ever. One minister without any administrative duties leaves & two with absorbing departmental duties take his place. It is a farce. Such a body cannot sit down to a prolonged diurnal consideration of policy. And it is on large questions of war policy & strategy that this Government is feeble. The new additions to the War Cabinet will not contribute any wisdom or strength on this side. Kingsley Wood possesses a commonplace mind & Bevin although a forceful personality & an intelligent fellow possesses the outlook & equipment of a trade union leader. He shows no breadth of mind – no great vision.

I am glad I am not in. The whole conception & direction I suppose of our campaign must be completely revolutionised. With a stubborn mind like Winston's blind to every essential fact which does not fit in with his ambitions you could do no good. And the rest you could not persuade. The Labour representatives are fighting the battle of Trade Unionism smashed by Hitler Mussolini & Stalin. They have no ideas as to a New World to follow the War. Winston is a Tory at heart. Kingsley Wood is a petty bourgeois. I should waste my strength and time in wrestling with this immalleable material. And my nights would be a sleepless nightmare. In a few weeks I should be broken.

I am convinced that I can be helpful if I can preserve my health & nerve for a few more months. The people are not ready to pay any heed to good counsel. They still cherish illusions of 'complete victory'. Maybe Hitler is not ready to agree to the only peace which a British Govt could accept. All this may sound UNHEROIC but I am convinced it is sound. We must all make sacrifices. But to sacrifice oneself on the altar of insensate ambition, social economic or political. The nation must have a sense of failure of the existing leadership & of the existing order. That means a long struggle for we are tough people with an enormous resource of self confidence born & bred in centuries of unbroken success. I cannot serve effectively in the intervening period. I do not possess the necessary store of physical strength to do so. Clemenceau waited until the fight was nearing the end. By that time every other leader had avowedly failed & there was no one left to challenge his decisions.

Just received your letter. So sorry to learn of J.'s painful experience with her teeth.

Fond love
D.

Dylan Thomas
Letters to Vernon Watkins, 1940

Malting House, Marshfield, nr. Chippenham, Wilts.
[envelope stamped 1940]

Dear Vernon,

God, yes, how awful it must have looked. But I didn't get the 2 quid. Mad things have been happening to letters: I've lost one before, about 3 weeks ago. I think this house must be marked, & the letters opened. Really. The house, as I told you, is full of musicians, all are young men, not one is in the army, one has a German name, there *was* a German staying here some time ago, and there have also been five lighting offences in about six weeks. Perhaps a lucky censor got your lovely present. I am so sorry, for you & for me. 2 crinklers. And at bank-bombing time too. I thought that your not answering my letter was because you'd been hijacked into the army. I couldn't realise *you* were waiting for an answer from *me*.

I can't imagine Gower bombed. High explosives at Pennard. Flaming onions over Pwlldu. And Union Street ashen. This is all too near. I had to go to London last week to see about a BBC job, & left at the beginning of the big Saturday raid. The Hyde Park guns were booming. Guns on the top of Selfridges. A 'plane brought down in Tottenham Court Road. White-faced taxis still trembling through the streets, though, & buses going, & even people being shaved. Are you frightened these nights? When I wake up out of burning birdman dreams – they were frying aviators one night in a huge frying pan: it sounds whimsical now, it was appalling then – and hear the sound of bombs & gunfire only a little way away, I'm so relieved I could laugh or cry. What *is* so frightening, I think, is the idea of greyclothed, grey-faced, blackarmletted troops marching, one morning, without a sound up a village street. Boots on the cobbles, of course, but no Heil-shouting, grenading, goose-stepping. Just silence. That's what Goebbels has done for me. I get nightmares like invasions, all successful. (Ink gone)

I saw, and of course liked for I'd known nearly all of it before, the Llewelyn poems. Have you any time for writing now? Will you let me see something new? I've collaborated in a detective story and am just about to begin a short story. I do scripts for the BBC, to be translated into, & broadcast to, Brazil. I've got an exciting one to do next, on Columbus. But I haven't settled down to a poem for a long time. I want to, & will soon, but it mustn't be nightmarish.

I just looked again at your last letter, and you said in it that bombs were falling on the cliffs. I hope they missed you. Where is the nearest air-raid shelter? Singleton? You must run very fast. In this house Caitlin & I have our bedroom on the top floor, and so far we haven't got up even when the German machines are over us like starlings. But I think we'll have to, soon. My mother wrote & told me that people are sleeping on the Gower beaches, in barns and hedges. I went to see a smashed aerodrome. Only one person had been killed. He was playing the piano in an entirely empty, entirely dark canteen.

What are our Swansea friends doing? Is Fred still crossgartering fruit and faces? drilling? objecting? I don't hear from him ever. Life & Letter, of course. My father said he saw him in an airbattle over the town, standing in the middle of the street, his long neck craned.

I don't know at all when we'll be back in the ruins. I'll have to go to London so often, once – & if ever – this job gets really going. I'd love to see you before you undrive your motorcycle. No chance of us meeting in London? We've never done that. That would be lovely.

Write soon. Forgive this unavoidable & rude-appearing delay. Sorry, very sorry, sorrier than I can tell you, about the death of the pounds.

Lower me immediately on the equinoctial list of dislikes.

Love from Caitlin & me.
Remember me to your people. I hope the bombs
won't touch the croquet lawn. We must all play next
summer.

DYLAN.

[No address: postmark from Chippenham]
[No date: probably August 1940]

Dear Vernon,

It was lovely to hear from you. Thank you for the rest of the lost
present. It was needed alright,: by others. I'm in debt, & need my job
quickly. Perhaps we're both marked. You translate Holderlein [sic] &
swear in German to the Home Guards; I have no visible means of
support, & have been known to call the war bloody and silly. I hope
there's a special censor for our letters: a man who keeps a miserable
family on the strength of attempting to decode our innocent messages.

I hope Dot will like Japan. Would she care for me to write to
Empson, asking him for addresses of some of his friends? He was
there for years, & knows a lot of people. He'd like to. Old Japanese pro-
fessors. Pale tea & poetry afternoons. I wish we were going there too,
I could do with a bit of inscrutability. Europe is hideously obvious and
shameless. Am I to rejoice when a 100 men are killed in the air?

Is the Pioneer Corps non-combatant? Was Fred happy about it?
Do you know his address? I'd like to write to him, even tho he won't
answer. I'll enjoy seeing his war-pictures: the veins of a leaf that blew
from a shelled tree; the crisscrosses on the head of a spent bullet. He
should do widespread camouflage work, & make Oldham look like the
back of a herring.

I can't do much work either. I go for long bicycle rides, thinking:
'Here I am on a bicycle in a war.' I play whist with musicians, & think
about a story I want to call 'Adventures in the Skin-trade'. I've finished
my poem about invasion, but it isn't shapely enough to send you yet.

Remember me to your mother & father.

Don't forget: cover the croquet lawn, bury your poems in a stout
box, & don't stare at the sky too much. The wrong wings are up there.

Thank you again. I'll come to Wales soon.

Love,
DYLAN

R.S. Thomas
'Local danger'

Later that year came the Munich crisis. The main railway line ran
through Chirk, and while the discussions between Hitler and
Chamberlain continued, hundreds of trains would go past during the
night on their way south, carrying weapons, no doubt, to defend
England from an attack by the Germans. Chamberlain returned with
his piece of paper, and the crisis passed. But the young curate wasn't
familiar enough with the way of the world to realise that Chamberlain
was only playing for time. He wrote in his innocence to his friends in
Carraroe insisting that God would not allow something as terrible as
war. But others knew better and the country began to get ready. And
indeed before the end of another year the nations of the world were at
one another's throats, and there came all the tribulations of gas masks,
the rationing of food and petrol and so on. The curate worked with
others for days preparing ration books for the areas around Chirk, and
the women began to gather black material to put over the windows to
hide the lights after dark. And yet at the same time the curate and his
sweetheart decided to get married, and the wedding was celebrated in
Llanycil on the shore of Llyn Tegid, an area of which both of them had
become very fond. It was a very small wedding, but he had asked the
owner of the hotel where they were staying to invite a harpist to play
for them and their parents on the previous evening, like a *neithior*, a
traditional Welsh marriage-feast. But the owner was an Englishman
and he did not succeed in getting hold of anyone, even though the
curate had been told by Euros, when he came to know him, that there
were plenty of harpists to be had in the surrounding area, if you only
set about it in the right way. The vicar did not want a curate who was
married, and so the problem of finding somewhere else arose. On the
other hand they did not want to move into lodgings. At last he heard
about a living in Maelor Saesneg which included a house. It was part
of the parish of Hanmer, but the young man did not know at the time
about that place's connection with Owain Glyndŵr. And yet, such
information would hardly have been enough to ease his *hiraeth*, after
he had moved fifteen miles further east. Now Wales and her hills were
further away than ever, and he would gaze hopelessly at them over
miles of flat, uninteresting land.

By this time the war had started in earnest, and although there
wasn't much local danger, the parish was in the flightpath of the
German aeroplanes as they made for Merseyside. Every night,

weather permitting, the aeroplanes would pass overhead on their way in, and they soon started getting on the curate's nerves, not because of fear so much as disgust and despair at the thought that they were on their way to drop their fiendish loads on helpless women and children. At the same time he noticed that he wasn't showing enough confidence and fearlessness in the presence of the girl he had promised to look after. Although Merseyside was some twenty miles as the crow flies, as he stood in the doorway with his wife to listen to the sound of the bombs in the distance and to see the flames lighting up the sky, he felt the occasional puff of wind going through his hair and lifting his wife's skirt. Sometimes the Germans would drop a few bombs in the area, after seeing a light somewhere perhaps, but without injuring anyone, thanks to the open nature of the land. One night he happened to be looking through the window when he heard a bomb screaming on its way down very close by. He waited for the explosion, but nothing happened. The next day it was discovered that the bomb had plunged to earth within a yard or two of a zinc-roofed cottage, where an old couple lived. They were fast asleep at the time, without realising that anything out of the ordinary had happened! The curate decided to erect an earthwork against the wall of the parsonage, opposite the space under the stairs, as a shelter, should more bombs start to fall. One night when he was leaving the church, which was next door to the house, he heard a terrible bang very close by. He ran inside and urged his wife to come and take cover under the stairs, and there they were for hours, while the enemy aeroplanes circled above their heads. They heard afterwards that there were Italians as well as Germans, and that they were having difficulty as they tried to get close to Merseyside. Many bombs were dropped in the area that night, and the hill-country in the vicinity of Minera was set on fire. On seeing the flames, they started to drop bombs there as well, and a shepherd who lived at the edge of the moorland got the fright of his life. So hateful was it to the curate to think of the destruction occurring almost every night, and such was his *hiraeth* for the hills in the distance (Moel Fama could be seen quite clearly to the north-west), that he decided to learn Welsh as a means of enabling him to return to the true Wales.

R.S. Thomas
Homo Sapiens, 1941

Murmuration of engines in the cold caves of air,
And, daring the starlight above the stiff sea of cloud,
Deadly as a falcon brooding over its prey
In a tower of spirit-dazzling and splendid light,
Pedestrian man holds grimly on his way.
Legions of winds, ambushed in crystal corries,
Conspiring to destroy him, and hosts of ice,
Thronging him close, weigh down his delicate wings;
But loud as a drum in his ear the hot blood sings,
And a frenzy of solitude mantles him like a god.

Alun Lewis
All day it has rained

All day it has rained, and we on the edge of the moors
Have sprawled in our bell-tents, moody and dull as boors,
Groundsheets and blankets spread on the muddy ground
And from the first grey wakening we have found
No refuge from the skirmishing fine rain
And the wind that made the canvas heave and flap
And the taut wet guy-ropes ravel out and snap.
All day the rain has glided, wave and mist and dream,
Drenching the gorse and heather, a gossamer stream
Too light to stir the acorns that suddenly
Snatched from their cups by the wild south-westerly
Pattered against the tent and our upturned dreaming faces.
And we stretched out, unbuttoning our braces,
Smoking a Woodbine, darning dirty socks,
Reading the Sunday papers – I saw a fox
And mentioned it in the note I scribbled home; –
And we talked of girls, and dropping bombs on Rome,
And thought of the quiet dead and the loud celebrities
Exhorting us to slaughter, and the herded refugees;
– Yet thought softly, morosely of them, and as indifferently
As of ourselves or those whom we
For years have loved, and will again
To-morrow maybe love; but now it is the rain

Possesses us entirely, the twilight and the rain.
And I can remember nothing dearer or more to my heart
Than the children I watched in the woods on Saturday
Shaking down burning chestnuts for the schoolyard's merry
play,
Or the shaggy patient dog who followed me
By Sheet and Steep and up the wooded scree
To the Shoulder o' Mutton where Edward Thomas brooded
long
On death and beauty – till a bullet stopped his song.

Alun Lewis
'A fine life'

Khaki and discipline and angry imperatives are apt to overawe and frighten – yes, frighten – the recruit. But it isn't so godalmighty, really. One of the corporals saw me reading a book of poetry the other day. He said, 'Do you like poetry?' I flushed and looked at him for a moment to see what he was playing at. Then I said, 'Yes. Why?'

'Oh, nothing,' he said. Then he looked at me like a little boy confessing a longing for your apples. 'I like it, too,' he said. 'I like writing it, at least. I never read any. I write a lot, though. Every letter I write to my girl I put a poem in it. Of course some of them are pretty soft, but now and again they're really good. She was proper nuts about one I wrote last week. Pretty intimate it was – about having a baby. She copies them up into a notebook. In INK. Tell me, can you have verses longer than four lines? Or have they got to be four lines?'

In any case, the Army is only an improvisation on a vast scale. There's bound to be some rough edging, and some pretty poor stuff, here and there. There are certainly plenty of friends. They come to you from Borstal and the Royal College of Music, from the Great War and the Spanish War, and everywhere else. It's a fine life in that way. There are a few snobs – crane drivers and navvies occasionally sneer at 'bloody clerks, bloody school-teachers'. But mostly it's democracy all right, mending the holes in its socks and sharing the parcel from home and showing photographs and being disconcertingly vulgar and humorous, ignorant and amazingly experienced, and calm, happy-go-lucky.

There are also Saturday afternoons and Sundays, if you're lucky not to get pinched for fatigues or guard duty. The mere in the valley of pine trees has a profound stillness. In the afternoon sometimes there are a few soldiers bathing there and lying in the sun. Young boys talking driftily about the A.T.S. girls, what they're like, 'If they've got to have A.T.S. why don't they have them all smashers?' – and about the blue dragonflies which flicker on the still water, abrupt electric turns, vivid colour, then utter stillness settled suddenly on a thin blade of green, the long thin pipe of the body dipped in the water, the four transparent wings extended and still; sleeping on the flat heart-shaped sensuously-thick lily leaves or more fittingly on the wonderfully white spiked petals over the golden open heart of the flower; or flying in pairs, tail to head fastened together; 'Look at them dragon-flies capitulating, the dirty dogs,' says one of Seurat's bathers, tiring of the A.T.S.

I wish I could write a poem about dragon-flies. It would be like a schoolboy's face as he watched the mercury for the first time, in the great glass beaker of water.

At evening the mere is utterly still. The tangled rustgreen underwater grasses cannot be seen from the top of the valley. Only the mirror of water, pure blue and magenta and intense clearness of evening; the mere holds it all. And I think of Dick and Bill and Gweno and home and watch the advent of the heron, its steady grey wing-sweep, its legs and neck out-stretched and calm, circling slowly the mere which it sees as I see it, a mirror of rest, a breast for the dark and silent visitant. But it is deterred by the laughter of soldiers and girls, and goes as I am going, elsewhere.

On the way back to camp I catch up with a hedgehog. He has thin, dragging hind legs covered with loose brownish-purple skin, four claws like tubercular roots, a little black snout, pointy, and beady intelligent eyes, hunched over a grub. His nostrils blow little soap-bubbles of terror and his breath hisses when I prod him gently with a stick. Sacrilege.

It's only because I am alone that I touch him like this. I wouldn't have yielded to such a private intimate impulse had I been in company. But alone we are more primitive, more natural. We regard our faces in the mirror and examine the colour of our eyes, and touch the downy hair on our arms, ruffling it.

Then I continue my way back over the downward sloping heather, and I am no longer alone. The forest is blue and hazy with warmth and distance, like lavender, and the sandy path runs forward to the cluster of tents on the open heath. I see only the distance, the forest, and I half forget my khaki and imagine myself an itinerant preacher, one of the old revivalists of the eighteenth century, of my own country, Wales. Hywel Harris perhaps, or Thomas Charles, crossing the mountains to the waiting hearth. Or a lover in a Hardy novel, fifty years ago, on this same path, Tess lonely and hurt, Jude instinctively seeking loneliness.

Do you know how quietly I sleep, on my groundsheet, between my three dirty blankets, in the crowded tent?

R.S. Thomas
'Others were brave'

Others were brave. Whether volunteering or conscripted, they went forth to the war, as their fellows had done hundreds of years. 'Would not have missed it for worlds.' Yes, action has its compensations. What does one do when one does not believe in action, or in certain kinds of action? Are the brave lacking in imagination? Are the imaginative not brave, or do they find it more difficult to be brave? What does a man do with his silence, his aloneness, but suffer the sapping of unanswerable questions?

★ ★ ★ ★ ★

Entered for life, failing
to qualify; understudied
for his persona, became identical
with his twin. Confronted
as the other, knew credit
was his for the triumph
of an imposture. Slipped easily
into the role for which
his double was cast, bowing
as low as he to appropriate
the applause. When volunteers
were called for to play
death's part, stood modestly
in the wings, preferring rather
to be prompter than prompted.

T.E. Nicholas
To a Sparrow
Swansea Prison, 1940

Look, here's another bread-crumb for your piping,
And a piece of apple as a sweetener.
It gladdens me to hear your steady pecking;
It's good to see your cloak of grey once more.
You've travelled here, perhaps, from Pembroke's reaches,
From the gorse and heather on Y Frenni's height,
And maybe on grey wing you've trilled your measures
Above fair Ceredigion at dawn's first light.

Accept the bread: had I a drop of wine
Pressed from a distant country's sweet grape-cluster,
We two could take, amid war's turbulence,
Communion, though the cell lacks cross and altar.
The bread's as holy as it needs to be,
Offering of a heart not under lock and key.

Dannie Abse
'The sudden shock of battle'

On the radio, we had listened to Churchill's stirring biblical rhetoric addressed only indirectly to Roosevelt. 'We shall not fail or falter. We shall not weaken or starve. Neither the sudden shock of battle nor the long-drawn trial of vigilance and exertion will wear us down. Give us the tools and we will finish the job.' That language, then, did not seem particularly inflated. It was 1941 and the diction of war will always be purple. Astonishingly enough, nobody I knew ever imagined we could lose the war. It was just a question of how long it would take us to beat the bastards. And if things did get desperate, as Dad said – as every-body said – the Yanks would come in sooner or later. They would not let us down. They were our rich cousins. We had 'a special relationship' didn't we? They were just Australians or Canadians with a different accent, weren't they ... surely? They would be helping us sooner or later by coming into the war. It would be more than lend-lease and giving us fifty clapped-out destroyers. But, Jesus, why didn't they hurry up?

The 'sudden shock of battle' came to our house in Windermere Avenue in earnest only a week or two after I had broken my collar bone. That night my father was out and it was a particularly bad raid. One could hardly distinguish the noise of gunfire from that of bomb explosions. We tried to ignore it all, my mother and I, as we sat before the coal fire, not talking much. When my father did come in he seemed excited. 'It's as light as day outside,' he said. 'You could pick up a pin.' He persuaded me to leave the blacked-out house for a minute and witness how the surrounding district was bathed in a luminous, eerie green. And indeed it was so. I have never seen anything like that sick light. It was the colour of gangrene. Flares were floating down like chandeliers – a number of small lights clustered around a big central green flare, and the pattern was repeated over and over.

'Incendiaries,' an ARP warden said and, indicating my arm which was in a sling, he urged my father and me to go to a shelter or at least to return inside.

'All right, Mr Davies,' my father said, 'don't fuss now.'

When the explosions rooted themselves nearer to our house, my father ushered us into the little cloakroom below the stairs, and he hung up a thick coat against the window lest glass should fly dangerously. Just in time, too, for there was the distinct whine of a bomb falling. The sound advanced, changed its note into a highpitched whistle. They used to say, in the war, that if you, could hear that whistle you would be all right – that some other poor bugger had his name written on it. No one is alive to contradict that fable. The poor bugger in this case who was literally blown to bits was the ARP warden who had only spoken to us a few minutes earlier. So our neighbour, Mr Davies, had been killed, and I remember hearing the thin scream of some woman outside in the street, now very close to us, for a hole had appeared in our wall and the ceilings were down. I lay on the floor in the smell of dust and plaster, and my shoulder was hurting again, and the green light crept indoors.

'Are you all right? Are you all right?' my father and mother were saying.

Soon after I was admitted to a small cottage hospital just outside Cardiff.

Meic Stephens
Homer

The first GI to venture down our street,
    a huge man, the same dap as Paul Robeson,
he walked with the panther gait of his breed,
    his boots and helmet, sunglasses and gun

like in the Pathé News. From Omaha,
    Texas, yessir, and among all the Yanks
billeted on us that blue-sky summer
    (they had comics, saxophones, gum and tanks)

the kids' favourite. Until one morning
    they were gone, and the street was deserted:
of his platoon there was almost nothing
    left, except his baseball bat – not needed,

I guess, as Homer ended his Odyssey
on the beach called Omaha, Normandy.

Goronwy Rees
'This strange purgatory'

As he grew accustomed to his surroundings, Lipansky began to realise
that not all his companions were mere visitors to this strange purgatory.
The opposite side of the tunnel was occupied by a series of cubicles
constructed roughly out of lath and sacking. Across their entrances
hung blankets which half concealed the interior and hung open to form
a doorway. Inside were beds, chairs, tables, in some even carpets.
Photographs and pictures decorated the cloth partitions and created a
feeble illusion of comfort and permanence. Some of the owners of these
residences stood in their doorways and chatted to their neighbours, as if
they were at home in their own street. They regarded the mere visitors
standing or stretched in sleep on the ground with a certain contempt, as
men of property regard tramps and vagrants. They looked on them as
mere temporary visitors, the daily traffic of their busy street, whom it
was interesting to stand and watch on an idle evening. Not all of the permanent residents spent their time in idleness and gossip, in mere street
gazing. Some had gone to bed and lay huddled beneath their blankets
on their bunks ranged in series one above the other; in the cubicle opposite him Lipansky saw the huge naked arm and frowsy head of a
sleeping woman. In other cubicles animated games of twenty-one or
housey-housey were in progress, in some the occupants lay on their
beds and turned the pages of brightly covered magazines, *Fashion Show*,
Glamour, *Woman's World*. In one cubicle a schoolboy pored over a heavy
volume and tried to do his homework.

The scene had the quality of a dream or a nightmare. These people
resembled those troupes of rats one sometimes sees at country fairs,
who in miniature houses run up and down stairs, turn sewing
machines or spinning wheels, execute all kinds of miniature functions.
It was hard to believe they were not human, but even harder to believe
that they were. Lipansky watched with fascination. He had never seen
anything of the kind before. In war, fighting men form the aristocracy
of their time and are spared the squalor of life of the civilians who act
as mere hewers of wood and drawers of water. Lipansky could not
help wondering whether just the same scenes were being enacted now
in his own country. He was glad to watch and rest. He was beginning
to feel the strain of his escape and it seemed to him that for the
moment he was safer in the shelter than anywhere else. His head bent
forward on his knees he continued to observe the life of his subter-
ranean refuge. The only reminder of the raid that reached him was an

occasional shudder that ran through the brick wall of the tunnel. The shelter seemed to shake and tremble under a heavy blow from above. These intermittent tremors only emphasised how far he was removed from danger. They were like faint ripples of a disturbance that occurred thousands of miles away.

As time passed, the shelter began to acquire a cosy, almost domestic air, as if ghosts had managed to create a home for themselves. A faintly sour smell of unwashed bodies guaranteed that these people were human; otherwise they were mere shadows of men and women. Yet the lives of these shadows were full of ghastly and realistic detail; the broken doll lying under a bunk, the chamber-pot thrust into the corner of a room, the middle-aged man lying under the blankets fully dressed, his white collar and black tie protruding as he read *The Star*. Later, uniformed women came round distributing cups of tea; only the regular residents were served and this also increased the impression that the other fugitives had broken in to some highly select and exclusive club.

Lipansky did not dare ask for a cup of tea. He was afraid his accent would betray him; besides, he had no money to pay for one. This reminded him that he had not yet searched the pockets of the guard's uniform. In the trousers he found a few loose coins. The breast pocket of the tunic was stuffed with papers, an emergency ration card, pay book, a book of clothing coupons, a wallet bulging with photographs; in the back of the pay book he found three pound notes. Lipansky returned the papers to his pocket. He was no longer an outcast, he had suddenly acquired an identity and had become a person of substance. Above all, he had papers, and this gave him a right to exist. He began to consider his next move.

Silence had now mastered the tunnel. Those lying or sitting beside Lipansky had fallen asleep, or sat patiently waiting for the All Clear. Then suddenly a stir of animation returned; life flowed back into these catacombs. Scattered groups of young men and girls began to enter, cheaply yet smartly dressed, the young men in double-breasted suits and gaudy ties and pointed suede shoes, the girls in bright artificial silk frocks, barelegged, and with brightly coloured kerchiefs round their heads, under which their hair flowed in untidy tresses down to their shoulders. They were heavily made up, in a way that almost shocked Lipansky, their limbs tinkled with bangles and bracelets; as they walked daintily on their high-heeled shoes among the bodies stretched on the tunnel floor they gave out a warm scent half natural and half artificial that lingered heavily on the air when they had passed.

These newcomers evidently had their homes and families in the tunnel. They were part of the settled population, and they regarded the intruders with the disdain both of youth and of natives. At the door of their cubicles they parted, murmuring 'Goo'-night Bert,' 'Goo'-night Sylvie,' 'See you tomorrow, chum,' and greeted their recumbent families with sulky words of greeting. The presence of these young bodies in the now fetid air of the tunnel disturbed Lipansky, especially as now, without much care for discretion, they began to make themselves ready for bed. And like winged messengers of the gods, the newcomers brought news from the upper air. A girl lingered at the entrance of a cubicle near to Lipansky, chatting to her mother who lay in bed within.

'Alfie'll be in soon. 'E's taking Gertie 'ome. She wasn't 'alf in a state. Smashing film, though.'

'Did you 'ear the sireens?' said her mother.

'Raid was still on when we came down. They 'aven't 'alf dropped a bucketful tonight. There's fires all over the place.'

''Ope Alfie's all right,' said the mother.

'Don't you worry, Mum. Alfie'll be all right. You know Alfie. Shouldn't be surprised if 'e don't come 'ome before the raid's over.'

''E didn't ought to be out so late,' the mother said in a worried voice. ''E's out late every night these days. Must be after twelve.'

Lipansky stretched himself. He was stiff from having sat so long. He rose slowly to his feet, taking care not to disturb his neighbours, and made his way out of the tunnel. At the head of the steps to the station a policeman halted him.

'Shouldn't go out now, chum. Raid's still on. Hell of a mess up there.'

'Got to get back,' mumbled Lipansky, averting his face, and hurried past up the next flight of stairs into the railway station.

What he saw bewildered him. The huge arch of the roof had been shattered by fire bombs, and jagged edges of glass protruded from the iron framework against a rosy sky that seemed to pulse and throb like a huge heart. The clouds in the night sky were illumined by the beams of the searchlights and tinged with crimson and the great hollow space of the station itself was filled with a rosy glare. Broken glass crackled under his feet. Through the far end of the station he saw the sky aglow with the reflection of many fires. The station was deserted, apart from a few railway policemen and belated porters who stood apathetically waiting as if the last train had left and none would ever run again. For the first time since he had escaped Lipansky really breathed the air of liberty. It was as if the world were being born again out of flame and ruin, and in the sky blossomed the first red rose of a new dawn.

He walked boldly past the policeman at the station gates. There seemed no danger of anyone trying to detain him at such a moment as this when the whole world was coming to an end. Outside the station he entered on an even brighter day. The rosy light that had bathed the interior of the station, giving its smoke-grimed walls the flush of ancient brick and marble, here became a hard crimson glare, painful and dazzling, in which buildings stood out raw and clear against intense black shadows. In the street a huge cavern opened at his feet and from a broken gas main in its depths a pillar of soft blue flame shot up with a roaring sound. In the depths of the crater men naked to the waist were working desperately and vainly to repair the damage, and from a broken water main a gushing torrent of water poured into the darkness of the pit with a roaring sound. The street was empty. Opposite the station a building was on fire and those on either side showed fronts that were ripped and torn like paper. The road underfoot was rough with fallen masonry and broken glass.

Lipansky had lost his bearings. In the intense bright glare he saw two policemen who barred the entrance to the street. Lipansky skirted the edge of the crater and walked to the other end of the street. It stretched away in a long vista of brightly lit shop fronts and the blackest of black shadows, and over the buildings in the distance he saw framed in flame and crowned with an aureole of fleecy cloud a great shining dome that overhung the blazing city. He crossed the road and turned up a narrow side street. Here the buildings were crowded too closely together to admit the bright glare that illuminated the sky above. Here it was dark and, strangely, the street was not deserted and the darkness was alive with shadowy figures that appeared and disappeared in the entrances of the shops that lined the pavements. These furtive figures gave an air of intense and secret activity. Then Lipansky realised that the buildings which they were entering and leaving so hurriedly were deserted and empty, their doors standing open on shattered hinges and their windows empty of glass. Those who ran up and down the street clutched bundles of food, clothing, household ware, snatched from the shops. No one lingered for long or made any organised search. They made quick sudden dashes into a shop entrance and then as quickly disappeared into the darkness.

Lipansky quickly decided. He walked slowly up the street, staring into the shattered shop fronts until he came to what he wanted, a shabby second-hand shop with its front blown in, its windows empty, and its contents scattered in wild confusion on the floor. In the darkness at the back a figure was hastily searching in the confusion at his feet by the single beam of an electric torch. Lipansky began to retreat as the figure straightened itself, but it took no notice of him except to say:

'What cheer, chum. Help yourself, don't mind me,' and continued its search.

Furniture, picture frames, old clothes, children's toys, bedsteads were piled on top of each other. Lipansky searched until he found a pair of old trousers and a jacket, a flannel shirt and woollen jersey, a threadbare overcoat and a greasy felt hat. His search took him some time, as he stumbled among the wreckage. In the meanwhile his neighbour had completed his task and emerged from the back of the shop clutching what seemed to be a metal box.

'So long, chum,' he said. 'I'm off.' He shone his torch on Lipansky and saw his uniform.

'On the run, are you? You'd best be quick. The cops'll be about soon. Or the flaming N.F.S., the bastards.' With these words he disappeared.

As he left, Lipansky heard the throbbing of planes and the sound gave him comfort and relief. His friends were returning to complete their destruction and attack for a second time the huge target of the burning city. Until the attack was over he felt he was safe. He stumbled into the darkest corner of the shop and there changed his clothes. When he was ready he buried his discarded uniform under a pile of debris and destroyed the guard's papers except for the ration card and the three pound notes. His new clothes fitted him well. When he had turned up the collar of the overcoat and pulled the brim of the hat over his face he felt that he would not easily arouse suspicion. There was only one thing that still worried him. His boots were too large and would quickly rub his feet into blisters. On a long journey they would be a serious handicap. But they were thick and strong and he would not easily find anything better by searching here. The only boots he could find were too small, but he continued his search until at length he came upon several pairs of thick woollen socks that he thought would protect his feet. He stuffed them into his overcoat pocket and prepared to leave.

As he left, Lipansky heard the throbbing of planes circling overhead. The sound was quickly drowned by the clamour of gunfire. Lipansky still waited. He felt that dressed as he was now he might safely join the looters and marauders until he had provided himself with food for his journey. Yet he knew that so far he had been lucky, and it would not be wise to strain his luck too far. A bomb exploded nearby. The shop and the street trembled, shook, recovered their balance and settled down uncertainly on their foundations. The explosion rolling and reverberating in the night decided Lipansky. He guessed that this second attack would not last long. The raiders would unloose their bombs on the fires and get away as soon as they could. When they had gone the city even though in ruins would come to life again, reorganise itself, try to control the fires and heal its wounds. The welcome interval of lawlessness and chaos would be over, the shadows that preyed on destruction would return to their holes, people would hurry from the shelters to see what was left of their homes, and the military police would have time to think of catching an escaped prisoner. The breach in the framework of law and order through which Lipansky had crept would quickly be repaired. And it was getting late. In a few hours it would be light. By daybreak he must find a hiding-place, as far from here as possible. He had no time to wait any longer.

He left the shelter of the doorway and followed the dark street away from the station. He walked amid the thunderclaps of the guns, broken by heavy detonation of bombs. When he emerged from his narrow alley into a broad main street he was again plunged into a blaze of light, the false noonday of the raid. Opposite, a large building was blossoming into flame and firemen were cordoning off the street. He heard the bell of a fire engine rapidly approaching. Lipansky allowed himself to be shepherded to the corner of the street by a policeman, passed through the little group of officials watching the fire and setting his face north began to walk at a steady pace away from the burning city.

Harri Webb
On Convoy

Over the Mediterranean light is failing
the soft grey sea heaves furrows long and slow
through the half-night the brave young stars are sailing
as over star-towed evenings long ago

whose wake still spreads a gentle perturbation
like the curved wave-scarp crumbling astern
among the tethered fleets of contemplation
forgotten in the roads of no return.

Square stubborn slow deep-laden moves the convoy
it will make port if we are strong and keen
yet who can stem the blurring waves of envy
for careless voyages that might have been

whose gilded hulks were stranded on the beaches
when gay brocaded tides were gathered in
baring the evil slime of muddy reaches
the face of truth upstaring with a grin.

Best to forget the plans for summer cruises
on darker deeper waters life now sails
forget the girls the minstrels and the muses
our useless sighs are swept away by gales.

This is the hard road all the world has travelled
and there is no escape among the stars
thought must not stray eyes must be ready levelled
we must stand steady when the gunblast jars.

We will go home the last squat tramp unloaded
if we go home and walk along the strand
by rotted planks and iron bolts corroded
fast fettered in the pale and jealous sand.

Offshore perhaps the galleons of illusion
spread their white sails a wanton seabreeze fills
but no more voyaging nor sea's confusion
for them that turn their eyes towards the hills.

There where the spent gales whisper in the grasses
with plains and tides one far blue dream of youth
where eagle screams ring down the empty passes
to rest at last and say, We once faced truth.

John Ormond
'The city split in two'

By the city, the mask of the city in snow,
By the city in fire, the city split in two,
Between the elements,
Between the snow and the fire I went,
Between her midnight and my own;
Where the town was taken and destroyed
And where the town still stood
In corridors of two ways of light
In streets where the red world met the white
I walked away from her death in the middle grove
Between my fear and my love.

Here buildings flowered red upon the air
And here a street, inaccurate and pale,
Lit but unconquered by the flame;
And here the fire burst tall
And there the snow furred on a wall;
Between two seasons of the soul,
One in its roaring end, the other asleep and slow,
I walked and watched the terror leap
But fail to destroy the further snow.

And as I turned to the only way to the sea
I passed where fire had had its way
And saw such faceless figures stalk,
The lost in blood, the torn, the terrible walkers
Seeking impossible safety blindly
Lost in the heart of the fire's fringe;
And from them stepped unscathed and strange,
One man living among the living dead;
And there he followed me,
There where I fell, he leapt, moved easily.

I waited for him. Here was one, I thought,
Who knew this part of what had been the city
Well, and would lead me
By some passageway underground.
But when I stopped and signed
To call him to come on
There as a roof and a wall tumbled red
Petals of fire like a rose,
Motionless he stayed under it, and did not move
Until I moved again, and then he followed on:

Through the arcaded gardens of inferno,
The narrow avenues, the mazes
Peopled by dead,
Their arms outstretched to embrace the fire,
The dead struck kneeling in homage
At the cry, the words of the giver of peace,
The dead as in stone but moaning in their age,
The children dead where the windows fell
To the familiar street
As if they had gladly watched the snow

Then suddenly were wise,
The white dust of the world upon their eyes.

And once I saw his shape
Stoop where a child lay beautiful and dead,
A golden-headed girl. He touched her head,
Lifted her up and laid her where
Fire left an alcove.
Then he came on
But would not walk with me
Though I beckoned again
And he coming ever nearer
Pointed on still
Until I saw his meaning
– Safety in separation from each other
Under the buildings' fire-drunk leaning
And falling, the steel veins bending
And falling under the unending wind of fire
Scattering the sky's broad arch of blazing snow.

And when at the edge of the town
He came towards the sea
Again the vortex snow spun endlessly
Over the shore, puffed up and winnowed down,
White poplar leaves blown red
Away from the angry breath
But still in the dome of fire.
The shuttling threads of snow worked in the air
To a hanging pattern of blood.
I waited for him, but he had disappeared.

Glad then to be alone
I started on the arc of the bay
For at the end there lay
The inland road to the hills,
Until I saw him come
Walking the lit waves
Near the shore
With his limbs in flame,
Leading three children,
Naked each one for the whip of spray.

As they came near I ran
And saw him leave them sink to drown
Washed by the tide and the bloody foam.
He waded to the sands
Ahead of me, and with fiery hands held out
Waited to greet me.

This man I saw with the bright body,
Had darkness in the holes that were his eyes.

Vernon Watkins
Sonnet of the Death of Alun Lewis

He was astonished by the abundance of gold
Light. In the street a beggar stretched her hand,
Dying. Then the shudder ran through him. Once he had
planned
To out-distance the sun in a chariot. But how might he hold
That instant, those uncurbed horses, and mix the mould
Her liquid shadow near the lotus and timeless sand?
A slighter man would have noticed the ripples expand
From the stark, regenerate symbol. But to him that cold
Figure was real. Ah yes, he died in the green
Tree. What was it, then, pierced him, keen as a thorn,
And left him articulate, humble, unable to scorn
A single soul found on Earth? O, had he seen
In a flash, all India laid like Antony's queen,
Or seen the highest, for which alone we are born?

Alun Lewis
The Earth is a Syllable

'What I say is, if you're in trouble, take it easy,' the ambulance driver
said. 'Always have done. Once I got a girl in trouble and I wasn't going
to get grey hairs over that. And now I've bust the gasket and she won't
budge and maybe the Jap is nearer than our own boys, but there you
are, you're no better off if your nose bleeds, are you now?'

He'd often thought he'd die; it was a familiar idea; why shouldn't he, if there's a war on and you're young and you try to be in it, some-where? It had taken him a long time to succeed. He'd got into the army easy enough, but the war seemed to elude him all the time. If he was in England it would be in France in hot summer weather and he'd be eating Wall's ice cream outside the barracks. If he was in India it would be in Egypt and he'd think of the Eighth Army glowing in the desert, attracting him like a moth to its fiery circle. He used to fancy himself flying there like a queen ant on her nuptial flight and shedding his wings when he alighted, and going to ground there. And now that he *had* caught up with it, here in Burma, well, it hadn't been much of a show. But he'd never liked the idea of Burma. He'd always known he'd die if he caught up with it in Burma.

'Can't you stop tossing and kicking those blankets?' the ambulance driver said. 'Wear yourself out quicker like that. Take it easy, I say. I've been in some bad spots off and on. Narvik for a kick-off, and Crete for a birthday, and a bloody narrow escape from going into Libya with Ritchie; thought I was lucky once, being sent out here instead. But I reckon it's all the same where I go. There's sure to be a war there.' He spoke very mournfully, a sort of thoughtful incantation. 'I've had more crump than crumpet this war. That's why I take it easy, mate. You got to last a long time, you know. A long time.'

The driver had given up trying to repair the damage to the cylinder head of his 15-cwt. Bedford; the tropical heat and the dust of the bumpy track that cavorted through the misleading jungle had dried up his water and blown the gasket. It was useless. They were on their way to the ren-dezvous where the wounded from the advanced dressing-stations were handed over to the main dressing-station ambulances. To-morrow they'd have to find out where the new rendezvous was; it changed daily, same as everything else changed daily; the situation was very confused, the Japs were said to have worked right round their left flank somewhere up the Sittang, and to have landed above Rangoon. To-morrow they'd have to find out where the new rendezvous was, if it still mattered.

He was lying on a stretcher in the back of the truck and it was a bit awkward because the truck tilted steeply, one side in the ditch so as to let the traffic pass up the track to the front, what front there was. The rear flaps were strapped up to give him some air and he could see the darkness of the jungle encircling them. It was dark and soft like a mass of congealed blood. If you put your hand in it, it would give like a sponge. If the Japs were there they'd be sleeping. They had to sleep. Or a snake or a tiger would get them, they weren't all that clever. Any case you could hear them if they were there, calling each other like owls, because they were lonely, maybe. And the jungle was utterly silent, dark and shimmering with darkness like ebony, and malevolent. And he was quite at peace. He'd been more nervous in India than he was here. It was lonely in India, no friendship there, nor any active hostility to brace you. Just loneliness and strangeness. It wasn't dangerous there: just nerves, that's all. You couldn't walk into a native village and have a good time there like you wanted to. QUIT INDIA they painted on the walls. Quit India, the silly fools. How can we? India is part of the world. It's the world we can't quit. No, it was just nerves in India. Riding back to camp after the pictures in a trotting tonga with bells tinkling on the skinny mare's neck, it was so dark it was like riding to your death. Just nerves. Here he was quite peaceful.

There was a sudden murmur in the jungle, a sigh, a growing perturbance. Dust. The wind puffed up with a hot dry sigh and the dust came riding in on them in a thick irritating column, into their eyes and mouths, making them swear, sweat and blink and extinguishing the petrol cooker on which the driver was brewing some char. His own lamp spat a high flame and cracked the glass and then subsided. He didn't move. He liked the dust storms by day, the whirling cylinder of tall red dust moving across the plain, the moving red towers that touched the blue sky. He didn't like it at night so much; now when he put his hand over his face his skin was dry and dusty like a statue in a dilapidated museum, like an embalming. The blanket was filthy, it set the skin of his fingers on edge, and he saw with sudden distaste that it was covered with hairs and dandruff under his cheek. It made him think of his wife, she'd written to say he'd left some hairs on his pillows the time he was on embarkation leave and she felt terribly cruel to shake them off, she said. But she was so beautiful and fresh always and the house always so clean and simple, with the sun or the snow always lighting it. She wouldn't like this dust.

'Well, we'll have to go without a cup of you an' me,' the driver said, grinning and sweating as he leaned over the tailboard to stow the cooker away. ''Tisn't the first thing I've done without by a long chalk. Christ, I've been without work before now. That's a real nasty thing; being without work. I don't suppose you've been without work, chum, being an officer?'

His mouth was bitter and dry and it hurt him when he smiled. It was the lump the shrapnel had taken out of his throat that was hurting now when he smiled. Life had been pretty heartless off and on, but you usually got a laugh out of it. When he'd written three novels one after the other and failed to sell any of them, and gone round to an agency for a job and the old clerk asked him if he could type and he said, 'Two fingers only,' and the clerk said, 'No good,' and he went to sea then as a trimmer. He'd never thought of dying in those days, though, it didn't seem a physical fact at all. Just something you wrote and theorised about. Not like this.

'Speaking for myself,' said the driver, 'I've found it a bloody sight easier with a war on. You don't have to bother now. It's all buttoned up. Food and clothes and dentists, trucks to drive, loads to carry, allowances for the missus. It's all laid on for you now. You don't have to bother.'

Yes, he thought, it's been pretty easy. You sink your scruples in conscription, and then there's always something interesting if you take the trouble of finding it. Infantry schemes, sleeping under hedges, swimming a river in full kit, being hungry, talking to a stranger. And since his regiment had been mechanised the tanks had him by the hair – the iron maidens – he'd never tire of pulling on the tiller bar and stamping on the clutch and pulling like hell on the gear lever and the thrill as she surged softly forward, grunting peacefully and bellying over a slope so sweet and easy. And the big 75 mm gun and the voices of your friends in your headsets coming over the air. And the queer consolation of the other things he'd tried and written off for failures and now recalled – the little meetings he'd tried to run, debates round a hurricane lamp on the FUTURE, talks he'd carefully put together on RECONSTRUC-TION, gramophone records he'd borrowed and played for the lads, the choir he'd tried to make something good of; naturally it was no good for a few odd men to sit round and discuss how to prevent another war, naturally they couldn't 'succeed'. Still, it was all right to remember it.

No. The terrible struggles had been quieter and less obvious than voyages and armoured regiments. They were just something inside you – simply whether to say Yes or No to a thing – to chastity or pity or love or drink with another man's wife. Maybe if you could avoid saying Yes or No to Life, and yet be free, you'd be stronger, better? Would you? How did the dust columns form? What did the Upanishads say? The Earth is a syllable.

'I'm turning in, mate,' the driver said. 'There ain't nothing I can do till a truck comes along. Get you back, then, if a truck comes along. It's so bleeding quiet in these parts, that's what I don't like. Makes you think we missed the road back somewhere, or missed the war or summat. I never did like the quiet. Give me a pub that can sell its liquor, not keep it. Give me a call if your pains come back, chum, though there ain't nothing I can do. Jesus, I'm tired. Goodnight, cocky.'

He stumped up the road a few yards to where he'd slung his mosquito net among the bushes. He sighed aloud as he pulled each boot off.

Now he was left alone and whatever he had he was alone with it. It was all right, as long as he was alone. Whatever he had he could manage it now. His lamp still burned calmly and it might last an hour yet. He didn't want the dark to come any nearer. He could see exactly where it started, just this side of his feet. And then it went on and on. The dawn is the head of a horse. He lay quietly among the crickets and the darkness and the moths came suddenly tilting head on against his lamp and righted themselves on his face, and flew on again. It was very still, except for the pain. There was a translucent golden influence at the core of his being. He could see his wife. She'd wanted a child before he left England, but it hadn't turned out that way. And now in a way he was glad. There was only her left, besides himself. She would understand. He'd tried bloody hard; he'd roughed it and now he was cut up a lot and he could smell the poison where his left shoulder and arm had been. But there was still her little house. That was all. He didn't want to go to Burma; he knew it would be a bad place for him. But all striving is a blind guess, and he wasn't in Burma now, he was in the night, in the common ground of humanity, and he wasn't alone now.

He wanted to get up and enter the darkness and enter the silent village under the hill and enter it with his wife alone. Not in a tank, for that was a schoolboy's thrill, nor in Burma, because it was a bad place for him. So he pushed himself up on his spare arm and sweated all over; Judas! it hurt. But he hated the dirt and hair on his blanket, and being hot in bed and he wanted to have this little walk.

So he went across the plain in the night and the darkness was hot and tepid and after a while he didn't know where the hell he was; but he knew he was all right; and he loved her so much that he knew he could throw the darkness over the hill.

The driver found him five yards away from the truck.

Alun Lewis
Burma Casualty
To Capt. G. T. Morris, Indian Army

I

Three endless weeks of sniping all the way,
Lying up when their signals rang too close,
– 'Ooeee, Ooee,' like owls, the lynx-eyed Jap, –
Sleeplessly watching, knifing, falling back.
And now the Sittang river was there at last
And the shambles of trucks and corpses round the bridge
And the bridge was blown. And he laughed.

And then a cough of bullets, a dusty cough

Filleted all his thigh from knee to groin.
The kick of it sucked his face into the wound.
He crumpled, thinking 'Death'. But no, not yet.
The femoral artery wasn't touched.
Great velour cloaks of darkness floated up.
But he refused, refused the encircling dark,
A lump of bitter gristle that refused.
The day grew bloodshot as they picked him up.

II

Lying in hospital he often thought
Of that darkness, whence it came
And how it played the enchantress in a grain
Of morphia or a nodding of the head
Late in the night and offered to release
The Beast that breathed with pain and ran with pus
Among the jumping fibres of the flesh.
And then he saw the Padre by his cot
With the Last Unction: and he started up.

III

'Your leg must go. Okay?' the surgeon said
'Take it' he said. 'I hate the bloody thing.'
Yet he was terrified – not of the knives
Nor loosing that green leg (he'd often wished
He'd had a gun to shoot the damned thing off)
But of the darkness that he knew would come
And bid him enter its deep gates alone.
The nurse would help him and the orderlies.
But did they know? And could a rubber tube
Suck all that darkness out of lungs and heart?
'Open and close your fist – slowly,' the doctor said.
He did so, lying still upon his back.
The whitewashed walls, the windows bright with sky
Gathered a brilliant light above his head.
Here was the light, the promise hard and pure,
His wife's sweet body and her wilful eyes.
Her timeless love stooped down to raise him up.
He felt the white walls part – the needle pricked,
'Ten seconds and you'll fade', the doctor said.
He lay and looked into the snowwhite skies
For all ten seconds means at such a time.

150

Then through the warped interstices of life
The darkness swept like water through a boat
In gouts and waves of softness, claiming him ...
He went alone: knew nothing: and returned
Retching and blind with pain, and yet Alive.

IV

Mending, with books and papers and a fan
Sunlight on parquet floors and bowls of flame
He heard quite casually that his friends were dead,
His regiment too butchered to reform.
And he lay in the lightness of the ward
Thinking of all the lads the dark enfolds
So secretly.
         And yet a man may walk
Into and through it, and return alive.
Why had his friends all stayed there, then?
He knew.
The dark is a beautiful singing sexless angel
Her hands so soft you scarcely feel her touch
Gentle, eternally gentle, round your heart.
She flatters and unsexes every man.

And Life is only a crude, pigheaded churl
Frowsy and starving, daring to suffer alone.

Alun Lewis
'The duties of the evening'

The colonel looked into the first Nissen hut.

'These bricks round the fireplace,' he said. 'I sent an order to all detachments that they be whitewashed. Why haven't you done it?'

'No whitewash, sir.'

'Get some. Christ. What are you here for?'

He picked up a pair of boots from one of the men's beds.

'These boots. Burnt. Look at the soles. Burnt through. Drying them by the fire. Is this man on a charge?'

'Er, no, sir.'

'Why the hell not? Nation can't afford to waste boots every time they get wet. Christ. Send him to me to-morrow under escort.'

'Yes, sir. I don't believe they are burnt, sir. The man has been waiting for a boot exchange for five weeks. He's worn them out –'

'I tell you they're burnt. Christ man, you're not a cobbler, are you?'

'No sir.'

'Then talk about something you know.'

By the time the old man drove off Captain Cochrane was utterly emasculate. He saluted with so pathetic and servile a gesture that the colonel didn't even return the salute. And so his day ended. The duties of the evening confronted him. Dinner in mess, then dance attendance on the old man's daughter. Poleworth was the name. Less respectfully, when the subalterns were hidden away in a pub, the name was sometimes garbled to Polecat. She certainly had a pungent odour. Still, hardy men said she was a good sport. She liked to play, they hinted, twisting the yellow ends of their moustaches. Captain Cochrane emptied his whiskey flask before deciding on his tactical plan. Marvellous thing, whiskey.

Curly took a walk after drinking his mug of tea and eating a piece of bread and marge and a Lyons' fruit pie. He didn't wash or brass up. He wasn't going to town. He wanted some peace of mind, along the sand dunes running from the harbour to the boarding house promenade where the ferro-concrete seaside resort began. Faintly, as though his tedious preoccupations had taken a musical form, the distant sound of hurdy-gurdy jazz songs blaring in the fun-fair touched his quietness, accompanying him unobtrusively as he climbed the loose sand. Thinking of the industry of pleasure he watched the sea, fuming like a thin grey smoke far far out beyond the mudflats, and it seemed as though the purpose of the town had been lost, the balance between sea and land ruined, the fundamental element forgotten. Pleasure had broken away from simplicity, the penny-in-the-slot machine had conquered the sea, people had turned their backs and were screaming with laughter. Watching the sea fuming and grey he found himself suddenly investing the solitary person walking slowly and with downcast head across the wet wormcast mud with all the attributes which humanity, he decided this evening, had rejected. He wanted to speak to this lonely person; it was a woman; heavy she was; heavy with the rejected attributes of humanity; pregnant she must be, and pale with a serious beauty, bearing so much in her.

Following his fantasy, he walked down from the dunes and across the slimy front towards the girl. He walked quickly, keeping his attention on her, refusing to allow the usual inhibitions to stop him accosting her.

Eva felt no particular strangeness at his approach. A little soldier with spectacles and curly hair like a wire brush. It was quite natural. She said good evening. She was glad he had come.

'I was standing on the dunes,' he said. 'And there was nobody but you anywhere at all. And so you became important to me, so that I came to ask you something.'

'Don't ask me anything,' she said.

'No, I don't want to,' he said thoughtfully.

'Will you take me back to the land?' she said, looking at him, holding her hand out to him uncertainly.

Her face was as he had imagined it, young and hollow, large hollow-eyed, luminous and vague with distress.

He took her cold hand and led her back to the firm land, the grass and rocks and walls and telegraph poles and houses. In silence.

'Have you ever tried to die?' she asked.

'Yes,' he said.

'What shall I do now, then?' she asked again.

'Walk,' he said. 'Pick a flower. Hurt your shin against a rock. Keep doing things like that for a bit. Do you like coffee?'

'Yes,' she said, thinking back to the taste of such things. 'Yes. I like coffee.'

'Shall we go and have some, and some chocolate biscuits, in the Marina?' he asked.

'Yes,' she said, very seriously. 'That would be nice.'

She looked at the people having coffee and peach melbas and spaghetti on toast at the little green tables, soldiers and girls, commercial men, ponderous wives on holiday with children past their bedtime. The waitresses rustling and slender and deft, rotund and homely and competent; the warm shaded lights falling on the flowery wallpaper. The strangeness and the fear gradually left her eyes like sugar melting in a lemon glass. She tasted the hot coffee slowly, and its warmth led her to smile.

'Why do you look so serious?' she asked Curly.

He looked at her all the time. She could see the gathering of his thoughts in the dark blue eyes magnified and concentrated by the curved lenses of his spectacles.

'Funny, you having blue eyes,' she said.

Looking at each other over the wispy coffee steam, each wanted to be confessed in the other, each desired to share a new yet ancient community of interest. Neither of them could think now of how different they were, the one from the other, how insulated by separate compulsions and circumstances.

'I live near here. Shall we go and sit by the fire?' she asked.

'I'd like to,' he answered ...

'It's only an electric fire,' she said, as he opened the glass door for her.

There were two photographs on the mantelpiece of her little bed-sitter. Curly noticed they were both men in uniform. Brothers? Or lovers? Also a sewing machine and dresses half finished. A reading lamp and *Picture Post* and *Lilliput* and a *Sunday Pictorial*.

'I haven't got a shilling for the meter,' she said.

He produced one.

'You're very good,' she said to him, putting the shilling in the slot, bending down as she spoke. 'You stopped me committing suicide and now you've given me food and money and – and what else?'

'What else?' he repeated, his sensitive mind crushed by the sledge-hammer blow of her casual confession.

'I don't know,' she said, standing up and smoothing her navy skirt down, picking bits of fluff off her knees. 'I don't know what I'm talking about.'

Her sick soul was in her eyes.

He stayed with her till late in the night, putting another shilling in the meter, going and queuing outside the chip-shop for some fish cakes for their supper while she set the little table and boiled the kettle and cut some bread and butter.

Tony Curtis
Incident on a Hospital Train from Calcutta, 1944

At a water-stop three hours out
the dry wail of brakes ground us down
from constant jolting pain to an oven
heat that filled with moans and shouts
from wards the length of six carriages.

We had pulled slowly up towards the summer
hills for coolness. They were hours distant,
hazy and vague. I opened the grimy
window to a rush of heat
and, wrapped in sacking, a baby

held up like some cooked offering from its mother –
Memsahib ... meri buchee ko bachalo ... Memsahib take –
pushed like an unlooked-for gift into my arms.
She turned into the smoke and steam.

I never saw her face.
As we lumbered off I unwrapped
a dirty, days-old girl, too weak for cries.
Her bird weight and fever-filled eyes
already put her out of our reach. By Murree Junction
that child would have emptied half our beds.

At the next water-stop my nurses left her.
The corporal whose arms had gone looked up at me
and said, 'There was nothing else to do.'
Gangrenous, he died at Murree a week later.
His eyes, I remember, were clear, deep and blue.

Gweno Lewis
'A regular camp-follower'

At the end of the rambling genesis of the poem 'Infantry' written in
December 1941 when Alun was getting used to being 2nd Lieut. A.
Lewis, 6th S.W.B., I found these lines of exorcism again:

> Today doesn't matter at all I should not break
> My heart with the nothingness of today.
> Blisters and early cold route march on frozen road
> The [illegible word] steaming on the beet fields, the
>   labourers in black
> The patience, sulkiness or rage of men
> The quietness of my gloom, not attending
> Upon the province of official tasks
> And talk and conference and tea.
> Yet all today I have been vulnerable
> And would have died quite easily,
> If my strange enemy had come.

I became a regular camp-follower during my holidays and at Easter
the Borderers moved to Felixstowe. The depression persisted and felt
like a weight dragging us down. I had to return to school and at the
station we wept as we held each other, he because he couldn't help
himself and I, because I couldn't help him. The battalion at this time
became a tank regiment and Alun, along with several other colleagues,
spent the summer term at a tank school at Bovington. And he began
to recover. Every week-end was free as there were no regimental duties
and there followed the long summer holidays at Southend (Sarthend
– as we used to say) and life went on for us in a state of deep and

abiding happiness. His strange enemy had withdrawn and he was safe again. He remained very well for the next twelve months.

Whenever possible most civilians had to undertake some form of war work and I used to do two shifts a week at the Control Centre at Mountain Ash, manning the telephones. So Alun always knew where to contact me. It was getting late one Saturday night when I felt sure the Borderers had already sailed for India. I knew Alun was one of the advance baggage party but when their actual departure was to be I had no idea. Then Alun rang up giving me a code name and the times of trains I was to catch immediately. I couldn't believe it! My colleagues on the shift emptied their pockets of all their spare cash, as I was totally unprepared for a journey, raced up the hill to get a few things and explain to the long-suffering Bombo that once more he must depend on my kind neighbours' charity and I was off, rattling through the night. Alun appeared at lunchtime the next day. I was just emerging from our room when he leapt up the stairs two at time, flung his cap, gloves and stick all over the place and we did our ritual war dance all round the room, which meant that we had managed yet again to defy time and the army.

After lunch we made our way to the Philharmonic Hall where Cyril Smith played Brahms' piano concerto; and the music stayed with us as we returned through the drizzle of this grey town to tea and margarine on toast. The blazing fire in the lounge was completely barred to us by the sleeping forms of commercial travellers. While we consumed our dismal tea, Alun stealthily appropriated the Sunday papers scattered around the floor and we were soon absorbed in their contents. When dinner was over we retired early as Alun wanted a leisurely hot bath in fresh water – the last he was to have for some time. He had a very bad cold and had had to be treated for a very heavy nose bleed which had lasted the whole of the previous day. He had given instructions at the desk for a 5.30am call and breakfast. At 3.30am I woke and looked at my watch and leaned over him studying his face as he slept. His sleep was deep and peaceful and there was something so angelic, so ineffable there, I felt my heart would break. I studied his high smooth forehead and the soft dark hair, his dark fringed deep set eyes and the little lines that ran away from them, deepening when he laughed and the hazel eyes disappeared altogether. The fine skin above the beard line was slightly flushed with fever; and his dear mouth still bore a scar from some game of hockey long ago. I prayed for the safe return of my dainty duck, my dearest dear, and, fearing to wake him, I switched off the bedside light and snuggled close. And suddenly, in the bright glare of the centre light stood the night porter. 'Five thirty, sir, breakfast is served in the dining room.' When Alun returned he hugged me tightly and we stared long and hard at each other as he left the room, stepping backwards. He saluted in the doorway and was gone. An overwhelming desire to howl welled up inside me and my throat contracted painfully. I groped for a handkerchief under the pillow and stuffed it into my mouth. It was his handkerchief I found and stained with blood. I cherished it as one would cherish a sacred relic.

When I checked out of the hotel later the clerk asked for my husband's food voucher. He had taken it with him by mistake. 'And how do I know he won't use it again?' she snapped. I nearly snapped back telling her why he wouldn't be likely to, when I remembered that 'careless talk costs lives,' and left.

The train home trundled down the Welsh Marches. It was a lovely autumn day and as we passed through the cutting approaching Abergavenny I went to the window and looked up, remembering, and miserably pondered on the hazards of separation and war.

Alun Lewis
Letter to Gweno Lewis, 30ᵗʰ September 1943

6ᵗʰ Batt. S.W.B.
September 30

It's hot and wet tonight buzzing with mosquitoes: and I know you won't have heard from me for ages and will be upset about my silence again. So I'm telling you that this is your odd husband, sweating and bug-ridden and brushing buzzing mosquitoes from his ears by his hurricane lamp among the mountains again. I'm sorry, Gweno, you had to go and marry me. It would have been so much simpler if you'd been charmed away by a fireside faun with a job of national importance such as doing statistical research or editing a literary magazine. Anyone rather than me, for I'm just some animation the world has set flowing and compelled to develop into and out of itself. I learn new things everywhere, all the time; new things form in me and bud and flower and flow out over the streets and deserts and roofs and fishing boats and beggars and poems I encounter or rather find myself amongst. And I know they are necessary and vivid, all these things, and they do something to me and in a deep unchained way I belong to them and see with their eyes and nerves. And also in a queer unchained way, I've made my peace with life and am willing to go on into and through and beyond. The only thing that prevents me is my body, which grows tired, and my mind which grows dull, and my heart which has a grief and a love that these things, these perpetual heres and nows do not permit to exceed them. And it gets conscribed and crowded – but there, someone has come into my tent and is prattling about battalion affairs and jealousies and itches – so I must stop.

Later.

And here I am, I keep saying to myself. After so much travel and motion, here I am. I feel uncertain about here. It was a tremendous emotional tug, a crying loyalty to the Welsh soldiers when I was away. I refused that job which meant 900 rupees a month and a real mental and physical challenge, because I wanted to be back with these boys. And now I'm here, I feel that it was sentiment and selfishness. They are lovely. Tonight, after playing soccer, I was having a bath in the straw sheds of the showers. There was a resplendent yellow sunset with a great rainbow flung over the sky; and a boy was singing beautifully as the water splashed over him. I couldn't see him, but only hear his voice.

And yet I want to be away, too. It's time I took a harder job in a way. Yet I'm frightened of leaving them. They seem to have some secret knowledge that I want and will never find out until I go into action with them and war really happens to them. I dread missing such a thing; it seems desertion to something more than either me or them. When I was leaving Karachi, one of the instructors said to me, 'You're the most selfish man I've ever met, Lewis. You think the war exists for you to write books about it.' I didn't deny it, though it's all wrong. I hadn't the strength to explain what is instinctive and categorical in me, the need to experience. The writing is only proof of the sincerity of the experience, that's all.

And the country is so beautiful now, the rich crops and the long fields of yellow sunflowers and red currant flowers and the peasants look so fertile, too. The rains make the burning cruel earth into a green gentleness of fruit and leaf. Soon it will all dry up again. I dread the long merciless months ahead.

Alun Lewis
Letter to Robert Graves, 6ᵗʰ May 1943

214565 Lieut. Alun Lewis,
6th Bn, South Wales Borderers,
India Command.

May 6ᵗʰ, 1943.

Dear Robert Graves,

Now that I'm actually writing this letter card I'm damned if I know how to start. You see I've got a very considerable request to make, and I never succeed in throwing myself easily upon another's charity. Still I think you'll be willing to help me. There's nobody else I want to ask.

It's about poetry. I've had a phase that, impersonally, I see is alarmingly prolific, and I've been sending poem after poem back to my wife ever since the ship swung into the stream. The obvious conclusion is that the poetry is bad: but because the impulse has been steadily serious and unambiguous, I think that some poems *may* be worth their weight in words. My publishers wouldn't discriminate: all they ask for is another volume: but I know very well that my own name (which, in a way, I care for) will be valued by the quality of the next collection I publish. Which is why I'm writing to ask you if you have either the time or the interest to read the bundle and advise my wife. For myself I can't judge: sometimes they seem to have some salt in them, othertimes they're as flat and insipid as the water at this camp. I would be *honoured* if you will consider my worth, nor will I be at all distressed if you find me wanting. There is such a leaven of naturally frustrated love and anxiety in me that I can't expect my poems to be 'pure'. And yet I do hear the only real music, sometimes, and try to write as I hear. We were camped for two months up in the Mahratta hills, beside a massive dam that held six miles of blue water, under a hill fort of great antiquity and splendour. My tent was by the lake; and at night there was nothing at all in the world but the great boulders of unhewn poetry to strive with. Before that I was in hospital with a broken jaw & dysentry and there too an occasional mistral or a dose of chloroform made one obstinate and heady, and resulted in some words. It is easy to write prose in India, there is so much to satirise or hate or shrug one's shoulders at. But poetry is harder to command, mainly I think because everything is somehow remorseless here, arid, pellucid and incurable. Politics at home is an inviting dance because things are more plastic and organic. Here I eschew them entirely, and have no sympathies with either side. The peasant remains, and it's in the villages that I've found what I'm always seeking. One morning I woke up just outside a remote hill village which I'd reached after dark the previous night on a reconnaissance. I was making for some battalion exercises. I woke lying on some tilled red earth. There was a zareba of dead thorns filled with lambs, a tree like a goblet with hay drying in the branches, a party of silent peasants walking barefooted across the valley, women returning with pitchers on their head, and the dawn grey on a precipitous steep, and over all a most innocent and empty sky. I had the queer certitude that I was waking in heaven. Not the heaven that doesn't exist, but the heaven of the peasant's mind, where all is silent and normal and tranquil, and the newcomer wakes and stretches his limbs and is neither questioned nor shunned, but tacitly allowed to become familiar with the simple continuity that exists. All of which is very reactionary: but it is there I find the poetry. The rest is all business. Particularly the Army.

We're in the whirl of big goings-on these days & have been ruthlessly handled. We were instructed without warning to hand in our tanks and train for a new role as infantry again. And we are doing so with a vengeance. The heat is the hardest to master. I've been on the coast for the last week; desultory palms & tepid water, bad food and decayed bungalows; and the Anglo-Indian horrors of Bombay available on Sundays from reveille to 2359 hrs. If you will read my poems, say in the late summer, (they won't be all in England before then) I may not be in a position to read your judgment, but my wife will stand by your advice in such a case. Her address is: Mrs Gweno Menerid Lewis, Bryngwyn, Aberffrwd Rd, Mountain Ash, Glamorgan. And that is the end of my space.

Yours very sincerely & unequivocally,
Alun Lewis.

Alun Lewis
Goodbye

So we must say Goodbye, my darling,
And go, as lovers go, for ever;
Tonight remains, to pack and fix on labels
And make an end of lying down together.

I put a final shilling in the gas,
And watch you slip your dress below your knees
And lie so still I hear your rustling comb
Modulate the autumn in the trees.

And all the countless things I shall remember
Lay mummy-cloths of silence round my head;
I fill the carafe with a drink of water;
You say 'We paid a guinea for this bed,'

And then, 'We'll leave some gas, a little warmth
For the next resident, and these dry flowers,'
And turn your face away, afraid to speak
The big word, that Eternity is ours.

Your kisses close my eyes and yet you stare
As though God struck a child with nameless fears;
Perhaps the water glitters and discloses
Time's chalice and its limpid useless tears.

Everything we renounce except our selves;
Selfishness is the last of all to go;
Our sighs are exhalations of the earth,
Our footprints leave a track across the snow.

We made the universe to be our home,
Our nostrils took the wind to be our breath,
Our hearts are massive towers of delight,
We stride across the seven seas of death.

Yet when all's done you'll keep the emerald
I placed upon your finger in the street;
And I will keep the patches that you sewed
On my old battledress tonight, my sweet.

Caradoc Evans
'Hitler in Aberystwyth'

God never meant me to live in the country. Here you see the same persons every day. You hear the same war grumbles although the war has not touched the farmers except to put more money in their pockets and exempt their sons. One never hears a word about the sacrifices of other people. The war is being fought for certain persons who are not in it, for certain persons who truly believe that their flesh is more precious than the flesh of the fighter, that the fighting men were born to hew a path for them ...

I do not know why I am alive. But of course no one knows that. But why am I on earth when so many very useful men are being removed?

The servant here, a German Jewess refugee, went for a walk yesterday and she met a man. The man said to her: 'I have five cows, seven pigs, and so on. Will you marry me? Let me know next Sunday. You will know me by my dog.'

Last Sunday afternoon preacher Methodist said: 'If you are sleepy, people, sleep. If I was not here very likely and most probably I would be in a big chair sleeping. Sleep, people. I will not say anything to startle you awake.'

Mrs Pugh who keeps the pub brings you your beer, takes your money, finds the key of her cash drawer, unlocks it, gives you the change, locks the drawer, and hides the key. Buying a beer is a long ceremony. By the time she has locked the drawer you call for more beer. Mrs Pugh is 83. Yesterday she spent in bed very weak and without appetite. The weakness must have come upon her suddenly. One day last week she was giving me her views on Capel Horeb and some of Horeb's members, especially Horeb's big heads. She hates Horeb. 'Church am I, Mr Evans bach. Capel and beer do not mix ...'

The favourite broadcaster is Winston Churchill. He was favourite even when Chamberlain was P.M. We like him because he casts out devils with energy and vigour. We like him for his sound English; every Welshman knows good English and likes it. When an eloquential preacher denounces sinners we are glad we are not sinners. When Winston Churchill denounces Germans we are glad we are not Germans. Faint hearts he strengthens and the timid man he makes into a warrior ...

I rise at about 7.30. I have my bath and dress and switch on the radio. Every morning I am subjected to the most futile and unctuous smug thing in religion. I suppose he has his fans. He must have otherwise the BBC would not employ him. The servant in this house listens in with me, and throughout she says:

'Well-well-well. Dear-dear-dear.' She says that all day at the things that please her and the things that don't ...

Mary Tycannol tells me that Hitler was in college in Aberystwyth. This much is certain. Miss Amold corroborates. O yes, everyone knows that Hitler was college Aberystwyth. He liked the old town so much that he gave special orders that though London be razed Aberystwyth must be saved ...

Preachers in Welsh capels never preach practical workable livable Christianity. They denounce the Egyptians of the Bible and other biblical bad men, they tell you to pray for the heathen and for Hitler, never to pray for yourself. Of course they pray for people who don't go to capel. They never denounce watered milk or dirty milk, cruelty to animals, cheatery and so on. I asked a farmer if he would take up his cross and follow Christ. He said he would. He said he was doing so. Would he give up his money for Christ's sake? This is what he said. 'Christ is not a twp. He does not want money. He wants no more than your heart and He has got mine' ...

Last Sunday evening preacher Methodist preached on the Hebrew law which ordains that a man should keep a corner of his cornfield for the poor and strangers. He said: 'How many of you farmers would keep a corner of your corn for the poor?' A very indiscreet question and the sermon was bad. So they said. There were two preachers last Sunday evening. One was from south Wales. He said: 'Prayer will not break the will of God.' Boys, bach, what nonsense. If prayer will not break the will of God, then prayer is no good at all. A man said to me: 'I pray hard against my enemy and suppose God loved my enemy – O damn.'

Lynette Roberts
Swansea Raid

I, that is Xebo7011 pass out into the chill-blue air and join Xebn559162 her sack apron greening by the light of the moon. I read around her hips: 'BEST CWT: CLARK'S COW-CAKES, H.T.5.' I do not laugh because I love my peasant friend. The night is clear, spacious, a himmel blue, and the stars minute pinpricks. The elbow-drone of jerries burden the sky and our sailing planes tack in and out with their fine metallic hum.

Oh! look how lovely she is caught in those lights! Oh!

From our high village on the Towy we can see straight down the South Wales Coast. Every searchlight goes up, a glade of magnesium waning to a distant hill which we know to be Swansea.

Swansea's sure to be bad; look at those flares like a swarm of orange bees.

They fade and others return. A collyrium sky, chemically washed Cu DH2. A blasting flash impels Swansea to riot! higher, absurdly higher, the sulphuric clouds roll with their stench of ore, we breathe naphthalene air, the pillars of smoke writhe and the astringent sky lies pale at her sides. A Jerry overhead drops two flares; the cows returning to their sheds wear hides of cyanite blue, their eyes GLINTING OPALS! We, alarmed, stand puce beneath another flare, our blood distilled, cylindricals of glass. The raiders scatter, then return and form a piratic ring within our shores. High explosives splash up blue, white, and green. We know all copper compounds are poisonous, we know also where they are.

Bleached, Rosie turns to fetch in the cows. I lonely, return to my hearth, there is a quiet clayfire with blue flames rising that would bring solace to any heart.

Caitlin Thomas
'Drunken Waistcoat'

The strangest thing that happened at New Quay involved Vera and Drunken Waistcoat. It's a story that has been told several times before: the shooting incident at Majoda that ended up with Drunken Waistcoat being prosecuted for attempted murder and Dylan giving evidence in the court case.

It was all very odd.

Dylan was late with his script for *The Doctor and the Devils*, which had been commissioned by Donald Taylor on behalf of Gryphon Films, and Donald was anxious to get the film into production. To help Dylan, Donald sent down a Russian-born secretary who worked at Gryphon, with whom Dylan was friendly; she had mothered him a lot, and helped him out with his typing.

One evening, after Dylan had worked all day on the script, we went down to the Black Lion, the pub we used every day in New Quay. Vera and her husband were there as well, and there were several other people in the crowd at the bar. A lot of drinking was done, and at some point the Russian secretary made several remarks that upset Drunken Waistcoat, who lost his temper. He was very rude and made some stupid comments about her being Jewish, which, in 1944, was rotten timing. She clawed at his face and he hit back, whereupon Dylan and the other men present threw him out of the pub. What none of them knew was that Drunken Waistcoat had recently returned from a very hazardous mission as a Commando officer, and he was more than a little battle weary. What's more, he had brought some of his weapons back, including a Sten gun and several hand grenades.

Drunken Waistcoat was also nursing a grudge: he was convinced that his wife had been living with us in a *ménage-à-trois* (which was a ridiculous thought) while he had been away, and that we had been drinking too much of their money (there may have been some truth in that). Anyway, he went off to another pub and brooded while we carried on drinking.

We returned to Majoda with Mary Keene, a friend of ours who was staying with us with her baby (she was the wife of Ralph, or 'Bunny', Keene, but at the time she was living with the painter Matthew Smith), and we settled down in front of the fire with some bottles of beer that Dylan had brought back from the pub. Suddenly, we heard some shouting outside the house and then a violent commotion, followed by a hail of bullets which ripped through those paper-thin walls. Mary and I dived into the room next door to see if the children were all right (they were fast asleep), and, moments later, the front door was kicked down and in burst Drunken Waistcoat, with his Sten gun under his arm.

Somehow, Dylan – who was unusually calm on this occasion – managed to take the gun away from him, at which point Drunken Waistcoat produced a hand grenade and threatened to blow us all to smithereens unless his gun was returned to him immediately. When he was later asked at the trial what he did then, Dylan replied, 'Naturally – I handed it back to him.'

There needn't have been any trial. Peace had been restored and tempers had cooled, and we were all settling down again when the police suddenly arrived (one of the neighbours had heard the shots and had dialled 999). So then, of course, there was a big investigation and Drunken Waistcoat was charged with attempted murder and we were all required to give evidence. It was one of those crazy things that happen in wartime; poor old Drunken Waistcoat was obviously in a bad state because of what he had been through, and none of us said very much against him. We all went to court and gave fairly weak evidence. I said that he had appeared very nervous and out of control. Eventually, he was found not guilty on the grounds that the provocation had been such as to temporarily deprive him of his reason.

Dylan Thomas
A Refusal to Mourn, the Death by Fire, of a Child in London

Never until the mankind making
Bird beast and flower
Fathering and all humbling darkness
Tells with silence the last light breaking
And the still hour
Is come of the sea tumbling in harness

And I must enter again the round
Zion of the water bead
And the synagogue of the ear of corn
Shall I let pray the shadow of a sound
Or sow my salt seed
In the least valley of sackcloth to mourn

The majesty and burning of the child's death.
I shall not murder
The mankind of her going with a grave truth
Nor blaspheme down the stations of the breath
With any further
Elegy of innocence and youth.

Deep with the first dead lies London's daughter,
Robed in the long friends,
The grains beyond age, the dark veins of her mother,
Secret by the unmourning water
Of the riding Thames.
After the first death, there is no other.

Dylan Thomas
Among Those Killed in the Dawn Raid was a Man Aged a Hundred

When the morning was waking over the war
He put on his clothes and stepped out and he died,
The locks yawned loose and a blast blew them wide,

He dropped where he loved on the burst pavement stone
And the funeral grains of the slaughtered floor.
Tell his street on its back he stopped a sun
And the craters of his eyes grew springshoots and fire
When all the keys shot from the locks, and rang.
Dig no more for the chains of his grey-haired heart.
The heavenly ambulance drawn by a wound
Assembling waits for the spade's ring on the cage.
O keep his bones away from that common cart,
The morning is flying on the wings of his age
And a hundred storks perch on the sun's right hand.

Lynette Roberts
Crossed and Uncrossed

Heard the steam rising from the chill blue bricks,
Heard the books sob and the buildings' huge groan
As the hard crackle of flames leapt on firemen
        and paled the red walls.

Bled their hands in anguish to check the fury
Knowing fire had raged for week and a day:
Clung to buildings like swallows flat and exhausted
        under the storm.

Fled the sky: fragments of the Law, kettles and glass:
Lamb's ghost screamed: Pegasus melted and fell
Meteor of shining light on to a stone court
        and only wing grave.

Round Church built in a Round Age, cold with grief,
Coloured Saints of glass lie buried at your feet:
Crusaders uncross limbs by the green light of flares,
        burn into Tang shapes.

Over firedrake floors the 'Smith' organ pealed
Roared into flames when you proud widow
Ran undaunted: the lead roof dripping red tears
        curving to crash.

Treasure was saved. Your loyalty broke all sight,
Revived the creed of the Templars of old;
Long lost. Others of the Inn escaped duty
                in black hats.

Furniture out, slates ripped off, yet persistently
Hoovering the remaining carpet, living as we all do
Blanketed each night, with torch, keys, emergency basket
                close by your side.

From paper window we gaze at the catacomb of books,
You, unflinching, stern of spirit, ready to
Gather charred sticks to fight no gas where gas was
                everywhere escaping.

Through thin library walls where 'Valley' still grows,
From Pump Court to dry bank of rubble, titanic monsters
Roll up from the Thames, to drown the 'storm' should it
                dare come again.

Still water silences death: fills night with curious light,
Brings green peace and birds to top of Plane tree
Fills Magnolia with grail thoughts: while you of King's Bench
                Walk, cherish those you most love.

Sarah Waters
'The Blitz'

The streets were deserted, and lightly fogged. In raids, like this, Pimlico
had an odd sort of haunted feel – the feel of having until recently
swarmed with lives, which had all been violently extinguished or chased
off. And when the guns stopped, the atmosphere could be even weirder.
Kay and Mickey had once or twice walked along the edge of the river
after their shift was finished. The place was uncanny: quieter, in its way,
than the countryside would have been; and the view down the Thames,
to Westminster, was all of humped, irregular masses – as if the war had
stripped London back, made a series of villages of it, each of them
defending itself against unknown forces, darkly and alone.

They arrived at the top of St. George's Drive and found a man – a

Police Reserve – looking out for them, waiting to direct them to the site. Kay raised her hand to him, and wound down her window; he ran over to the van – ran lumpishly, because of the weight of his uniform, his hat, the canvas bag that was strapped to his chest and swung as he moved. 'Around to the left,' he said. 'You'll see it all right. Keep well out, though, because of glass.'

He ran off, then, to flag down Partridge and say the same thing to her.

Kay went on more cautiously. As soon as she turned into Hugh Street there began to come, as she knew there would, specks and smuts upon the windscreen of the van: dust, from pulverised brick and stone, plaster and wood. The light from her headlamps – which was poor enough, because the lamps were dimmed – seemed to thicken, to cloud and swirl, like stout settling down in a glass. She leant forward, trying to see, driving more and more slowly, hearing the crunch and snap of things beneath her wheels; afraid for the tyres. Then she made out another faint light, fifty yards ahead: the beam from the torch of an ARP man. He slightly raised it, hearing her come. She parked the van, and Partridge drew up behind her.

The warden came over, taking off his hat, wiping beneath it with a handkerchief, then blowing his nose. Behind him was a line of houses, dark against the almost-dark of the sky. Peering through the swirling dust, Kay could see now that one of the houses had been almost demolished – its front compressed, reduced to rubble and beams, as if under the carelessly placed boot of a roving giant.

'What was it?' she asked the warden as she and Mickey got out. 'HE?'

He was putting his hat back on, and nodded. 'Hundred pounder at least.' He helped them get blankets, bandages, and a stretcher from the back of the van, then began to lead them over the rubble, shining his torch about as he went.

'This place caught all of it,' he said. 'Three flats. The top and the middle we think were empty. But the people from the other were all at home – had been in their shelter and were just coming out again, if you can believe it. Thank God they never made it to the house! The man's pretty cut about with glass from one of the windows. The others were all more or less knocked flying, you'll be able to tell how badly. One old lady's got the worst of it: she's the one I think you'll need the stretcher for. I told them all to keep in the garden till you arrived. They ought to have a doctor look at them, really; but Control say the doctor's car's been caught in a blast –'

He lost his footing, then righted himself and went on without speaking. Partridge was coughing because of the dust. Mickey was rubbing grit from her eyes. The chaos was extraordinary. Every time

169

Kay put down her feet, things cracked beneath them, or wrapped themselves around her ankles: broken window-glass mixed up with broken mirrors, crockery, chairs and tables, curtains, carpets, feathers from a cushion or a bed, great splinters of wood. The wood surprised Kay, even now: in the days before the war she'd imagined that houses were made more or less solidly, of stone – like the last Little Pig's, in the fairy tale. What amazed her, too, was the smallness of the piles of dirt and rubble to which even large buildings could be reduced. This house had had three intact floors to it, an hour before; the heap of debris its front had become was no more than six or seven feet high. She supposed that houses, after all – like the lives that were lived in them – were mostly made of space. It was the spaces, in fact, which counted, rather than the bricks.

The rear of the house, however, was more or less intact. They went through a creaking passageway and emerged, bizarrely, into a kitchen, still with cups and plates on its shelves and pictures on its walls, its electric light burning and its black-out curtain up. But part of the ceiling had come down, and streams of dust were tumbling from cracks in the plaster behind; beams were still falling, the warden said, and the place was expected to collapse.

He took them out to the little garden, then went back through the house to the street, to check on the neighbours. Kay put up the brim of her hat. It was hard to see, through the darkness, but she made out the figure of a man, sitting on a step with his hands at his head; and a woman, lying flat and very still on a blanket or rug, with another woman beside her, perhaps chafing her hands. A girl behind them was going dazedly about. A second girl was sitting in the open doorway of a shelter. She had a whimpering, yelping thing in her arms – Kay took it at first to be an injured baby. Then it wriggled and gave a high-pitched bark, and she saw that it was a dog.

The dust was still swirling, making everyone cough. There was that queer, disorientating atmosphere that Kay had always noticed at sites like this. The air felt charged, as if with a rapidly beating pulse – as if still ringing, physically vibrating – as if the atoms that made up the house, the garden, the people themselves, had been jolted out of their moorings and were still in the process of settling back. Kay was aware, too, of the building behind her, threatening its collapse. She went very quickly from person to person, tucking blankets over their shoulders, and shining her torch, looking into their faces.

Then, 'Right,' she said, straightening up. One of the girls, she thought, might have a broken leg or ankle; she sent Partridge to look at her. Mickey went to the man on the step. Kay herself went back to the woman who was lying on the rug. She was very elderly, and had taken some sort of blow to the chest. When Kay knelt beside her and felt for her heart, she let out a moan.

'She's all right, isn't she?' asked the other woman, loudly. She was shivering, and her long greyish hair was wild about her shoulders; probably she'd had it in a plait or a bun and the blast had ripped it free. 'She hasn't said a word since she lay down. She's seventy-six. It's all on account of her we were out here at all. We'd been sitting in there' – she gestured to the shelter – 'as good as gold, just playing cards and listening to the wireless. Then she said she wanted the lavatory. I brought her out, and the dog came tearing out behind us. Then the girls started crying, and then he comes out' – she meant her husband – 'with no more sense than to start running round the garden, in the black-out, like a fool. And then – Honest to God, miss, it was like the end of the world had come.' She clutched the blanket, still shivering. Now that she'd started talking, she couldn't stop. 'Here's his mother,' she went on, in the same loud, chattering, complaining way, 'and here's me, and the girls, with God knows how many broken bones between us. And what about the house? I think the roof's come off, hasn't it? The warden won't say a word, wouldn't let us back into the kitchen, even. I'm afraid to go and look.' She put a jumping hand on Kay's arm. 'Can you tell me, miss? Are the ceilings down?'

None of them had seen the front of the house yet; from the back, and in the darkness, it looked almost untouched. Kay had been moving her hands quickly over the elderly lady, checking her arms and legs. She said now, without looking up, 'I'm afraid there's rather a lot of damage –'

'What?' said the woman. She was deaf, from the blast.

'I'm afraid it's hard to say, in the dark,' said Kay, more clearly. She was concentrating on what she was doing. She thought she'd been able to feel the jut of broken ribs. She reached for her bag and brought out bandages, and began, as swiftly as she could, to bind the lady up.

'It's all on account of her, you know –' the woman started again.

'Help me with this, if you can!' Kay shouted, to distract her.

Mickey, meanwhile, had been examining the man. His face had seemed black to Kay, at first; she'd imagined it covered with earth or soot. Once she'd shone her torch on it, however, the black had become brilliant red. His arms and chest were the same, and when she'd moved the light over him it had sent back dainty little glints. He had shards of glass sticking out of him. Mickey was trying to get out the worst before bandaging him up. He was wincing as she did it, and moving his head as if blind. His eyes were half-closed, stuck together with thickening blood.

He must have felt Mickey hesitating. 'Is it bad?' Kay heard him ask.

'It's not so bad,' answered Mickey. 'It's made a bit of a hedgehog of you, that's all. Now, don't try and speak. We've got to stop up those holes. You'll never be able to drink a pint again, otherwise; it'll all come sprinkling out.'

He wasn't listening, or couldn't hear. 'How's Mother?' he said, over the end of her words. He called hoarsely to Kay. 'That's my mother.'

'Do try and not speak,' said Mickey again. 'Your mother's all right.'

'How are the girls?'

'The girls, as well.'

Then the dust caught in his throat. Mickey held his head so that he could cough. Kay imagined his cuts reopening as he shuddered and jerked, or the glass that was still in him moving in deeper ... She was aware, too, of the buzz of planes, still sounding monotonously overhead. And once there came the slithering, splintering sound of a falling roof, from a street nearby. She worked more quickly. 'OK, Partridge?' she called, as she tied off the bandage. 'How much longer?'

'Nearly there.'

'And you, Mickey?'

'We'll be ready when you are.'

'Right.' Kay unfolded the stretcher she'd brought from the van. The warden reappeared as she was doing it; he helped her lift the lady on and tuck the blanket around her.

'Which way can we take her?' Kay asked him, when she was in place. 'Is there a way to the street through the garden?'

The warden shook his head. 'Not this garden. We'll have to go back through the house.'

'Through the house? Hell. We'd better go right now. Ready to lift? OK. One, two –'

As she felt herself rise, the old lady opened her eyes at last and looked about her in amazement. She said in a whisper, 'What you doing?'

Kay felt for a firmer grip on the arms of the stretcher. 'We're taking you to hospital. You've hurt your ribs. But you'll be all right.'

'To hospital?'

'Can you lie still for us? It won't take long, I promise. We must just get you out to the ambulance.' Kay spoke as she might to a friend – to Mickey, say. She had heard policemen and nurses address injured people as though they were idiots: 'All right, dearie.' 'Now then, Ma.' 'Don't you worry about that.'

'Here's your son coming, too,' she said, when she saw Mickey helping up the bleeding man. 'Partridge, are you ready with the girls?

OK, everybody. Come now. Quickly, but softly.'

They trooped raggedly into the kitchen. The light made them wince and cover their eyes. And then the girls, of course, saw how filthy and cut about they were – and how dreadful their father looked, with the blood and the bandages on his face. They began to cry.

'Never mind,' their mother said, shaken. She was still shivering. 'Never mind. We're all right, aren't we! Phyllis, turn the key in the door. Bring the tea, Eileen. And cover up that tin of corned beef! Just to be on the safe – Oh, my Lord!' She had reached the door that led from the kitchen and seen the chaos that lay beyond. She couldn't believe it. She stood with her hand at her heart. 'Oh, my good Lord!'

The girls, behind her, let out screams.

Kay's feet slid about again, as she and the warden tried to manoeuvre the elderly lady over the rubble. Every step they took sent up a new cloud of dust, feathers, soot. But finally they got her to the edge of what was once the front garden. They found a couple of schoolboys swinging from the handles of the ambulance doors.

'Need any help, mister?' the boys said, to the warden or, perhaps, to Kay.

The warden answered them. 'No, we don't. You clear off back to your shelter, before you get your bloody heads blown off. Where are your mothers? What do you think those planes are, bumblebees?'

'Is that old Mrs Parry? Is she dead?'

'Get out of it!'

'Oh, my Lord!' the woman was still saying, as she made her way through the wreckage of her flat.

The ambulance had four metal bunks, of the kind used in shelters. There was a dim light, but no form of heating, so Kay tucked another blanket around the elderly lady and fastened her into the bunk with a canvas belt, then put one of the hot-water bottles under her knees, and another next to her feet. Mickey brought the man. His eyes were gummed shut completely now, with blood and dust; she had to guide his arms and his legs as if he'd forgotten how to use them. His wife came after. She had started picking little things up: a single tartan slipper, a plant in a pot. 'How can I leave all this?' she said, when the warden tried to get her into Partridge's car so that she could be driven to the First Aid Post. She'd started crying. 'Won't you run and get Mr Grant, from out of his house across the road? He'll watch our things. Will you, Mr Andrews?'

'We can't let you bring it,' Partridge was saying, meanwhile, to the girl with the dog.

'I don't want to go, then!' cried the girl. She gripped the dog harder, making it squeal. Then she looked down at her feet. 'Oh, Mum, here's that picture you had from Uncle Patrick, all smashed to bits!'

'Let her take the dog, Partridge,' said Kay. 'What harm can it do?'

But it was Partridge's decision, not hers; and there wasn't time, anyway, to stay and debate it. She left them all arguing, just nodding to Mickey in the back of the van, closing the doors, then running round to the front and wiping off the windscreen: for in the twenty minutes or so that the vehicle had been sitting idle in the street it had got thickly coated with dust. She got in the cabin and started the engine.

'Andrews,' she called to the warden, as she began to turn, 'watch my tyres for me, will you?' A puncture now would be disastrous. He moved away from the woman and the girls and shone his torch about her wheels, then raised his hand to her.

She went cautiously at first, speeding up when the road grew clearer. They were supposed to keep to a steady sixteen miles per hour when carrying casualties – but she thought of the elderly lady with her broken ribs, and the bleeding man, and drove faster. Now and then, too, she'd lean closer to the windscreen to peer up into the sky. The drone of aeroplanes was still heavy, the thumping of the guns still loud, but the sound of the engine was loud, too, and she couldn't tell if she was driving into the worst of the action or leaving it behind.

Wynford Vaughan-Thomas
'Anzio'

As the BBC Correspondent on the Beachhead, I also kept a diary and made a tour of the forward positions during the first few weeks in April. These notes jotted down hurriedly on the spot or immediately after returning from the front to the battered Press villa on the water's edge near Nettuno may help to recreate the strange atmosphere of danger, boredom, dirt, courage and humour which never left the Beachhead perimeter.

Here is a night spent at the mouth of the Moletta stream, which marked the extreme north-west position of the British sector, held in late April by a battalion of the Wiltshire Regiment.

> This strangely calm sector at the mouth of the Moletta is a
> blessed relief to troops who come to it direct from a spell in
> the wadis. In spring the wild flowers are scattered in thou-
> sands amongst the sand dunes while the sea looks invitingly

near – though death to bathe in. The Boche wants no trouble here: the American combat engineers told the British as they left, 'You leave that guy alone and he won't get mad at you.' The men camp in dug-outs amongst the dunes and on a warm night a single nightingale pours its heart out somewhere in the sweet-smelling bushes.

The forward platoon of the Wiltshires lived within fifty yards of the enemy, and I went on hands and knees down a shallow crawl trench to visit them. Their position was just a series of sand-bagged holes sunk amongst a tangle of shrubs and small trees, but by peering cautiously through a slit between two of the sandbags I could see the wire in front of the German line: it seemed so close that there was no need of the warning to talk in whispers.

A youngster of nineteen murmured quietly to me, 'Come and see our German.' I wriggled farther forward still, crawled beside him into his look-out post and immediately sensed a foul reek, sickly sweet, like a pile of rancid butter left too long in the sun – the unmistakable, clinging smell of an unburied corpse. There he lay right under our noses, for it was impossible to get out to bury him; all the Wiltshires could do was to sprinkle creosote over the body at night and try to get used to the stench. Few people could get it out of their nostrils and out of their memory. 'Two more out there amongst the minefields.'

I crawled back into the next sap. 'Listen,' said the sergeant, and in the quiet of the evening with no gun firing for miles around I heard a hoarse cough and a shuffle of feet. 'It's old Ted,' said the sergeant. (Ted, from the Italian *Tedeschi*, is the new term for the 'Jerries' out here.) An eerie business to hear your enemy, the man you are supposed to kill, scuffling around in a slit-trench as cramped as your own, feeling as you do the evening nip in the air, thinking as you are thinking of the chance of getting leave and escaping from it all. It's easy to feel venomous about Old Ted when he comes charging towards you with a gun in his hand, but when he coughs and scuffles, unaware that he's been overheard, he becomes suddenly human, a fellow man caught in the same predicament as yourself.

Maybe this is why the sergeant suddenly turned to me and whispered, 'You ought to have been here on Hitler's birthday: they had a high old time, singing 'Lilli Marlene' and yelling their heads off – plumb crazy or just bomb happy. It takes you that way sometimes when you've been having a real basin-full up in the wadis.' Then the sergeant had his brainwave; 'Tell you what. Put your mike up here on the parapet and tonight the bastard will come out wiring – I'll guarantee you a winner. He cusses something horrible, bangs away at the old wiring posts and whistles; proper Blackpool it is out there sometimes. If we don't open up on him you'll get the recording of a lifetime.'

Carried away by the sergeant's enthusiasm I placed the mike on the parapet, crawled back along the trench with the mikelead and joined Bob Wade, our engineer, in a small dug-out where he crouched over his recording gear. We waited like hunters in their 'hide' by a water-hole in the

African bush, for our victims to come out within mike-range.

The strange, inconsequential sounds of the Anzio night were all around us. A sudden chattering from a Spandau began somewhere ahead of us in the darkness and ceased as pointlessly as it began. The dirty blanket that served as the dug-out door was carefully pushed aside and the sergeant squeezed in with two cups of cocoa, thick and sugary but consoling in their warmth, as we gulped the scalding liquid down, and then thawed out our numb fingers around the cup. The sergeant checked on his watch – 'They're putting down the big stonk on the Germans north of the "Boot" in a few minutes, come and watch.'

We followed the sergeant out into the trench and looked towards the north-east; the night was very clear and full of stars.

There was a swift flash from somewhere away along the sea-coast, then another and another until the whole sky seemed lit by sheet-lightning which, after a few seconds' interval, was followed by the overwhelming thunder of the guns. The noise seemed to roll in on top of us – an awe-inspiring rumpus of cracks, crashes, thumps and then the muffled thuds of the shells exploding out in the distant German lines. Over five hundred guns are now crowded into the Beachhead, and our artillery fire is so perfectly syn-chronised that, in the central sectors, every single gun can be brought to bear on one selected target and send five hundred shells smashing down on it in a matter of seconds. Flare after flare went up from the German side of the line to the north. The barrage ceased as suddenly as it had begun.

'What are they firing at?' I asked the sergeant.

'Who knows? Some poor bastard's copping it.'

Our war is confined to the few yards of soil around the mouth of the Moletta, and the most cosmic-seeming events can be taking place a few miles away and we still neither know nor care. But in the silence that follows the barrage the nightingales began to sing, a lone bird at first, then a whole chorus of them until the air seemed to throb softly with their trillings and flutings.

A young sentry standing muffled beside us said, 'Lovely, bloody little birds, the more guns there are the more they sing. I can tell 'em – they sing like that near Horsham where I come from.'

The sergeant would have none of this. 'Wait till you've heard 'em every mucking night, the bloody sound they make will get into your bones. We had a lad with us who let them get on his nerves so much that he loosed off with his rifle every time he heard them sing – he was "bird-happy", if ever I saw a man.'

Is it the racking contrast between the nightingale, singing free above the earth, and the muddy, crawling life the soldier has to lead below, that makes this bird song so difficult to bear? We went back into the dug-out, listened on our headphones, dozing and yawning ... until a grey half-light crept past the curtain. Dawn was at hand and still we had no message from the sergeant. I could stand it no longer and crawled forward again to the line of pits where we had left the mike. I found the sergeant and his men in a state of restrained fury.

'He never came out, Old Ted didn't; the beggar's let me down, that's what he's done, proper let me down. I'll never forgive him for this; he's got no right to do this to me. I'm really disappointed in Old Ted, I really am.'

'Should have sent him a contract!' came the laconic mutter from one of the men.

[...]

The pattern of the great set-piece assaults of World War II never varied. Always we felt the strange silence creeping over the dark landscape as zero hour approached, then the violent shock of the guns tearing the silence ruthlessly apart, followed by the slow, insect-like crawl forward of the tanks with the small, huddled figures of the infantrymen bobbing amongst the shell-holes! The dense pall of smoke blots out the front, the crackle of machine-guns erupts from somewhere inside it, the crump of bombs and shells echoes in the heart of the smoke cloud, and the watchers wait, with fear and anxiety in their hearts, for the first news back. Success? Or have all our long preparations, all the careful staff-work, the minute analysis of intelligence reports and the cunningly devised cover-plans gone for naught in the first half-hour of battle?

We know the routine by heart, and yet who could have the heart to stay away? Even those who had no business there, from high-up generals to war correspondents, went as far forward as they could in the early hours of 23rd May. We huddled against the walls of a ruined farmhouse near Isola Bella. Away to the westward the flashing of gunfire on the skyline marked the British holding attacks on the Moletta: they were a vital part of our assault plan and convinced the enemy that we were going to make our break-out along the old battlefields of the Albano road. Von Mackensen kept his main strength around the Factory and Carroceto until it was too late to save Cisterna.

The dawn was strengthening, dull and with a threat of rain, but we still spoke in whispers, afraid to break the silence around us. Over 160,000 men were close at hand, waiting, watching and, maybe, wishing desperately that the minute-hand would at last mark zero hour and that they were out of the tension of fearful anticipation.

Few men carried small books of verse in their pockets in this war as they did in the last. *The Shropshire Lad* seemed to have no place in the world of the Nazis, but some words of Milton's, learnt at school, persisted in running through my head:

Oh, how comely it is and how reviving
To the Spirits of just men long opprest,
When God into the hands of their deliverer
Puts invincible might ...

The GIs getting ready for the advance had other things on their minds
than apt quotations from the poets.

Raymond Williams
'Normandie, July 1944'

The hay meadow sloped down to the little apple orchard. At the edges
of the uncut grass there were hundreds of bright buttercup flowers. In
the high hedge behind which they were drawn up, wild roses had
climbed in long briars, some beyond the support of the hedge and
now tumbling down its sides. Their own long gun barrel was pushed
in among a spray of one of the smaller white roses.

Through the long black binoculars – Paul's binoculars as he still
thought of them – Bert could make out the corner of a roof beyond
the apple trees. The road must run alongside the orchard and behind
the high-banked hedge of the meadow. It was hot now under the
midday sun. He pushed back his beret, which was rubbing along its
band on his sweating forehead. He unwrapped and sucked a boiled
sweet, feeling its sharp chemical taste on his palate. He looked again
through the binoculars, slowly sweeping the probable line of the road
and then staring into the shadows of the orchard. Everything was as
still and peaceful as in any country summer. This meadow and
orchard in Normandie could be anywhere between Ross and
Hereford, on a scout camp.

'Cossack?'

The crackling voice was at a distance in the helmet lying on the turret
by his right hand. He pulled off the beret and put on the helmet, which
at once, with its radio crackle, seemed to cut him off from the world.

'Cossack,' he acknowledged.

'Confirming your lead on my arm.'

'Roger. Wilco. Out.'

He looked along the line of the hedge at the other tanks. The new
young lieutenant, Angell, was fifty yards away in Condor, with
Cormorant twenty yards beyond him.

Angell had arrived only yesterday, replacing Harvill who had been
killed, walking to breakfast, by a sniper outside Tilly. The troop had

hoped that with a new commander they would be reserve for a few days, but then there had been this flap with reports of two SS Panzer divisions – one of them the famous *Totenkopf*, the Death's Head – counter-attacking along the seam of the bridgehead, between the British and the Americans. Everything had then been pushed forward, though the centreline of the German attack was still uncertain. There was a rumour that they had broken through to the west and blown up a huge dump of diesel barrels. Somebody had said that headquarters there were already packed up and facing the sea, engines running. You could believe anything or nothing, in this mixed-up battle in which there were no real lines. Yet along this whole sector there was not even the sound of gunfire, though there was something heavy and very distant, probably bombing, away to the east.

Bert crawled down past Paddy and Sam in the crowded gun turret and crouched behind his driver.

'When we go, Tom ...'

Tom pulled off his helmet.

'When we go, flap down, right?'

'Bugger that.'

Bert nodded. None of the drivers liked driving on periscope, with the armoured flap down, but it was much the safest way. He put his hand on Tom's shoulder.

'I'll guide you like you was a pram, boy.'

'Aye, stuck in the first bloody hedge. And you know bloody well I can't see these banks in the periscope.'

'Open your eyes a bit you will.'

'It isn't, I can't see they're there, I can't judge the drop.'

'We've still got a few teeth left after your last roller-coaster.'

'Then tell me in time, for Christ's sake.'

Bert patted his shoulder. Tom was already closing his flap, adjusting his periscope, and tightening his hands on the two long steering tillers. Bert squeezed the elbow of Harry the radio operator, sitting beside Tom in the small forward compartment. Then he pushed back up past Paddy's legs.

'One up the spout, Paddy?'

'Yes, Sarge.'

Sam was already on the machine-gun, alternately whistling and chewing. Bert rose in the turret. There was no signal yet. He looked the other way to Dai in the turret of Conqueror, twenty yards along the hedge. He held his hands out parallel and then widened them. Dai nodded and put up his thumb.

There were voices again on the radio net.

'Sunray to Three. Sunray to Three.'

'Three.'

'I gather that in the next race the favourite may not even start. But the going is firm to good.'

'Wilco, Sunray. Out.'

Angell put down his microphone and lifted his arm, pointing across the meadow. Bert checked with Dai and then spoke down to Tom.

'Start engines. Then go like a bat out of hell, boy, till we're in by the cider.'

There was no acknowledgement, only the sudden shattering roar of the big diesel engine behind them and the cloud of foul smoke. They lurched forward through the hedge and into the meadow. Conqueror was even quicker away, through a hedge gap, and was widening the arc across the field. In the turret of Cossack all three were holding on as the speed increased. The long grass was hiding bumps in the meadow and they were thrown this way and that.

'There'll be eggs for sure,' Paddy shouted.

'Yeah,' Bert shouted back.

He was staring through the orchard at the building which was now coming more into view: a low farmhouse, with a stone barn beyond it.

'If the bloody chickens make off, there'll still be eggs.'

'Right, Paddy.'

There was no sign of other movements as the two tanks raced across the meadow. The shape of the orchard now looked different, elongated towards the west, but Dai in Conqueror was already adjusting to this, going wider.

'These things were never made for fighting in fields and trees,' Sam said, as much to himself as to the others.

Bert was still staring forward.

'Tom, that bit of broken fence, you see it, this side. Get close in to that and then crawl up to the road hedge.'

They heard the engine slacken, and then there was a fast spectacular sliding turn in beside the fence.

'Bloody Brooklands,' Sam said.

Bert looked across, to see Conqueror disappearing beyond the bend of the orchard.

'Come in, Conqueror.'

'Conqueror.'

'Dai, we're out of sight but okay. Get to the road hedge if you can but do not go to the house, do not go to the house.'

'Conqueror wilco and out.'

Cossack had stopped by the broken fence. The apple trees close to them were heavy with small green unripe fruit.

'Crawl now, Tom.'

They went very slowly forward, but there was still a puff of blue smoke. There was a gate twenty yards along the hedge from the orchard. Bert stared through the tops of the high hedge and then got Tom to creep along to the gateway.

'Engine off.'

The low roar coughed and cut out. Bert took off his helmet. All the noise still trembled in his body but slowly the peace of summer came back.

'Shall I go for the eggs, Sarge?' Paddy asked.

'Not just yet, mun. I'm going to look around.'

He climbed from the turret to the engine cover and then jumped down to the long grass. He moved under the hedge to the gateway and looked cautiously out along the road. It was clear and empty in both directions and the hedge on the far side had been recently layered. He was able to look out many miles to the south, over the low wooded hills. It was deep green and peaceful as far as he could see, though as he moved to a different angle he could see smoke a mile or so west: ordinary woodsmoke, it looked. He found a position where the tank could command the road in either direction, and guided Tom into it. As Tom switched off he lifted his cover and put his head out. His face was dark red and running with sweat.

Bert put a foot on the heavy track and climbed up the front past the gun. He reached across for his radio.

'Dai?'

'Yes.'

'Anything?'

'There've been vehicles into the yard. Two or three and recent. But most of the yard's beyond the barn, I can't see it.'

'Wait.'

Bert sat in the warm sun on the turret and looked through the binoculars towards the farmhouse. He had only a very partial view through the trees, but he could see no movements of any kind. He was about to jump down again when the radio crackled.

'Sunray to Three.'

'Three.'

'Will you tell your bloody men to keep radio discipline?'

'Three wilco. Out.'

There was a short pause and then the expected call.

'Three to Cossack, Three to Cossack. Keep radio discipline.'

'Sarge!' Paddy shouted, pointing down through the orchard.

There was a puff of black smoke just beyond the farmhouse, and the sound of a powerful engine. Then almost at once there was a burst of machine-gun fire.

'Three to Cossack, I say again, Three to Cossack. Keep radio discipline.'

Bert slid down into the turret.

'Traverse right.'

Paddy swung the big gun. Sam had already realigned the machine-gun. Bert grabbed the microphone.

'Dai, was that you firing?'

'No, but there's a Tiger in that yard, probably two. And Billy's been hit.'

'Have you got him?'

'Just about. Hang on, Bert –'

There was another burst of machine-gun fire and then the unmistakable sound of tank tracks moving.

'Dai, listen. Dai. Back out now, back out. I'm putting smoke in.'

There was no reply. When the radio crackled again it was Angell.

'Cossack, report your situation, report your situation.'

'Engaging. Out. Dai. Dai.'

There was still no reply from Conqueror.

'Tom.'

'Sarge.'

'Covers down, back twenty yards, then round the back of the orchard.'

'Sarge.'

The diesel roared in acceleration. With its noise and the cover of the radio helmet Bert was now cut off from all the sounds in the orchard.

'Dai. Come in, Dai.'

Two voices cut in as he was waiting.

'Cossack, identify your situation and await orders.'

'Cossack, this is Sunray. What the bloody hell are you doing?

The tank was lurching now from its turn, moving towards the back of the orchard. Bert held on with difficulty. He released the microphone switch and told Sam to tap Tom's shoulders and get him to slow down. Then he pressed the microphone switch and said curtly:

'Request radio silence. Emergency. Out.'

'Christ!' Paddy shouted.

He had taken off his helmet and was at the sights of the big gun. Bert had already seen what he was shouting at. There was a sudden

182

high column of black smoke from the back of the orchard, its base just beyond their view. Bert ripped off his helmet and tried to look through the binoculars but he could not hold them steady.

'Sarge!' Paddy shouted, frantically traversing the big gun left. Bert saw the big Tiger tank at almost the same moment. Its gun was facing at an angle from them, towards the column of smoke.

'On!' Paddy shouted.

'Fire!'

The explosion shook the turret but Bert at once reloaded.

'Fire!'

It had required the second armour-piercing shell, which struck between turret and hull. The engine of the Tiger was now on fire, and its crew were jumping out on the far side.

'Sam.'

But Sam was already spraying the area of the Tiger with machine-gun bullets. Several of the bullets, Bert saw, were hitting and ricocheting off the trees. He looked across to the meadow-hedge running back from the orchard. What he wanted to see was men running or sheltering there: the five men from Conqueror. But there was nothing of that kind, only the blue black column of smoke, now thickening into the clear blue-and-white sky. As he watched there was a sudden explosion, followed immediately by others.

'The bloody ammo going,' Sam said, looking down at the stacks of shells that surrounded them in the crowded turret.

'Shut your gob!' Paddy shouted.

'Right,' Bert said.

He paused and consciously breathed. The Tiger was still burning but it had not brewed. He picked up the microphone.

'Tom, engine off.'

'Sarge.'

It was extraordinary how quiet it seemed, as the big tank engine cut out. The explosions from Conqueror had stopped. The meadow and the orchard were quiet again, under the spreading pall of black smoke. The silence seemed to last for several minutes.

Bert looked carefully at the column of black smoke. At near ground level it was billowing towards the orchard, as if in a north wind. But at about thirty yards up it was blowing the other way, as if from a light south-east breeze.

'We didn't lay our own smoke,' he said to Paddy.

'There wasn't time, Sarge.'

'Sure. But if we laid it now, along the line of the orchard, I could get to Conqueror and see.'

Paddy turned and looked at him. Bert saw the broad pink face smeared with grease and dirt, the staring blue eyes under the curly ginger hair.

'No,' Paddy said.

'Not the tank, Paddy. Just me slip along on foot.'

'That's what I said no to.'

'Did you, you insubordinate bugger?'

'And that's what I meant. No.'

Sam had turned and was watching them.

'Watch your front with that gun,' Bert said, sharply.

'Don't worry,' Sam said. 'I heard Dai. One Tiger, probably two.'

'Yes and that's why we can't go on in the tank.'

'We should get the bloody hell out of here,' Sam said.

'With the same objection. We'd be a sitting duck all across the field.'

'Not if we laid smoke and then drove flat out.'

'The wind's too uncertain for that far.'

'Well, we can't go into the bloody orchard and find him. And we can't stay here for ever.'

'We can stay for a bit. Remember they're probably as confused as we are.'

'Confused, that's a bloody fancy word for it,' Paddy said.

'All right. Confused and scared.'

'The bloody SS?' Sam said. 'Not those Death's Head bastards.'

'Yes,' Bert said. 'Fascists get frightened too.'

'Fascists are Italians. These are Germans.'

'And confused and scared,' Bert said. 'They probably only went into the farm for some eggs.'

He smiled at Paddy as he spoke. Paddy smiled broadly back.

'So this is what we do,' Bert said. 'In two minutes we lay smoke, lots of it, along the edge of the orchard. Then I run behind it, see if there's anybody alive there. Two minutes after I've gone you lay smoke again. For Christ's sake don't forget that. Then fast through, beyond where Conqueror is but down the line of that hedge. If I can bring anybody I will. If not, or if I'm not back, wait one minute and then through that hedge and keep its cover back to the others.'

'I still –' Paddy began.

'It's an order.'

Paddy shook his head but in the same movement began picking up the mortar smoke bombs. The radio crackled.

'Three to Cossack.'

'Cossack.'

'Cossack, disengage. Disengage.'

184

Bert smiled.

'Wilco. Out.'

He put aside the helmet.

'Right, Paddy, you're in command. Explain it now to Harry and Tom.'

'Sarge.'

'And Sam, no firing unless they fire. We don't want them on us too soon.'

'If they're there. I'm beginning to doubt it.'

'Good. Now the smoke.'

They fired six smoke bombs along the edge of the orchard. As the white smoke billowed out Bert climbed from the turret to the engine cover and then dropped lightly to the grass. He stopped to unhook a grenade from his belt and removed the pin, holding the lever tightly in his fist. Then he sprinted across behind the smoke, trying to hold his breath as some of it drifted towards him.

Coughing and with smarting eyes, he could momentarily not see the base of the black column, which was still thick and high in the air. Then suddenly he saw Conqueror, its near track broken, its gun lurched and pointed to the ground. It was blackened at the turret and across the engine cover; the green paint on the hull was mostly peeled but some still sizzled. One of the crew was lying directly under the barrel of the gun. One or two bullets had torn through his steel helmet and the back of his head was shattered, though there was little blood.

Bert ducked round the back of the tank. A corpse burned to an almost shapeless blackness lay under the engine cowling. Another body, still retaining some of its shape, hung halfway out of the turret, overcome there while trying to escape. He looked quickly around and even called, quietly: 'Dai.' But he was almost sure that Dai was the shapeless body under the engine, and there was no other human sound or sight. The driver and the radio operator must have been trapped inside; there could be no hope for them. He looked for identity tags on the corpse by the engine, but it was too thoroughly burned. He ran back and got the tags from the first body, turning it over. It was, as he had expected, Billy Edwards. His lips were drawn far back, showing all his teeth, but his face was otherwise unmarked.

The second smoke began landing behind him. He ran into the cover of the burned-out Conqueror. He could hear Cossack's engines now, and got ready to jump up. He was still holding the grenade, as if convulsively. He must remember to throw it before he climbed up the hull.

Suddenly there was a shell whistling above him and the crump of high explosive somewhere beyond the farmhouse. He could not understand who was firing it but there were then two more and their direction was unmistakable: from behind their squadron. Turning furiously, he supposed that the report of enemy presence at the farm had been passed to the field gunners, who would be shelling the map reference. As yet, fortunately, they were overshooting, but it was in any case time to get out. The bastards could at least have waited until Cossack was back.

Cossack was coming now through the smoke, veering wide. He ran out, waving his arms, but at just that moment there was what sounded like a heavy slap, and then a booming secondary explosion. Cossack was swung round by the impact, towards the orchard, and was then hit again. He saw the white heat as the armour-piercing shell entered its first stage. Meanwhile the field-gun shells were now coming in a barrage across the farm and orchard, the high explosive rattling among the trees.

Cursing and shouting wildly he ran towards Cossack. The turret was opening but the driver's cover was still closed. He saw Paddy's head and shouted up to him, unheard in the noise. He climbed up the hull and grabbed at Paddy's shoulder. Paddy did not turn but shouted:

'That second bugger was there!'

'Come out, Paddy! Jump!'

Paddy did not answer. He moved down into the turret again. Bert pulled himself right up and looked into the turret. Sam was sprawled on the littered metal floor. Harry and Tom were motionless in their seats. He leaned in and grabbed at Paddy.

'Leave it!' Paddy shouted. 'I think Sam's still alive.'

'She'll blow any minute,' Bert said.

Paddy was hauling at Sam's shoulders, trying to get him upright, but it was a dead weight and he could get him only half up, jammed against the gun breech. Bert reached in and pulled at Sam's shoulder but could get no real weight on it.

'Paddy, come out. Now!' Bert shouted.

'Fuck off!' Paddy shouted back, still trying to wrestle Sam's body across the breech.

There was a sudden sheet of flame, and a new explosion, as the fuel tank blew. Bert was thrown down to the grass but not before he felt across his face a flame that was more like light than touch or immediate hurt. Still shouting to Paddy, he struggled up. He was just reaching for the hold on the hull when a shell landed between Cossack and the burned-out Conqueror. He felt a sudden hammer-blow on his right knee, again without immediate pain. As he hung on to the hold a third tank shell hit Cossack. This time he saw the flash from the black shape of the Tiger in the orchard. The flame in Cossack seemed to explode, and there was a rush of choking black smoke. He saw Paddy's arm come up through the turret and then fall back. The billowing black smoke rose all around him.

Bert's face was stinging and scraped, now. His sight was blurred and he found he could see only from his right eye. His right knee was beginning to pulse, as if separate from him. Instinctively, but still shouting Paddy's name, he ran crouching for the hedge and pushed himself deep under it. The last thing he remembered was the strange dry taste of earth in his mouth.

Dannie Abse
"'All change!'"

The mechanical voice of the loudspeaker floated disembodied across the station clock that had stopped long ago in the year 1933. The sinister German voice mingled with the Guards in black uniforms and the sorrowful Alsatian dogs cocked up their ears. The voice over the crackling loudspeaker shouted, 'All change at Auschwitz-Dachau.' The engine gave a shriek of pain and the dogs would not look. Near the Refreshment Room stood a hygienic-looking shed containing a few gas chambers, inside one of which a stray passenger now found himself.

The rest of the passengers sat in the train, their luggage on the rack of pain. These suitcases were labelled Munich, Berlin, Vienna, Madrid, Prague. When the engine gave its plaintive shriek in the still air, no passenger moved, no passenger spoke. They merely sat, the hooked-nosed ones, gazing straight ahead, waiting for the train to move out. Not looking at the pictures lining the carriages. Neither that of Hitler addressing a huge crowd, nor aeroplanes over Barcelona, nor troops goosemarching through Austria. Nobody looked, nobody spoke, nobody waved a last farewell.

A Guard came and opened the door. 'All change!' he screamed. They changed into skeletons. Skeletons row after row sitting bolt upright in the carriages of Time.

The loudspeaker crackled again. The next train to arrive at platform two will be the London train.

The engine pulled in.

'There they are,' said Uncle Bertie.

Leo bundled out of the train, mother and father after him, smiling.

'All change!' a porter shouted.

Tony Curtis
Soup

One night our block leader set a competition:
two bowls of soup to the best teller of a tale.
That whole evening the hut filled with words –
tales from the old countries
of wolves and children
potions and love-sick herders
stupid woodsmen and crafty villagers.
Apple-blossom snowed from blue skies,
orphans discovered themselves royal.
Tales of greed and heroes and cunning survival,
soldiers of the Empires, the Church, the Reich.

And when they turned to me
I could not speak,
sunk in the horror of that place,
my throat a corridor of bones, my eyes
and nostrils clogged with self-pity.
'Speak,' they said, 'everyone has a story to tell.'
And so I closed my eyes and said:
I have no hunger for your bowls of soup, you see
I have just risen from the Shabbat meal –
my father has filled our glasses with wine,
bread has been broken, the maid has served fish.
Grandfather has sung, tears in his eyes, the old songs.
My mother holds her glass by the stem, lifts
it to her mouth, the red glow reflecting on her throat.
I go to her side and she kisses me for bed.
My grandfather's kiss is rough and soft like an apricot.
The sheets on my bed are crisp and flat
like the leaves of a book ...
I carried my prizes back to my bunk: one bowl
I hid, the other I stirred
and smelt a long time, so long
that it filled the cauldron of my head,
drowning a family of memories.

Tony Curtis
A Visit to Terezin

Here are the houses.
There is a light there, and listen
– someone sings.
How clean the streets, yes?
A tidy people, we have observed,
with their own pride.

Here is their bakery and, do you see,
a cobbler, carpenter, the butcher
with their own beliefs
in the killing for meat.
We come to the school. Later we will
be entertained by their orchestra.
A race is redeemed by music, I think.

Look at the children's pictures. You see –
houses with fences. The chimneys smoke
– there are families inside.
A giant – look at his club, his boots.
Wnere there are children, there will be giants.
And always butterflies, look, so many colours,
they use all the colours,
as large as kites, as large as clouds.
Where a child's mind flies, yes?
This one has played the gallows game.
Or it could be a door.

Lord Elwyn Jones
'Margit'

Most of the families who lived in the terraced houses of Old Castle
Road were Welsh. There were a few English like our next door neighbours, the Pedleys and the Bodmans. The Irish O'Sheas lived two
houses away. A pious Jewish family lived at the other end of the road.
One Friday evening when I was walking home from school an elderly
Jew asked me to come into his house to light the gas lamp in his
kitchen. It puzzled me greatly. I had no knowledge then that on their

Sabbath pious Jews forswore all such activities.

I never sensed any racial animosity in Llanelli. I do not recollect any anti-semitic feelings in either of the two schools to which I went. Harold Benjamin was one of my friends at school. His older brother Isaac had been a friend of my older brother Gwyn. Harold won a scholarship to Oxford and took a brilliant First there. He became a solicitor and sent me some briefs when I started at the Bar, when briefs were most welcomed, as did R.I. Lewis, another Jewish school-mate. Like the Welsh, the Jews believed in education and, however poor, made sacrifices to give their children this start in life.

There were marked class differences in the town, though no one asked you who your father was. The assumption that every person is as good as another was at the heart of our social behaviour. In moments of exaltation in Wales, I have felt that Thomas Traherne in the seventeenth century expressed its essence when he wrote: 'You never enjoy the world aright, till the sea itself floweth in your veins, till you are clothed with the heavens, and crowned with the stars: and per-ceive yourself to be the sole heir of the whole world, and more than so, because men are in it who are every one sole heirs as well as you.'

★ ★ ★ ★ ★

I shared the evening lectures at King's with Richard Latham, a friend who had won brilliant Firsts at Melbourne and Oxford. He had a Jewish business friend, Wilfrid Israel, who owned a department store in Berlin. Just before the war, when the persecution of the Jews became increasingly violent, Mr Israel tried to get as many Jewish chil-dren as he could out of Berlin to England. Richard organised the English end, Polly and I, – we were married by this time – chose Margit from a sheet of photographs. She was only fifteen. We agreed to be her guardians and learned her story later. Her father was a graphic designer, a Christian who refused to divorce his Jewish wife and renounce his children in compliance with Nazi decrees. When in 1939 his studio in Cologne was looted and burned and he was beaten up by the Nazis, he decided to take his wife, son and daughter to Berlin in the hope of being able to establish a new home there.

In 1938 all Jewish children were forbidden to attend German schools. Margit's parents found a place for her in a Jewish art college in Berlin where she studied design and textiles. Part of the course involved visits to Israel's store to study materials. On 10 November 1938 came the terrible *kristalnacht* (crystal night). The Nazis looted and burned all Jewish business premises. Margit was in the Israel store at the time. I have asked her what she remembers of those events. She told me that she had tried in vain to obliterate them from her memory. She wrote: 'I escaped down a rear staircase during the fire. I ran home and looked for the all clear signal from my mother. A prearranged handkerchief "code" on the balcony was put up by my mother if the Nazis were in the flats. When the handkerchiefs were out we just kept on walking.' By such devices Margit survived. She wrote:

> In May 1939 I left for England. A letter came from Polly and Elwyn in April to welcome me. It was my passport to life. [Margit still has the letter.] I left on what was to be the last Jewish children's 'transport' out of Berlin and Le Havre. I remember my parents were not allowed to come to the station to see me leave and that I was permitted to take very little with me. Little else remains in my mind of the sad and miserable journey. I was met by Polly at Waterloo Station in London. Later I discovered that shortly after my departure my parents and my brother were arrested by the Nazis and disappeared into concentration camps. Afterwards I learned that my brother had been gassed in Theresienstadt Camp.

Polly remembers vividly going to meet Margit and bring her home. The arrival platform was crowded with German Jewish children. Some were extremely young, some were clutching shabby toys. All were pale, thin and exhausted. Each child bore a placard bearing identification details in large letters and the name of the sponsor. Polly spotted Margit. She bore the description 'Margit "Sara" Reiter'. The Nazis added the name 'Sara' to every Jewish girl's name, while 'Israel' was added to boys' names. They were compelled to wear a yellow star. None of the children spoke English. Margit, when she arrived at Harwich, was asked where she was born. She replied 'Köln'. The immigration officer said: 'No, not Köln, child. Cologne.' She burst into tears. Beautiful, steady and intelligent, Margit became one of our family and helped to bring up our first two children, Josephine and Dan.

She married Brian, a Catholic whom she met in the Lake District, where Polly had been sent in October 1940 to have our second baby. Brian was in the navy during the war and served in the north and south Atlantic. In due course he became headmaster of a notable English school. Margit's father and mother survived the war although her mother had been subjected to inhuman medical experiments in a concentration camp. Margit's marriage has been a happy one. She and her husband respect each other's religion as Margit's parents did. They are now grandparents, and Margit named her first child Josephine, after our eldest.

Tony Curtis
Crossing Over

Three days out from England,
The summer-calm Atlantic lulled us with sun
And the last U-boats lay deep like drowsy fish
Waiting for the music of pistons.
Cloudless and hot, so we let the POWs take the air
And a stretch on the after-deck, hundreds of them
In murmuring huddles, bleary and pacing those confines.

Above them, a row of American aircrew headed home,
Perched on the rail facing the bows, away
From the grey dregs of that beaten army.
Those sheepskin and leather flying jackets
We so envied, worn loose now in the heat.
They flexed their arms like boxers lifting weights,
Punching each other in play.

And when those strong young men
With their war-tightened faces
Turned to go to the mess, we saw why
They'd broadened their backs above the Germans.
Every man's jacket proclaimed *Berlin Dresden Cologne*
Each raid commemorated with a painted nose-down bomb –
Six, eight, eleven missions through the shrapnel.

As we docked at our final berth those fliers
Were soused in bourbon and grew louder,
As men come through it all, against the odds,
Will shout their lives out to the sky,
Slapping backs, jitterbugging man with man,
Then blowing up their last French letters
To launch them as love zepplins towards Manhattan.

Dannie Abse
'The camp'

In April 1945, when the war seemed almost as good as over, our firm was called together. Would any of us volunteer to nurse and treat critically sick prisoners in a camp that the Germans had abandoned? We were not told the name of that camp. Of course I volunteered. But unlike Russell Barton, Titch, Eric Trimmer, Hargraves and others, inexplicably I was not accepted. 'They must think I'm a duffer,' I told Titch gloomily.

Soon after, Titch and the rest were flown from an RAF camp near Swindon. Their destination hell. Some called it Belsen. They flew from RAF Lyneham on April 28th, the day the Italian partisans hung Mussolini and his mistress head downwards from meat hooks in a Milan garage. Two days later Hitler committed suicide and my friends in Belsen heard his emaciated victims cry pleadingly, 'Herr Doktor, Herr Doktor.' They were covered, those barely living skeletons, with sores and ulcers and infested with every kind of body parasite. Hargraves contracted typhus and became seriously ill.

None of this I knew until much later when I guessed that I was not allowed to join the Belsen team because I was a Jew. Meanwhile, on May 8th, it was Victory Day. With Nan I joined the effervescent singing crowds in Trafalgar Square who were wearing paper hats as at a party.

I often think about my not going to Belsen.

Dannie Abse
Cousin Sidney

Dull as a bat, said my mother
of cousin Sidney in 1940 that time he tried
to break his garden swing, jumping on it,
size 12 shoes – at fifteen the tallest boy
in the class, taller than loping Dan Morgan
when Dan Morgan wore his father's top hat.

Duller than a bat, said my father
when hero Sidney lied about his age
to claim rough khaki, silly ass;
and soon, somewhere near Dunkirk,
some foreign corner was forever Sidney
though uncle would not believe it.

Missing not dead please God, please,
he said, and never bolted the front door,
never string taken from the letter box,
never the hall light off lest his one son
came home through a night of sleet
whistling, *We'll meet again.*

Aunt crying and raw in the onion air
of the garden (the unswinging empty swing)
her words on a stretched leash
while uncle shouted, *Bloody Germans.*
And on November 11th, two howls
of silence even after three decades

till last year, their last year,
when uncle and aunt also went missing,
missing alas, so that now strangers
have bolted their door and cut the string
and no-one at all (the hall so dark)
waits up for Sidney, silly ass.

Alun Lewis
Raiders' Dawn

Softly the civilised
Centuries fall,
Paper on paper,
Peter on Paul.

And lovers waking
From the night –
Eternity's masters,
Slaves of Time –
Recognise only
The drifting white
Fall of small faces
In pits of lime.

Blue necklace left
On a charred chair
Tells that Beauty
Was startled there.

Post-War, Cold War, New Wars

Nigel Heseltine
Hero of his Village

Though you are missing from the shelf
where your family coffins rot in the vault,
your cross is on the church wall
decorated with a button or two from your coat.

So the children coming with the hymn-
books in their hands see that you died
for liberty or some cause and hang
above where the parish magazine is displayed.

Though there is nothing of you but the buttons,
those in the cricket-team you taught to bowl
remember you; the girls you looked aside from
lest you become entangled, married now
look beyond their solid husbands, remember you well.

Though you left no child, nor a wife
nor ploughed land save once on leave
as relaxation; though the parson leaving
his church in a hurry now never sees
your cross, yet given a proper occasion the man
could preach a sermon on your dying that would make
futile in comparison the longest life.

Christopher Meredith
Averted Vision

Edwards knew that he ought to be dead.

He was used to the smell and the sea was calmer. Calm sea and star-froth, then unfamiliar constellations. The spewstench from the hold but then just turn your head and there were lungfuls of pure air with salt for flavour, the dark sea broken with the glitter of points of starlight.

The day before he'd been sick when the underbalasted coalship had pitched in the huge swell.

Christ, he'd thought. This is the worst thing in the world. Worse than the dysentery. Then, shut up you dull bugger – you're alive.

★ ★ ★ ★ ★

Lovat looked at the stars. He was used to the dark and could see the blue or red tinge of some of them, thought he could detect, here and there, the faint films of nebulae. He wished he knew more about it, thought he would have to get a book. But then, some luck and another month or so and they'd be home.

He hung his head back and stared up straight. The fixed stars shifted with the ship's movement. A point of light came into being as it crossed the edge of his field of view and then vanished when he tried to look straight at it. He looked slightly away again and it reappeared. Averted vision, that was called. Something to do with how the eye works in the dark. Look away slightly and faint objects get clearer. He remembered reading that.

He felt his tommy gun slide away on his knees and grabbed it with a start. He looked across the hatch, but Edwards had his face turned away, looking out to sea.

Lovat looked up once more.

★ ★ ★ ★ ★

Like them, Edwards thought. They all ought to be dead.

He didn't look down into the hold where his feet dangled above the sleeping prisoners.

They must think it too. Every day he thought, why am I still alive? In the hold beneath his swinging heels where there should have been thousands of tons of coal, the prisoners lying in one another's dried vomit must be glad to be alive. But they were only second line stuff, clerks and all. They were only moved in after the front line men had – finished. So perhaps they didn't realise that they ought to be dead.

He looked at Lovat.

He didn't know he ought to be dead either. Came too late.

Sorry, Private Lovat. We all know how much you wanted to do your bit, what? But it finished ten minutes ago.

What a shame. But never mind. Help me disinter the pieces of my friends and give them Christian whatsits. The many men so beautiful. Fragments whirling in the void like stars. And help me, Lovat, on the fence at Sham-shu-po.

Show them who's boss, the pillock of a subaltern says, *just till things calm down a bit.*

And do you love that, Lovat, strutting with a gun?

Edwards realised he was gripping his machine gun very tight.

198

★ ★ ★ ★ ★

Stare straight at a faint object in gloom, Lovat thought, and it vanishes. Huge catastrophes on the other side of space tricked into oblivion by some technical hitch in the retina.

Staring at the invisible far sun, Lovat felt the tension draining from his limbs, his eyes getting heavy, seeming to drag down his face.

His father, waving the scissors, said, 'Keep your nose clean and your head down, and for them as sneers at your trade, tell them barbering's preferable to barbarity.'

He wiped the two sinks in front of the mirrors, checked the floor for yesterday's clippings.

'And don't tell your mother about the johnnies. It's a good sideline and comes natural with the trade. People often fancy a bit of the other after a trim and a nice bit of smelly stuff on the bonce. Frustrated conception's no sin. Frustrated people – now that is something that can end up nasty.'

Handy to have a trade. In the army it would come in useful, like playing the trumpet, they said. Help you avoid the bad bits. Ballocks. You end up cutting everybody's hair *and* loading the bodies onto the lorries, standing around by the fence with a gun, acting hard. The peaked cap studiously looking away after he tells you, in his indirect way, to do something nasty. Still, not long. This is a trade mission, sort of. Japs for coal. This is how civilisation reasserts itself. Clear up the bodies and screw the best deal you can out of them before they can have their young men back. Just hang on. Live through it and we might get back to our own side of the planet. Keep you head clean and your nose. No. That wasn't it.

★ ★ ★ ★ ★

Edwards watched Lovat, who was sitting with his feet hanging in the opposite corner of the hatch, fall asleep. There was little light, but Edwards saw the head sink forward. The imitation of death. The many men so beautiful and they all dead did lie and a thousand thousand slimy things.

Edwards glanced away at the glittering on the black ocean. About and about in reel and rout. And when they reared the elfish light feel off in hoary flakes. How was it?

He couldn't see Lovat's eyes but imagined the lids rolling down, the pupils up. Ah sleep it is a gentle thing beloved from pole to pole, so take your nightshift sentry-go and stick it up your.

Something moved, sliding on Lovat's knees. A dull glimmer.

The tommy gun clanged on the steel ladder as it fell into the hold. It hit the rungs several times as it must have turned end over end.

Edwards was up and part way down the ladder when he heard a strangled shout.

He looked up and called, 'Lamp, wanker.'

Lovat's torch flickered over the edge of the hatch.

'Shit. It nearly went once before.'

'Down here quick before they twig.'

Edwards hung out on the ladder with one hand and held his gun in the other. Somebody groaning. Lovat passed him, panting, the torch-beam jiggling.

The thin ray moved over the still figures, picking out the promontories of hips and shoulders.

'No fucker woke.'

Edwards saw Lovat stoop, pick up the gun and look at the man who had his hands on his face. Lovat looked towards the ladder.

'Come and have a look at this, Taff.'

★ ★ ★ ★ ★

Fucking cunt. Why did you go and lie there for? Nobody wanted you in Singapore. Nobody wanted you under the bastard hatch. You taking up astronomy or something?

He pulled the prisoner's hands away from his face.

The man was still conscious. One eye was closing with a swelling. The nose was spread across the other cheek and his upper lip had split in a very clean straight line. The front teeth were smashed and the man, looking frightened up at Lovat with one eye, gargled blood.

★ ★ ★ ★ ★

No fucker woke? You must be greener than I thought.

Edwards looked at the still forms as he came down the ladder and moved slowly towards Lovat.

That's right. Keep your heads down.

He glanced at the injured face in the pool of torchlight and looked round the hold once more. The smell of vomit and coal.

'Well done, Lovat.'

'He's only a Jap.'

He's a Jap, I'm a Taff. Who the fuck are you?

'Well we can't leave him like that. He's being fucking repatriated day after tomorrow.'

'They aren't in a position to complain though, are they?'

Edwards looked round at Lovat whose face was dimly lit from below. A light that makes faces demonic, but Lovat looked merely scared.

'Get the fucker up. See if he can walk and get him aft and patched up.'

Lovat put the gun down, thought, picked the gun up, put the torch down and pulled at the prisoner's upper arm. The man got to his feet, a little unsteadily, holding his head back as if he was afraid part of his face might slide off. He was wearing only shorts. Edwards watched the torchlight jiggle as Lovat followed the man up the ladder.

Fucking marvellous. Leave me in the dark.

Edwards got up behind them quickly and went back to his place at the corner of the hatch.

Three hundred odd of them. The promontories of hips and shoulders.

The path of weak light flickered in his mind.

For a charnel dungeon fitter. Why am I still?

★ ★ ★ ★ ★

Lovat pressed the muzzle of his gun into the man's back as they walked aft.

Just like the films. Except he's very tall. Thin, from the camp of course. They were supposed to be little and yellow and wear thick glasses. They were inscrutable heathens.

He looked at the tall man's starved back. What muscle there was was sculpted by the upward angled torchbeam. The notched spine was clear.

They fuck up people like Edwards. Looks forty, but he's twenty-four. Time I'm twenty-four all I want to be is a barber flogging rubber johnnies to customers wanting to enjoy what comes natural after a bit of preening. There's pleasure in that exactness. The precise clipping, the perfectly razored back of the neck, the carefully angled hand-mirror allowing him to inspect your razorwork while you discuss the match. Stepping into the yard of an evening with a packet of Players, watching Orion or whatever arcing up over the shed. Keep your head down and your nose clean. Or keep your nose on your face, anyway.

Unpleasantly, Lovat felt himself smiling.

Clean. The peaked cap giving me a long hard look. How? Do you really expect me to believe? Seen your sort. Quiet, and then they get a taste for it. Really, now it's all finished too. You'd change your tune if you'd seen half the.

Edwards was half way round the bend. Stuttered sometimes and said he'd been six stone when they took him out of it for his last leave.

They did that. Peaked caps and heathens. And who would count them the other end? Who counted?

Lovat glanced back. They were passing between the rail and some superstructure. Edwards was no longer in sight.

Lovat whispered, 'Stop.'

He moved inboard of the prisoner and nudged his shoulder with the muzzle so that they faced one another, Lovat with his back to the bulkhead, the man with his back to the sea. In the upturned beam Lovat saw that the bruises had ripened. The closed eye was buried in a fold of swellings. The unharmed eye looked startlingly ordinary, a dark brown, the tiny map of blood vessels in the white. Almost, Lovat thought, intelligent. Almost, even, real.

Staring straight at the man's face, Lovat snapped the torch off. He continued staring but the face had disappeared.

* * * * *

Edwards knew how it would be. Lovat would come back. Edwards would say, that was quick. Lovat would be quiet a moment and then say. Edwards would say nothing. Lovat would say why. Try to. And that would be all. And a thousand thousand.

Edwards held his gun loosely across his lap. A tenseness passed through him as if he would vomit and he unclipped the magazine, threw it to one side. He relaxed.

The torchlight danced on the deck towards him, flickered momentaily across one pair of walking feet.

Above the far thrumming of the engines and the purling of water around the hull, Edwards had heard nothing.

Tony Curtis
The Grammar

They were never dull, those half-remembered,
half-composed men, our masters.

We joined with them in some conspiracy
(the grey-trousered 'Fifties needed authority)

and the hurts they did us dull down the years,
those classroom NCOs from some distant war of tears.

Some had survived, like Jenkins Chem whose face
was one big scar from when his tank bought it at Falaise.

Others missed the show, or dodged the chance to fight:
they lived through peacetime's sterile wank.

Perhaps they took it out on us, the celebration
fruit of victory over Hitler and the Japs; a generation

not long enough on the branch, fallen,
rotten on coffee and juke-box rock 'n' roll.

We made them the stuff of boyhood myth, and all
colluded in that corridored game they played.

We had the hatred of all arty things
an all-male institution brings:

Roberts Music played us Chopin, the poof,
but set us shivering with that Mussorgsky stuff.

Ethy the Art taught us nothing at all. Smutty
Michaelangeloes, we'd draw in his David's classical balls

And rather die than meet him behind the board
– hands on flies, backs to the wall.

Maths when Bonzo Davies would chalk backwards on a dap
BONZO – and print it on your bum with a public whack.

And all the time the skirmishings ran on:
their job to keep us under the thumb;

our skill in changing words of the hymns
and silent, riotous farting in the assembly gyms.

Then stinging ears, arse canings.
A system of rude awakenings.

Those well-remembered, rarely-composed men, our masters,
coloured in our formative years, the clever bastards.

Gillian Clarke
Oranges

So many of them among the stones,
each like a float over a lobster pot
coming in numerous as the drowned.

Up early at the Little Harbour,
we found the treasure we'd sought
all the Saturdays of childhood.
First gold brought generously
to a mean Britain. I remember
the water calm as milk licking
the sand with little oily tongues.

We filled our sleeves,
gathered our skirts to make sacks,
bumped uncomfortably homeward.
Crates like the smashed ribcages of sheep.
Across milky water the wreck
was languorous, her tilted deck
rolling with Atalanta's gold.

Salt at first bite, then bitter pith
and a sharp juice. My tongue searched
for the cloying concentrate I knew
or the scent the miner spoke of,
an orange broken at snap-time underground
breathed a mile away
if the wind's in the right direction.

Dannie Abse
Not Beautiful

In all hiroshimas, in raw and raving voices,
    live skeletons of the Camp, flies hugging faeces,
        in war, in famine, he'd find the beautiful.

Being saintly, his vocation was to find it
>   at the dying bedside, in the disrobing dead.
>   And what he did, they said, you should be trying.

Well, once, while dissecting a nerve in a cadaver
>   my cigarette dropped, fell into its abdomen.
>   I picked it up. I puffed out the smoke of hell.

Yet still was not fit for time to come: the freehold grave,
>   things run over like slush all bloody and throbbing –
>   for though they were dumb, not beautiful, I said.

It's the parable again of the three wise men:
>   the first who, with finger and thumb, tweaked his nostrils,
>   and the second who pressed his eyes to his palms,

whilst the third, the wisest, cried, 'Oh what beautiful,
>   white teeth have these vermin which died.' *Homo sum,*
>   etc., but the third was divine (as they said).

One sees the good point, of course, and may admire it;
>   but, sometimes, I think that to curse is more sacred
>   than to pretend by affirming. And offend.

Dylan Thomas
'Knocking down air-raid shelters'

[NOISE OF DRILLS AND DEMOLITION FADE NOISE INTO BACKGROUND]

ALFRED: Gives you a funny feeling, knocking down air-raid shelters. I helped to build this one.
WORKMAN: Looks a bit ricketty, too ...
TED: I used to make wireless sets and as soon as I'd finished 'em I'd pull 'em to bits. Always. Must have made scores of sets and never listened in more than a couple of minutes.
ALFRED: That's different.

TED: Course it's different. I used to try to get Moscow and
                South America on sets I made. Only got Germany
                on air-raid shelters. But I learned something new all
                the time I was fiddling about with coils and con-
                densers and things. There was some point pulling
                them to bits and starting again ...

[A CRASH]

ALFRED: One for old Hitler ...

[ANOTHER CRASH]

WORKMAN: One for old Franco ...
TED: ... Hope we all learned something new now. Knock
                all the shelters and pillboxes to bits, and start all over
                again. But not to build new shelters. We've had
                enough of that.
ALFRED: Don't no need no shelters for atom-bombs. Give me
                a nice old fashioned 200 pounder.
TED: If a bomb had your name on it, you had it coming
                and that's all. Atom-bombs got everyruddybody's
                name on 'em, that's the difference. But there aren't
                going to be any atom-bombs. There can't be. It
                doesn't make sense. We're not children.
ALFRED: I feel young enough sometimes, on a Saturday night.
TED: No, I mean, *we're* the Government, aren't we. It's we
                who got to say, 'No, there's not going to be any funny
                business any more.' And just *see* that there isn't
                either. If people all over the world say, 'We don't
                want atom-bombs, we want all the things that atomic
                energy can make not what it can bust up,' then that's
                how it's going to be.
ALFRED: You shouldn't talk politics when you're working ...
TED: If a man can't talk politics when he's got a pneumatic
                drill in his hand, when can he then ...

[UP NOISE OF DRILLS ETC., MUSIC WHILE YOU WORK]

Goronwy Rees
'A sinister enchantment'

But we were driving towards the Ruhr; we were soon out of the unravaged countryside and evidence began to collect of the consequences of war and defeat. I began to understand the man who said that war may be hell but defeat is worse. For in most of Germany at that time, and certainly in its industrial areas, it seemed true to say that even the most elementary conditions of civilised life had ceased to exist. Wherever the war had been, it had remorselessly ground to pieces the whole structure of organised society and all we could see around us was the ruin and rubble that remained. Even Tamplin's headlong progress was halted by broken bridges whose arches and girders projected crazily into the sky and by roads that were a continuous series of potholes and craters; our journey became slow and erratic wandering along whatever highways and byways still remained open to us, like lost travellers painfully exploring some landscape of the moon. And all around us, at every turn, was the same monotonous repetitive vista of gap-toothed buildings, houses brutally torn apart, endless miles of fallen and broken masonry, and a few bent and solitary figures scratching in the ruins for anything that might be useful to them in the struggle to survive. It was a landscape as mournful and fantastic as those Piranesi drew of the ruins of ancient Rome, in which a few tiny human figures are dwarfed and overshadowed by the colossal fragments of a ruined world.

As we penetrated deeper into this scene of devastation, which had once formed the greatest industrial complex in Europe, moving slowly forward as if through some dense jungle of shattered stone and brick and steel, rain began to fall, the sad grey drizzle of a world that had come to an end. When we entered Düsseldorf on a Sunday afternoon, it was pouring from a leaden sky, the colour of dead ashes, and in this downpour the ruined empty streets had the mournfulness and melancholy of some tragic funeral dirge, as if we had come to attend a burial ceremony. But we were the only mourners, for the streets were totally deserted; in this dead city there was nothing any longer to support life, neither food nor water nor shelter nor heating and ever+yone who could leave had already left; only the rats still scuffled in the rubble. We drove to the offices of the commander of the local Military Government detachment, who occupied the only building in the town which seemed to be relatively undamaged; that is to say, it had a roof and its walls were still standing and its broken windows had been repaired, though it was as grimy and cheerless as the ruins themselves.

As we walked down the passage we crunched underfoot the little piles of broken plaster that had been shaken from the walls.

We found the local commander at work among a litter of papers in his naked ground floor office; from his window he had a view, through the rain, of the ruins which constituted his empire. He was a lieutenant-colonel who only a short time ago had commanded a battalion which was enthusiastically engaged in completing the final downfall of Germany; now, with equal enthusiasm, he was doing what he could to mitigate the effects of her defeat. The breast of his tunic was covered with ribbons and in all the miles around him of dirt and devastation, he was the only object that was spruce and clean and shining. By one of those magical transformations, like a scene in pantomime, which occur in war, he now found himself the administrator and absolute ruler of an area containing over one million human beings who had suddenly been deprived of the means of existence. He might just as well have been dropped from the skies in the middle of tropical Africa and told to get on with the job of governing some primitive tribe living on the edge of starvation.

Indeed, he would have been better off, for there at least he would have found some form of tribal organisation through which he could have given his commands. But the tribal organisation of the Germans had vanished overnight; the whole complex interlocking structure of State and Party and local government had been swallowed up in defeat and with it had disappeared all the men responsible for working it. So far as local administration was concerned, the lieutenant-colonel might just as well have been operating in the desert, and to a more rational man the task in hand would have seemed so grotesque and futile as to be not worth attempting; but he was not a rational man, particularly because he seemed quite unaware of the irony of his endeavours to succour a people whom a short time ago he had been doing his best to destroy. When the Political Adviser suggested that there might be dangers in adopting so wholeheartedly the cause of our defeated enemies, he asked rather angrily whether it was the intention that they should be left to starve, or in winter to freeze, to death. He was not concerned with the preoccupations of political advisers; his only, his obsessive interest in life, it seemed, at that moment was the baffling problem of how, without transport, he could bring enough coal into the city to allow the Germans to get to work again; for without work they could not live. Until that moment I had not really understood that without fuel and transport it is impossible for men to exist in cities.

But the lieutenant-colonel also had another obsession as well as coal, without which the Germans, or what he sometimes referred to as 'my people', would also lack all the other means of subsistence. Kafka says somewhere that the worst horror of war is that it dissolves all the established rules and conventions of life; after a few weeks of trying to control its results, the local commander in Düsseldorf would have agreed with him. For his area, like other areas of Germany, was at that moment overrun by thousands of foreign workers, Frenchmen, Poles, Czechs, Russians, who had been the slaves of the Reich and now, suddenly released and at liberty, were determined both to keep themselves alive and take their revenge by plundering its corpse. At night the countryside was alive with bands of what were politely called 'displaced persons', who with considerable reason felt themselves entitled to pillage, plunder, rape, and murder with impunity; for what crimes could they possibly commit worse than the crimes which had been committed against them, and who more than they had the right to act on Bacon's dictum that revenge is a kind of primitive justice? The lieutenant-colonel found himself faced with moral problems of a kind he had never envisaged; he had solved them on the simple principle that of all evils the complete absence of any form of law and order is the worst, worse even than the lack of the means of subsistence, and that his first task was to re-establish them, even though individual justice might be compromised in the process. When the lieutenant-colonel talked about coal and food, he talked like a Marxist; *Erst kommt das Fressen, dann kommt die Moral.* When he talked about morality, he made one think that perhaps, after all, it is not merely a consequence of material conditions.

It was fascinating to listen, in that dingy office, while the rain poured down outside, to the representative of Military Government explaining his problems, with a passion and eloquence which were certainly not native to him; they were the product of the appalling situation in which he found himself. He was like a man who finds himself lost in a dark and impenetrable forest and is determined, if necessary, to hack his way through the undergrowth with his own hands; but now he looked to the Political Adviser as one who might throw some light into the darkness which surrounded him and give him some help in his task. But the Political Adviser was essentially an honest man. He had the sense to know that in our absurd ivory tower in Lübbecke we knew far less about these matters than the local commander himself did, and that in his place he could do no better than he was doing. So he contented himself with saying that he would report the condition of affairs to London, and that he thought this might make some difference to those politicians who, following in the footsteps of Mr Morgenthau and Mr Noel Coward, still thought that the fundamental problem in Germany was how to be beastly enough to the Germans;

and to this the lieutenant-colonel answered simply that if there were such people who had office or influence, they should come and do the job themselves and not leave it to British soldiers.

It was with a certain feeling of shame that finally we left him in his office to address himself to what at that moment seemed a hopeless task, with an enthusiasm which did him so much honour; while we drove off gropingly in the darkness to find our way to the luxuries and comforts of a Corps Headquarters, where the Political Adviser was received with the lavish hospitality befitting his rank but so repugnant to his taste. The Corps Commander, silvery haired, with an aquiline face and a manner which a tragic actor might have envied, was giving a very good imitation of a Renaissance prince enjoying the pleasures of his latest conquest, and was anxious to show that in him the exuberance of victory was refined by the discrimination of taste. Certainly in his freshly furnished and furbished *Schloss*, from which all traces of war had been effaced, or in its green and peaceful park, it became almost impossible to believe in the dark picture painted for us in Düsseldorf, of a population not merely ruined but abandoned and betrayed and a country devastated and denuded and systematically pillaged by bands of brigands who would have been affronted by the mere suggestion that Germans could have any rights against themselves; indeed, we might well have thought the local commander guilty of sentimentality or exaggeration if we had not heard the same account at every post we visited in the course of our journey.

But indeed as we continued on our journey it seemed to acquire something of the unreality of a fairy tale, of a journey through a country which had fallen under a sinister enchantment, like that journey of Manawydan and Pryderi in the third book of the *Mabinogion*, through a land in which 'where they used to see the flocks and the herds and the dwellings, not a thing could they see: neither house nor beast nor smoke nor fire nor man nor dwelling, but the houses of the court empty, desolate, uninhabited, without man, without beast within them'. Over large areas the country had precisely this air of abandonment; 'not a soul could they see. In mead-cellar and in kitchen there was nothing but desolation.'

Only where it might have been least expected, and in its least expected forms, did life seem to continue. In a huge hangar abandoned by the *Luftwaffe* we visited a vast camp of men, women, and children who had been transported to the factories of the Ruhr when the Germans occupied the Ukraine. By night many of them joined those bands of bandits and marauders who roamed and pillaged the countryside; by day also they went into the woods and fields and lanes, but the only plunder they brought back with them were green branches plucked from the trees and flowers picked in the fields, with which, under the immensely high girders of the hangar roof, they wove for themselves green and leafy little huts and cubicles in which each family made a home of its own. Entering the hangar, one suddenly had the impression of being in some huge green conservatory, as at a flower show at Chelsea or Shrewsbury, filled with the hundreds of little green-leaved huts into the foliage of which their inhabitants had also woven the fresh flowers they had picked that day, and under their arched roofs their tenants lay or squatted while their food cooked in whatever served them as a family pot; for these citizens of the Soviet Union, conscripted into National Socialist Germany, treasured above all their individual family life and stubbornly refused to share in any form of community feeding. Rations had to be distributed each day to each family, who then cooked their own meals in whatever way pleased them best.

Walking among them was like visiting some huge gypsy encampment set down in the heart of Europe in the improbable setting of that abandoned hangar; it made one feel that the war had transformed Germany, and indeed the whole of Europe, into a vast transit camp, in which all permanent relationships had been dissolved and men and women tried desperately to improvise the best substitute for them which conditions would allow. It was as if all that remained to these people were their little huts of boughs and branches which reminded them of a home and homeland which had been destroyed. And we saw these same people, or their brothers and sisters, once again later on our journey, when driving along a dusty road alongside a railway track we overtook one of the few trains that were to be seen in Germany at that time. It dragged slowly and painfully along, overloaded by its weight of passengers, who crammed every compartment to overflowing, stood on the running board clutching the window frames, lay on the roof strumming their balalaikas and singing their Ukrainian songs, which rang so strangely across the German fields. They had wreathed the engine and carriages with the same green branches out of which they made their huts in the hangar, and when the train jolted to a stop they flung themselves from the carriages and from the roof into the fields to collect fresh flowers and foliage. These people had been liberated from one dictatorship, which had collapsed, and were travelling across Europe to return to another, which still survived. In the interval they were free, nomads wandering across Europe without home or habitation. Thousands of others were in the same condition, moving from west to east or from east to west. We seemed to be in the world of Saint-John Perse's *Anabasis*, as if the age of the *Völkerwanderung* had returned.

211

John Davies
Pursuit

I've been reading letters my father sent
after D-Day, the edging inland
through Normandy under fire from mosquitoes
then rain, sleep chopped in fragments.
('All the guns in France won't wake me')
and, after stand-to, breakfast canned.

'We have come back from the front.' Censored,
stray shellfire bursts through anyhow.
A lot's buried. He bathed 'in our English Channel',
sang 'Lledrod' in an apple orchard.
I'd ask if Collinge made it, Smith,
but all those guns wouldn't wake him now –

and at least one risk made him blunt:
the abbey at Mont St. Michel 'is treacherous
without a guide. There are secret passages
so one can easily get lost.' *About the front ...*
I'd have probed, though we are too slow
to ask the past much, slipping from us.

Still turning the dark side from his family,
he stored the letters in this book he'd keep
safe. He knew us, I think. We knew
the half of him. What he let us see
was the orchard, light cover, you'd have
to guess the dugout seven feet deep,

and I know now that when we let
silence speak it didn't, would not
speak for us, marching to the old tune
Sons and Fathers that we couldn't forget.
So looking at my daughter
suddenly I need to say something but what.

Owen Sheers
War Wound

It looks old, this scar,
this trickle of raised flesh
running the length of her shin.

Yet I know it still opens daily,
seeps into her talk,
bleeding memories

of the shard that entered her leg,
and stuck out,
a gun metal fin:

of the oiled sea made slow,
with waves that heaved
and swallowed men whole:

of the officers undoing their ties
before jumping, leaving
the bed-ridden patients,

some quiet, some screaming.
And of how she saw it;
a scar across the ocean,

a disturbance on the radar,
an explosion flipping out shock waves
that never stopped.

Sheenagh Pugh
Bolshies

In the last days of a lost war,
a man occupying a Brussels office
made time for spite; signed an order
to send one final trainload down the line
to the death camps. And his secretary

typed it, and a clerk bespoke the train,
and policemen who had no heart for the job
loaded the prisoners anyway.

But then it was all down to the lads
on the line: the drivers, the signalmen,
the track gangs, and all of a sudden
points seized up; urgent repairs took days,
you couldn't lay your hands on spare parts.
Wrong-set signals sent the train trundling
in circles while the bolshie branch rep
wheeled out his trusty, well-oiled excuses.

And when peace finally turned up
ahead of the spare parts; when the prisoners
could all change trains, and the bosses commenced
awarding themselves medals, the lads went back
to looking out for each other, fiddling time-sheets,
arguing over demarcation lines,
doing their best to baulk each jack-in-office
who tried to make the trains run on time.

Stevie Davies
'The Fatherland'

LAKE PLÖN, 1958, MAY 1945; MINSK, 1941

Michael read the morning news over his morning egg. A case going on
and on in a Schleswig-Holstein court brought by a Jewish dentist
against a well-respected teacher, who had indignantly defended in a
restaurant the right of Modern Youth to paint swastikas on synagogues. Suez was proof, said the teacher, that the British lion had lost
its roar; France was rotting in disorder; the Arabs would smash Israel;
the US was too fat and lazy and stupid to become a soldier nation
again. That left the Fatherland, which within a decade would be ready
again to confront its Hour of Destiny. *Far too few Jews went into the gas
chambers*, the teacher informed the dentist. *They forgot to gas you too.
Those were the days. They will come again. Remember I told you so.* And

the waiters put down their plates to applaud.

Is this a free country or is it not? demanded the teacher in court. *Does freedom of speech mean something or doesn't it?* The judge allowed him to rant on. The court wept at the teacher's noble sentiments: he would rather cleanse the streets, lick them clean with his tongue, than go crawling to a Jew. The race laws had been based on sound reasoning, he claimed. The court erupted in prolonged applause.

Adenauer ignored filth, protected rats. And here in Schleswig-Holstein, where the rats had found haven, Michael read today of the election of SS General Heinz Reinefarth to the State Assembly – 'the butcher of Warsaw', no less. He eyed the picture, which was small and indistinct, but the face was memorable. Only when he brought his eyes close to the page, obeying an instinct to stare into the depths of the rehabilitated butcher, did the bland face disintegrate into a random rash of dots. There were no depths. Where could you look these days without recognising some *Gauleiter*, Hitler Youth leader, Propaganda Ministry bigwig, strutting high in office, a face you knew? Fatter now, plusher, older, oleaginous, but the same brazen face.

Isolde Dahl: some such Wagnerian name had adorned the child his one-time friend disowned. The name churned up depths; it dredged him, bringing up filthy matter. The woman was a beauty, opulently made, with a strikingly oval, open face. He had seen his son hover over her as she sat by the lake, her skirts spread out around her in a blue flare, as if she had a lapful of gentians. He had seen Wolfi not daring to approach. *Keep it like that, Wolfi.*

The coffee Wolfi had left percolating on the stove gave out an aroma of the deliciously mundane. That steadied him. He poured and drank.

Michael cycled to Ruhleben, since the weather was so fine. He free-wheeled past Lake Suhr, looking over to 'The Trout' camp. Old Dönitz and the final frenzy. He came in to the music room with his usual brisk step; set down his briefcase and hung his coat on the peg. The pair bending over the piano moved back, embarrassed.

'Miss Dahl. Good morning.'

'*Guten Morgen.* Your son found me playing ... Chopsticks, I'm afraid, on your piano, and ... he's shown me a few notes.'

She looked up briefly and caught Wolfi's eye; Michael registered the shy intensity of his son's rare smile. Wolfi said, 'Miss Dahl should learn properly. She has a natural feel for ... Chopsticks,' and the young people burst out laughing, then quenched it.

'Well, I must get down to work,' said Michael, feeling hollow.

The young woman nodded and left. Wolfi picked up a cello by the neck of its case and followed her out. Michael looked through his list of pupils and set out the sheet music he would need that day. The girl was disturbing. And the room felt queasy, disorientated.

The two of them there, she in that bilberry-coloured soft dress, leaning over the piano, he in the blue shirt Quantz had ironed for him the night before: they seemed dressed to match, as if in uniform, their heads close, collusive. Sex undoubtedly played its moonshine tune across the gap between them. He sat down on the double piano stool and flexed his fingers to play; but failed to play. He looked at the backs of his hands, then laid his palms on his knees, rubbing them to and fro in mental inertia. He turned slightly, scanning the room over his shoulder. Everything was the same. Tall windows with blinds admitting flying buttresses of dusty light; that bare table at the centre. Captain Pauckstadt's operations table, where nicotined fingers had reached to fiddle with counters on an hourly shrinking map. It was the same colossally empty room.

★ ★ ★ ★ ★

Kube whispered: *bodenlose Schweinerei*. Bottomless bestiality. He had complained to HQ, Kube hissed, he was prostrate, he was helpless, Kube said, what could he do? At Lvov the pit was covered but blood kept gushing out, 'how shall I say it ... like a geyser.' Kube said burying alive or half-dead was common. Wounded Jews worked their way out of their graves. The ground heaved, they were reborn, only to be shot and buried again.

Don't tell me, prayed Quantz. *Spare me this.*

Up they came. Up however hard you worked to pack them back down. The earth had lost its stability and turned into a churning sea. The people climbed down into the pit with gentleness and dignity. Naked, families soothed their children with calm, and lay down in the interstices between bodies to be machine-pistoled by the SS task forces.

Quantz was to report to Canaris.

'Spare me another trip,' he pleaded. 'Spare me.'

'But we must know.' The admiral had splashes of coffee on his tunic; his white hair was unkempt. He looked past Michael at the dachshunds. 'You will kindly execute commands. I am asking you only to observe; it is necessary.'

'Send someone else,' begged Michael. 'I'll be no good to you.'

Quantz was a witness, a travelling eye without the comfort of an eyelid.

Dahl had boasted. Boasted how he suffered from no pity, no ruth, no insomnia. 'Hard work, you have to be hard, work for men, real men, hard men, hard on us, cream of the cream, best blood.' On and on. He bragged how he took care of his kit even in the most foul of circumstances, not a hair out of place. Brayed a hee-haw laugh like a donkey. It appeared to be an acquired laugh, for Quantz had not heard it before: a Heydrich whinney.

Dahl's immaculate boot seemed a thing possessed of a will of its own, as it kicked the elderly man down into the pit. He had seemed to poise on the edge of that pit full of his people, hands clasped over his genitals. He had peered in, then turned to stare Dahl in the eyes. His hands left the vulnerable genitals and opened at his sides in a gesture of ... not beseeching but as if professing the most profound bafflement. He screwed up his eyes like a person who needs spectacles. Perhaps he did. The victims had been relieved of their watches and glasses a short distance back, leaving time and space a blur.

The old man, suddenly a figure not of pathos but of judgment, opened his mouth to speak. Whereupon Dahl reached over, tweaked his beard, said something like, 'Get a move on, Israel, we haven't got all day,' and booted him into the pit ... and shot, shot over and over again, shot regularly, as if measuring time like a clock. Michael reeled down a path into the woods, retching, vomiting. He could still hear the firing, getting fainter as he stumbled on.

Later, under the spell of drink, Dahl waxed lachrymose.

'You lads are lucky to have us to do your dirty work for you,' he bragged. 'Where would you be without us? And we have families of our own, you know. We are not without tender feelings. But our weakness we have overcome, rooted out.'

He had a new wife, he told Michael with pride, and showed a photograph. Two blond sons, and another on the way. Kissed the photograph devoutly. Said how he missed them; asked after Effi and Wolfi.

'Cat got your tongue? What's up? Got to you, hasn't it? This is nothing. Have a swig. What you've seen is nothing, man, compared with some of it. Toughen up – you have to be iron. We have overcome,' he added heroically, 'all effeminate feeling.'

Michael had begged Canaris to allow him to return to the navy, preferably on ship-board. The admiral must have realised his insides had gone to mush; he could be little further use. Canaris himself appeared less and less convincing as he became a stooped, haggard valetudinarian, living on reputation as an archaic god dangles by a mere thread of myth.

'Spare me,' Michael had pleaded. But memory did not spare him, for in what he was forced to witness and made no effort to stop, he must be accounted complicit. The venerable Jew surfaced, broke through the soil, got up and followed him like a hound. He was always there, observing Quantz.

But the Little Admiral was hanged, relieved of his memories.

★ ★ ★ ★ ★

There was no Kiel left. He came upon the smashed city as if dreaming awake. No Kiel. And Effi, Effi had died six weeks before in an air raid. Wolfi scavenged from the cellar of the ruined house. He did not recognise his father. His father scarcely recognised him.

'Will you come with me?' asked Michael.

His son acquiesced. Wherever there was food and shelter, the lanky, pragmatic ex-child would go. They returned together to Plön.

Dönitz and his government were said to be nicely set up in a castle owned by the Duke of Mecklenburg and Holstein, overlooking the picturesque waters of Kiel Bay, whence they proceeded by limousine to Flensburg for council meetings at ten prompt each morning, to discuss the government of a state garrisoned by four foreign conquerors. Michael heard that the admiral wore his dress uniform and grew more imperial by the day. But Michael had metamorphosed into his own double, in mimesis of a cultured Englishman: quiet, reliable, a musician and interpreter. He pronounced his Christian name the English way, and blessed his parents for supplying such an ambivalent label.

Michael and his son walked by the lake, the young man tagging behind, a dumb animal on an invisible leash. The compass of Michael's consciousness had shrunk to the life of the rediscovered boy; Wolfi could not help but seem like a minor destiny. What Michael had neglected, he had been permitted to redeem and he pledged himself to care for him. He watched how warily the lad walked, putting his feet down as if the nerves of the soles were tender.

'What is it, Wolfi?'

The boy shook his head. He was dry-eyed, sombre. He walked like someone whose roots hurt, that was it. This was the feeling Michael had when he looked at the strange way he walked. The boy had been torn up, bombed out and suffered mother-loss, and though the roots would heal and he was already adapting, the endings must tingle, like phantom nerve-pains from lost limbs.

★ ★ ★ ★ ★

The English girls and boys came and went. Michael forgot the view over his shoulder. He chatted to a new child, who showed real musicianship. Rachel's touch was fine, her sense of tone-colouring unusual. She had seemed less than promising when she sat down on her half of the piano stool, monosyllabic, crouched in to herself.

'How far have you got?' he asked her.

'Schubert,' she mumbled, which was not an answer. He asked her to show him what she could do, expecting little.

Her frozen gaze melted at the keyboard, She stretched her arms and, relaxing her hands over the keys, let her fingers ripple. She played from memory, fluently, magnanimously, without show or artifice.

'Well,' he said. 'Who taught you?'

'Our mam.'

He began a dialogue at the bass end of the piano and they improvised against one another. As the bell went, she turned up to him a soulful face with dark, liquid eyes that were dragged back reluctantly from far away and seemed to ask where the time had gone; why the one good thing had to be over?

'You will do well, Rachel. Have you enjoyed it?'

She nodded miserably. The music had perished with the magical hour.

He walked back across the quadrangle, past the flagpole and its rigging, behind a group of matrons, teetering on their high heels. He watched their calves, straightening the seams of their nylons with his eye. Their heels clicked on the tarmac. They cast a common shadow, with hydra heads and spider legs, which seemed to clamber down the shadow of the rigging in the late afternoon sunlight. Their tongues wagged. He caught a wisp of their hugger-mugger conversation, which was, *A kike Hitler forgot to gas.*

John Tripp
Pay Detachment, Exeter

This was where the dregs went
down to the bottom of the barrel
when the regiments spewed them out.
We had bad feet, squints, glass eyes, unhappy childhoods
and the look of rodneys on the run.
But we could add up shillings and pence,
write vouchers to destitute wives
when their men scarpered. We played cards
and drank applejack from the farms.

I knew then
none of us would enter the Ministry
or speak to the Cymmrodorion.
We were not
the 20th Valeria Victrix, proud under Trajan,
defending the western limits of empire.

We were what our time had made us
coming in at the end of a war:
small, insignificant, and wary
of speeches and flags.

Taurus Intelligentsia Frustrat
(Bullshit baffles the mind)
was our motto in pidgin-Latin
over the door of the bogs.

John Tripp
Dering Lines '45

I

He was my first sight of evil,
a masterpiece of cunning:
Sergeant Hopkin, blonde as an actress
with small pig eyes like blue ice,
marched us up to the butts
to pick mushrooms for his mess.
I tried to pick toadstools, but was afraid.
Then we'd lie flat on the turf and click triggers
at invisible planes. Rifle Ack-Ack they called it.

'You, come here' said Hopkin, jabbing a finger.
'You're shooting like a frog
at those bloody Messerschmitts.'
His red lips were always moist,
he kept sliding his tongue around them
while his poor brain flamed and would one day break
on its path to insanity.

II

Dead sheep littered the ranges
burst open by grenades, and farmers cursed in Welsh
as we trudged through their cattle pancakes.
The skulls of the poor sheep were everywhere.

Summer rain screened the Lines
sunk deep in raw country,
boots crunched on concrete
in our trap in the hills.
We wiped guns and shone brass,
bending to sadists with stripes on their sleeves:
'You're a fuckin shower. You're frogs. Wot are you?'
'Frogs, sergeant.'

Boredom was worn like a second skin
as we darned socks and sewed buttons,
whitewashed the cokeshed, saluted anything that moved;
once, six of us hacked a lawn with knives.
We slept on pallets where beetles lived
inside the straw, snug in the warm.
We were a mix of bully-boys from the ports
and callow bundles of shock from Ebenezer.

Our mentors were old sweats:
brave Rats who fought Rommel
now cynical and venomous, growling for their tickets.
Here the crack Welsh regiments of the line
with the skulls of Rorke's Drift in their cupboards
ran down to a skivy remnant.

I was young, respectable as a curate,
flummoxed by foul language and strapped
inside my Baptist straitjacket.
There I learnt to drink draught Bass,
jig with fast Naafi girls
and fritter my lean 19th year
among the reek of latrines and bolt-oil
in the bleak scooped uplands of Epynt.

John Tripp
Burial Party

Probert told me. The lieutenant was blown
to bits on the grenade range
looking for a dud. 'Jesus
it was a fuckin mess,' Probert said.

Poplars dripped. The box draped with a Jack
was lifted off the wet gun-carriage;
the bearers almost dropped it
as one of them slid in the slime.

Four of us had dug a hole in a copse
on a slope not far from their house.
Our capes were soaked, our boots were caked.
There was this drizzle, continuous, and much
slithering about in mud as the box
was lowered. The widow's black stockings
were splashed with mud. Buglers lined up and blew
a short Last Post – piercing and eardrum-banging
on the dawn air. Riflemen discharged their blanks
as the little knot of mourners
waited for the thing to end.

We covered him up, flattened out the earth,
slung spades and rakes on a jeep,
lit cigarettes and sludged back in the rain
through the sopping Breconshire fields.

'I'm going to get pissed tonight'
said Probert. Pity was a four-letter word
we never used, and all I could feel
was an emptiness, the beginning of pity.

Leslie Thomas
'The train from Kuala Lumpur'

They had to wait all day for the train. There had been shooting from the lineside and trouble with the bandits in places spaced widely between Kuala Lumpur and the north.

There was Brigg, Tasker, Lantry, Sinclair, and Waller, the infantry-man who was going to get off the train half-way down the country to go back to his unit. At the station they sat until the columns of sun-light standing from openings in the roof to the floors, had banked and gradually become rafters of the same roof. Tasker went to sleep curled up on two suitcases. Sinclair took Lantry to see the engines.

Waller said to Brigg: 'I went to hospital in Penang.'

Brigg said: 'I know. About your kidneys or something.'

'The nurse, the girl you know, told you? You saw her?'

'That's right,' said Brigg.

'She's lovely,' said Waller. 'Is that where you were all night?'

'Yes,' said Brigg smugly. 'All night. Thanks for telling her.'

'I went to see the doctor,' said Waller. 'I thought if I could start building up a medical case I might work my ticket, or get down to Singapore, or somewhere else where I didn't have to have my teeth chopped out.'

'What did they say?' asked Brigg.

'Mumbled about, as usual. If you told them you were going to have triplets they'd not disbelieve you. And I thought it would *look* better if I reported it when I was on leave because it's not the time anyone would normally try to pull a fast one, is it? They'd think you were too busy enjoying yourself and if you went to hospital then it must be genuine.'

'What do you do next?' asked Brigg.

'I've got to tell my own M.O. I've got a note,' said Waller. 'And I'll take half a dozen salt tablets, the ones they give us up here because of the salt we lose sweating. That'll make me spew like mad and they'll think there is something really wrong. I'll be down there pushing a pen yet.'

It was dark before the train went out. The small pilot engine probed bravely before the express, searchlight out in front, down through the black, jungled country, With nothing to see only the poor peeping lights of villages every ten or twelve miles.

Brigg lay, on the bottom bunk this time, which was better, jolting with the track, staring up at the middle bunk low over his forehead. It was hot, and sometimes Tasker, who was above him, passed down a bottle of pale beer.

Sinclair, by counting the rhythm beats of the train, could tell each mile as it went by. Brigg listened to the hasty talking of the wheels too. When he was a child he remembered listening like that as they went to the seaside and saying to himself: 'Soon-be-there. Soon-be-there. Soon-be-there.' He did it now. But moved his wet lips without sound to 'Soon-be-home. Soon-be-home. Soon-be-home.'

That's all he wanted now. Not even Phillipa, because she was running away from him with every roll of the wheels. He knew that was how she had intended it. To give him one night, a night of plenty and love, which was fine, except that she called him sergeant.

Now he must not consider her any more. Or Lucy, sweet Lucy, who had taught him love in return for rhymes. Now there would be Joan and home. Joan-and-home. Joan-and-home. Joan-and-home.

The first bullet came through the roof and went like a drilling wasp through the toe of his boot standing on the floor by his bed. He frowned at it, for he could not see the ceiling, and the buzz from his boot and the hole suddenly in it made him think stupidly that something was trying to get out from inside it, forcing its way through. Once at Panglin he had stamped through a parade with a crushed and suffocated beetle, the size of a small mouse, imprisoned in his boot, in the channel under his toes. Now he thought there was another in it and was boring through to the surface.

Then Tasker and Lantry fell from above him like rocks.

'Shots!' croaked Tasker. 'They're shooting!'

Another bullet sawed through the side of the compartment and blew the nozzle from a fire extinguisher on the wall, sending a soda fountain of spray all up and around.

Brigg found himself on his hands and knees on the floor. The long alleyway was full of crouching, colliding figures, like animals in a pen. Brigg put on one boot, but took it off again and left them lying there. He had both hands gripping the stock of his rifle. Somebody was moaning: 'Oh Christ. Oh Christ.' From the front of the express came a great heave as though the engine itself were throwing up.

They were all tipped forward on their faces in the gangway. All the voices were frightened, mixed, and then drowned by a vivid bang from the front of the train and a drumming din that shook the carriages as though the express were rubbing its skin against the jungle trees. The men were rolled and spilled about, then levelled out and left hugging the floor and each other as the train made a final hit, and bent itself off the track, back on, and then off again the other side like a crumpled straw.

It stopped and it was like the inside of a drum in Brigg's compartment. The air was full of dust and darkness, and the fire extinguisher was still gurgling. No one moved. They were piled on each other as though they were dead and in a mass grave. From the darkness came coughs and sobs. Then a stream of machine-gun bullets did a savage trepanning of the front part of the carriage, opening up the roof like a lid.

'Get out!' howled someone. 'They'll be chucking grenades in.'

They scrambled and escaped in a panic from the coach and into the next one. This was lying tilted, screwed upwards with the windows facing the treetops. It was full of civilians, all thrown and lying in the deepest trough. Brigg could not see them but he could hear them moaning and sense them moving. He heard the sound of breaking canes and he realised it was the bullets coming back.

'Down,' he shouted in a voice that surprised him for its clearness. He felt the soldiers fling themselves on their stomachs around him. Somehow he landed on his back and tried to wriggle over as the bullets bit overhead and the glass in the windows exploded. He realised how illogical it was as he did it, but there was something awful about lying face up to bullets.

When the volley had gone by there was a slow silence as though it had killed everyone. But Brigg could feel the men on either side of him panting. Then, down in the trough where the civilians were, someone struck a match and held its light trembling to the face of a young Chinese girl who stared in death with such horror that it seemed as though she had seen the bullet coming to her. It had struck her through the cheek, and blood was covering the bottom of her face and her neck like a clean, fresh garment.

'Put it out!' shouted Tasker. 'Put the match out.' Brigg saw him fling himself forward and slide down the inclined floor to punch the match away from someone's fingers. The person began to scream and then they all started, sounding like an awful wind.

A grenade rattled along the far end of the corridor, bouncing and sounding like a ball on the floor. A train steward scrambled along the aisle, away from it, like a playful monkey, but it blew up too soon and turned him in a dead somersault. The blast flew over Brigg's head like the beating of wings.

The firing was not continuous. The bandits seemed to be waiting and picking out targets. Brigg cursed the Lewis gunners on the armoured truck because they weren't returning the fire.

It was Waller who got up. 'Come on,' he said. 'They'll bloody slaughter us here. Get out and on the ground.'

They went with him because they knew he knew best. They stumbled along the corridor, over the sickening bundle of the steward, and followed Waller through the gap that the grenade had made in the side of the carriage. Close and quick they dropped on to the wet grass by the line, and slithered around behind the rearing wheels of the wrecked train.

Even from there they could see how thorough the ambush had been. There was steam and smoke and glowing fire coming from places as far as they could see along the broken back of the express. Only a few feet from them, in the ditch by the lineside, was a dead airman, and on the other side a woman was sobbing over someone lying in the grass.

By a soldier's instinct most had not known they possessed, each man was still armed. Wailer had a sten and the others rifles. They were still frightened.

They took the signal from young Waller and crept along, spider-fashion, towards the head of the train. They had to slide across the airman just as they had the steward, and his body was still rubbery and warm.

Brigg realised he was still without his boots. The heavy wetness of the grass was making his socks soggy. They dodged along in single file until they reached the front of the train. All they could hear was the hiss and puff of steam and the sharp eating noise of fire.

At the front of the train, by the first staggering coach were some soldiers and airmen crouching against the wreckage. Waller called softly to them, preventing them shooting them down for enemies.

Up there they could see what had happened. The little pilot engine was lying crumpled some way down the track, outlined in the orange fire which cradled it. The express was hanging half off the track, gasping, with its head resting against a clump of strong trees. They looked like a buffalo and calf hunted and gunned. Brigg instinctively glanced at Sinclair. Sinclair said: 'Good engines too. Both good.'

There had been unusually few servicemen on the train. No one had taken charge. A sergeant from the Dental Corps was in the group at the front, but he said he couldn't do anything because he had smashed his front teeth. It made him sound like a comedian. Someone said that the armoured truck at the back was off the lines. The Dental Corps sergeant said that he had seen some Gurkhas on the train. But he did not know what had happened to them.

Waller took charge. He was trying to sort them out behind the wreckage when another stream of bullets rattled like rain along the coaches and they all rolled down into the ditch at the side of the track. 'They're not all that close,' whispered Waller to Brigg when they were down there. 'They can't be sure how strong we are, and they're keeping a bit of distance. Otherwise they'd be all over us by now. Every now and then they send somebody up to chuck a grenade. We'll get the next bastard.'

Brigg felt himself steadied by Waller. If he was as frightened as they were, he didn't show it. He moved around among the fifteen men and sent them sliding on their bellies over the sleepers, under the coaches.

Moving along twenty yards over the flints between the track, Brigg flattened himself behind a big metal wheel of the leading coach that was still flush to the railway line. It gave him good cover and there was a loophole for his rifle and another for him to see. He began to feel less cold with fear. He waited.

Suddenly a scampering shadow rose up only a few feet ahead of him, resolving from the anonymous black of the scrub. Brigg shot him down like a cowboy shooting from behind a wagon wheel.

He even remembered the safety catch, thumbed it forward, felt the trigger around his finger like a metal worm, and then the firm jolt and bang as the weapon went off. The man reached up as though trying to catch something in the sky, then fell stiffly on to his face.

'Ha!' shouted Brigg. 'Ha! Ha! Ha! Ha!' He was almost hysterical with the excitement of killing his first human being. 'Ha! Ha!'

'Wrap up,' snorted Waller. 'Shut your mouth, will you.'

A patch of darkness which had been standing motionless moved quickly and became men running at the train. They screamed as they ran. Everybody began firing then, shooting from the tracks, from the shelter of wheels and the piled wreckage. Brigg loosed off half his magazine before he realised that the sparks coming from the running men were guns that they were firing too. He felt the earth shudder under him like someone shaking a carpet and saw the dirt spray and bounce two feet away. A man was rolling on the track near Brigg and screaming. Waller, lying with his snub sten to his shoulder, pushed another flat magazine into its side and processed it through like a chocolate bar as he sprayed the ground ahead.

Brigg was shooting like a madman now. At least they couldn't say this lot were from the arseholing Chinese laundry. The bitter smoke was thick all around, and the noise numbing. His ears were senseless from the explosions of his own rifle, and his cheekbone bruised with its kick against his face.

The attackers fell back, on the ground and crawling away through the trees. Waller told everyone to stop firing. They did, and saw red darts towards the middle of the train, and heard the clapping bangs.

'Those Gurkhas must be up there,' said Waller. 'We'll shift up towards them, I think. The closer we get the better.'

They left two men dead: the Dental Corps sergeant, apologetic without his teeth, was one, lying on the track. None of the Panglin soldiers had been hurt. Brigg saw Tasker's face near to him, round with excitement, and with no fear. Sinclair was wiping his glasses carefully and Lantry slotting a fresh magazine into his rifle. Brigg felt warm and heroic.

'I got one for sure,' said Brigg.

'I know,' agreed Lantry. 'The first one. I saw you get him.'

'Shut up,' said Waller again. He led them at the back of the track behind its slightly humped back.

The Gurkhas were grouped around one of the centre wagons. A warrant officer was with them and they had got a lot of the people out of the exposed coaches and had them lying down behind the embankment. They had driven off a sharp attack, and now everything was quiet and waiting.

There was no change in the expressions of the dark men as the British soldiers joined them. They were all small and the warrant officer was like a little boy. He looked them over.

'Any jungle soldiers?' he asked briefly. He caught Brigg's arm and turned his sleeve around, but seeing the yellow lion, the Singapore garrison flash, he released him. He did the same to Sinclair and released him.

'No jungle soldiers?' he said.

'I am, sir,' said Waller. He turned his shoulder to show the Malaya district insignia. The Gurkha nodded. 'East Anglia brigade, sir,' said Waller.

'Good,' nodded the Gurkha. 'So far they come only from front. Over there.' He nodded towards the frontal shadows. 'But soon all around. Over us everywhere. You take your men up at the back and cover from there. Except one. We need one.'

Waller nodded at Sinclair. 'You stay then,' he said. Sinclair blinked behind his glasses. 'Yes. What do I do?'

He was sent with one of the Gurkha riflemen to the end of the train where the armoured truck had come off the line. Two men were already there, lying watch across the tracks, and another was altering the Lewis gun stand so the guns could be brought down horizontally even though the truck was tipped upwards. At the Gurkha's signal Sinclair climbed up on to the turret, behind the twin guns. They had them fixed now, so that the arc of fire could sweep the ground all along the side of the train. There was a small searchlight positioned alongside the gun. They pointed to that and made it clear that Sinclair had to operate it.

He stood behind the unlit light and found the switch and the swivel operator and smiled in his studious manner at the Gurkha, who nodded back. The Gurkha who had walked along the track with him now stretched himself across the lines with the other two. The little man who had been fixing the gun, crouched behind it and swung it experimentally. Sinclair trod on something soft and looked down to see it was the hand of one of the original crew, who was sitting dead alongside his cold partner down inside the armoured car.

The rest of the Panglin men, and the other oddment soldiers, and airmen, were strung out on the embankment now waiting for the attack from the rear.

Brigg felt his heart punching the ground. 'Surely all the noise, all the shooting, would have made someone realise we're in trouble,' he said to Waller.

'Who's someone?' asked Waller, still squinting across the brief patch of open grass ahead to the wall of trees.

'Well, anyone,' said Brigg. 'Isn't there anyone around here at all?'

'You realise in this country,' said Waller softly, 'that there is *never* anyone around. It's a good bet that the nearest army unit is twenty or thirty miles away. So they're out even if the boys in the armoured truck sent out a radio message. And twenty miles through all this muck is as good as a hundred unless they can get to the railway. The last town on the line with a road going to it was miles back. You can bet on that too. That's why they picked this spot. They're not daft, you know. I told you the other day they've been in the jungle for years. They know all about it.'

'But surely there's a village nearer than that?' whispered Brigg.

Waller still did not move his face. 'There might be,' he agreed, 'and when they heard all the banging going on, d'you know what they did? They stuck their bloody heads under their pillows, or their wives, or something, and tried not to listen. Because they have to live with this, mate, all the time. And they're terrified. Just like we are now.'

They stared. Then Brigg said: 'The only hope is if another train comes along. The overnight leave trains always cross somewhere.'

'The timetable is all out,' said Waller. 'We were hours late starting. I shouldn't count on that. Besides which they might have taken the track up further downline too.'

'Sinclair could tell us,' whispered Brigg hopefully. 'He'd know to the minute. He knows all the times. Shall I go and ask him ?'

Waller laid his hand heavily on Brigg's forearm and tightened it. Brigg looked where Waller was looking and saw the shadows moving from the trees. In another second it was happening again.

From both sides they ran. Just as the Gurkha warrant-officer had said. There were shots from the front first and at once Sinclair's searchlight threw itself across the scene, fanning over the grass and the fluted trees and lighting up the yellow faces as the bandits ran.

'Fire at will,' ordered Waller softly. Brigg glanced at him, as though he had said something theatrical, unreal. But Waller was stern and bent across the short length of his sten, using it from the shoulder as he lay against the climbing ground. He began firing it in vicious, short bursts. Brigg returned to his rifle, suddenly conscious again of the danger, yet still shocked by the calmness and authority of the infantry-man who had once confessed how frightened he was.

But there was no time to think. They came at the crippled train and the soldiers firing into them brought some to their knees, and others thudding like stones on to the ground. But it was a big bandit gang. The Lewis guns on the askew armoured truck were throwing bullets in a wide curve following the track of Sinclair's searchlight.

Sinclair stood upright, turning the searchlight with a mechanical coolness back and fro across the banks on both sides. As the beam swooped over the back of the train and flew over the attackers in front of Waller's men, Brigg realised how many enemy there were. They lay flat as the light came across, and charged again as it went by. But Sinclair flicked it back immediately, beautifully, catching them stark in the beam. Their many faces were fixed by it.

'Christ,' breathed Waller. 'They're like a football crowd.'

He began firing steadily again. One of the airmen at the end of the rank stiffened and stood up, before flopping over like a clown. But the attack was held. In the front the Gurkhas were holding too. Then the battle vanished into the darkness as the bandits went back to the trees. 'How many did we get, d'you think?' Brigg asked Waller. He felt jubilant at remaining alive, and yet having killed.

'Why don't you go out and count them,' suggested Waller without rancour. 'One thing's for certain: they'll be back in a minute. They're going to sort us out.'

'Perhaps they *won't* come back,' said Brigg, afraid of Waller's certainty.

Waller did not answer for two minutes. Then he said quietly: 'Here they are now.' And louder: 'Ready. Fire at will.'

This time there was no way to stop them. They shattered the searchlight with an immediate burst of fire. It flew around in Sinclair's hands like a toy drum. The Lewis-gunner fell across his guns immediately, and began to swing on them in death like a man lounging across a gate. One of the Gurkhas below the armoured truck jumped the side like an ape, but they were waiting for him too and they shot him as he reached the top, curling him over so that he dropped and jammed in the already crowded hatch.

Next two bullets hit Sinclair, striking him in the lower chest and pitching him silently out of the armoured truck and into the ditch beside the railway.

Brigg did not see it. He was terrified now. They came on with such force that nothing could stem them. While Waller was alive he stuck his ground, firing from the hip. But Waller died with a surprised start, falling over his hot gun and slewing sideways.

Brigg ran sideways along the ditch. A sort of comedian's exit trot, tripping over bodies and guns and mud, and shouting apologetically all around, to friend and foe: 'Going for help! I'm going for help!'

The bandits had almost overrun the train from both sides now, with some of the Gurkhas holding out from inside one far coach. The shots were fewer, grunts and sobs and bodies falling were all sounding in the darkness. From it all, Brigg with almost juvenile ease slipped away, jabbering in terror, and running straight through the trees from which the bandits had emerged to make their rear attack. He was going for help. Where he was going he did not know. But he was going.

Sinclair regained a little life in the ditch, stirring in the mud made muddier by his leaking blood. The shooting was all done, it seemed, but he could hear rapid movements and voices and someone crying.

The crying was very near. On one elbow he pushed himself into a sitting position, although it was very painful.

The train was fiercely on fire now. Twenty yards from his ditch he could see the girl who was crying. She was a Malay teenager, plump like a puppy. One of the Chinese was standing in front of her, one hand carelessly holding a sub-machine gun and the other pulling open the front of the girl's dress. She stood still and weeping, unable to move for fright, while he casually tore the linen away from her body.

Sinclair watched while the bandit unbuckled his belt and threw open the buttons on his trousers. The girl's body reflected the fire; it glowed on her fatty breasts and her young neck. She put her hands to her face, but still did not move away from the man. The bandit pushed out his free hand and quite gently threw her backwards on to the ground.

There was a dead man in the ditch with Sinclair. Near his sightless head was a sten gun. 'Dirty little dogs on leads,' thought Sinclair. 'They were all the same.'

He positioned the sten on the bank of the ditch and manoeuvred it carefully, in bitter pain with each movement and feeling the blood leaving him in quicker flow. He pulled the trigger and tried to get a curving action on the weapon as he did so.

The effect was astonishing. The streaking line of bullets almost cut the bandit in half at the waist. He tore apart like one of the sacks they used to use for bayonet practice at Panglin on Saturday mornings.

Sinclair fell back into the ditch. He could think as lucidly as ever, and he could actually feel the lumps of the two bullets working about inside him like indigestion. He thought of praying, or quite seriously of trying to sing the chorus of a childhood hymn. But it had, frankly, been so long since he had imposed on God at all, that it seemed a bit unreasonable to bother Him.

He made himself more comfortable and thought of Mr and Mrs Boot at Royal Oak, feeling the platform quake as the Paddington expresses steamed by. He mentally ticked off the names of the Battle of Britain class locomotives and was pleased that he was well enough to remember them all. Then he thought about his place on the embankment back home, by the gradient climbing to Rugby. Those good, cold nights, watching the big ones working along the steel. Oh, what a damn shame.

He heard the steam and a train whistle drifting through his haze. It brought him sharply back. That was a real whistle, no death dream. With all his strength he listened and heard it again and the shouts. In agony he twisted his wrist around and looked at the luminous dial on his watch.

'Hah,' he noted with satisfaction. 'The one-ten from Kuala Lumpur.'

It was 5.29am by his watch. By five-thirty he was dead.

Dannie Abse
A Night Out

Friends recommended the new Polish film
at the Academy in Oxford Street.
So we joined the ever melancholy queue
of cinemas. A wind blew faint suggestions
of rain towards us, and an accordion.
Later, uneasy, in the velvet dark
we peered through the cut-out oblong window
at the spotlit drama of our nightmares:
images of Auschwitz almost authentic,
the human obscenity in close-up.
Certainly we could imagine the stench.

Resenting it, we forgot the barbed wire
was but a prop and could not scratch an eye;
those striped victims merely actors like us.
We saw the Camp orchestra assembled,
we heard the solemn gaiety of Bach,
scored by the loud arrival of an engine,
its impotent cry, and its guttural trucks.
We watched, as we munched milk chocolate,
trustful children, no older than our own,
strolling into the chambers without fuss,
while smoke, black and curly, oozed from chimneys.

Afterwards, at a loss, we sipped coffee
in a bored espresso bar nearby
saying very little. You took off one glove.
Then to the comfortable suburb swiftly
where, arriving home, we garaged the car.
We asked the au pair girl from Germany
if anyone had phoned at all, or called,
and, of course, if the children had woken.
Reassured, together we climbed the stairs,
undressed together, and naked together,
in the dark, in the marital bed, made love.

Dannie Abse
After the Release of Ezra Pound

In Jerusalem I asked
the ancient Hebrew poets to forgive you,
and what would Walt Whitman have said
and Thomas Jefferson?   *[Paul Potts]*

In Soho's square mile of unoriginal sin
where the fraudulent neon lights haunt,
but cannot hide, the dinginess of vice,
the jeans and sweater boys spoke of Pound,
and you, Paul, repeated your question.

The chi-chi bums in Torino's laughed and
the virgins of St. Martin's School of Art.
The corner spivs with their Maltese masks
loitered for the two o'clock result,
and those in the restaurants of Greek Street,
eating income tax, did not hear the laugh.

Gentle Gentile, you asked the question.
Free now (and we praise this) Pound could answer.

The strip lighting of Soho did not fuse,
no blood trickled from a certain book
down the immaculate shelves of Zwemmer's.
But the circumcised did not laugh.
The swart nudes in the backrooms put on clothes
and the doors of the French pub closed.

Pound did not hear the raw Jewish cry,
the populations committed to the dark
when he muttered through microphones
of murderers. He, not I, must answer.

Because of the structures of a beautiful poet
you ask the man who is less than beautiful,
and wait in the public neurosis of Soho,
in the liberty of loneliness for an answer.

In the beer and espresso bars they talked
of Ezra Pound, excusing the silences of an old
man,
saying there is so little time between
the parquet floors of an institution
and the boredom of the final box.

Why, Paul, if that ticking distance between
was merely a journey long enough
to walk the circumference of a Belsen,
Walt Whitman would have been eloquent,
and Thomas Jefferson would have cursed.

Spring, 1958

Dannie Abse
The Sheds

Articulate suffering may be a self-admiring,
but what of the long sheds where a man could only howl?
How quickly, then, silhouettes came running
across the evening fields, knee deep in mist.

Or what of nights when the sheds disappeared,
fields empty, a night landscape unrhetorical
until the moon, as pale as pain, holed a cloud?
As if men slept, dreamed, as others touched on lights.

Dannie Abse
Case History

'Most Welshmen are worthless,
an inferior breed, doctor.'
He did not know I was Welsh.
Then he praised the architects
of the German death-camps –
did not know I was a Jew.
He called liberals, 'White blacks',
and continued to invent curses.

When I palpated his liver
I felt the soft liver of Goering;
when I lifted my stethoscope
I heard the heartbeats of Himmler;
when I read his encephalograph
I thought, *Sieg heil, mein Führer.*

In the clinic's dispensary
red berry of black bryony,
cowbane, deadly nightshade, deathcap.
Yet I prescribed for him
as if he were my brother.

Later that night I must have slept
on my arm: momentarily
my right hand lost its cunning.

Dannie Abse
Demo against the Vietnam War, 1968

Praise just one thing in London, he challenged,
as if everybody, everything, owned a minus,
was damnable, and the Inner Circle led to hell;
and I thought, allowed one slot only,
what, in October, would I choose?

Not the blurred grasslands of a royal, moody park
where great classy trees lurk in mist;
not the secretive Thames either, silvering
its slow knots through the East End –
sooty scenes, good for Antonioni panning soft
atmospheric shots, emblems of isolation,
prologue to the elegiac Square, the house where,
suddenly, lemon oblongs spring to windows.

Nor would I choose the stylised catalogue
of torment in the National Gallery.
Better that tatty group, under Nelson's column,
their home-made banners held aloft,
their small cries of 'Peace, Peace,' impotent;

236

also the moment with the tannoy turned off,
the thudding wings of pigeons audible,
the shredding fountains, once again, audible.

So praise to the end of the march,
their songs, their jargon, outside the Embassy.
Yes, this I'd choose: their ardour, their naïveté,
violence of commitment, cruelty of devotion,
'We shall not be moved, We shall overcome' –
despite sullen police concealed in vans
waiting for arclights to fail, for furtive darkness,
and camera-teams, dismantled, all breezing home.

Tony Curtis
Veteran, South Dakota, 1978

If you were in demolition
taking out the bridges
as the marines fell back.
If you were ordered to cut down
the women and kids,
leave everything dead.
If you swung round like
the workings of a clock
and scythed the three officers instead,
fragged them good –
if all that's true, then I'm with you.

But if saying this is your trick,
your way of living
with the fact you'd really
killed those peasants
(given the war and the VC
and not knowing
one gook from another
and it's making a better story that way)
then this party is flaking off
from your head like used skin
and I'm far from home
and reason and the neat confusions
that make poetry.

John Davies
Borrowing the Mauser
for Rich

'Let's shoot,' he says,
the ex-trumpet player parachuted
out of adolescence to Vietnam.
His head plays solo still.
So will he ...?
'Buy a trumpet? practice a little,
pretty soon you'll want to join a band.
If you're not careful,
you could end up happy.'

We visit his father's place.
Wesley of the intrepid socks,
recoiling from retirement,
has bought a stump grinder
or metal Sumo grunting.
On building lots, shredding
what's left of trees,
it roots out the old, makes space
for brandnew walls.

Wesley has his Mauser.
The yellow stock kept polished
in memory of D-Day
gleams, its muzzle a clean whistle.
And shells? Over the tabletop,
he fires a brass burst
then claws back half.

Though green's making up lost ground
at the mine brooding
on spent bricks and shells,
metal would keep its edge
if it could, every bar and strut.
Wire grips snapped fence-posts,
figuring what to keep, how
much it's better to give up.

We two press against the recoils.
Blasts blank thought.
Can't see our hits, too far,
and there are still shells left
when he says, 'That's it',
heads back to the car.

I smoke. He flicks the tape,
Nat Adderley. Whose trumpet's
soaring clears the air, branches
then leaves
itself and reforms like
a tree fluttering
the sun to small bright pieces.

Leslie Norris
A Small War

Climbing from Merthyr through the dew of August mornings
When I was a centaur-cyclist, on the skills of wheels
I'd loop past The Storey Arms, past steaming lorries
Stopped for flasks of early tea, and fall into Breconshire.
A thin road under black Fan Frynych – which keeps its winter

Shillings long through spring – took me to the Senni valley.
That was my plenty, to rest on the narrow saddle
Looking down on the farms, letting the simple noises
Come singly up. It was there I saw a ring-ousel
Wearing the white gash of his mountains; but every
Sparrow's feather in that valley was rare, golden,
Perfect. It was an Eden fourteen miles from home.

Evan Drew, my second cousin, lived there. A long, slow man
With a brown gaze I remember him. From a hill farm
Somewhere on the slope above Heol Senni he sent his sons,
Boys a little older than I, to the Second World War.
They rode their ponies to the station, they waved
Goodbye, they circled the spitting sky above Europe.

I would not fight for Wales, the great battle-cries
Do not arouse me. I keep short boundaries holy,
Those my eyes have recognised and my heart has known
As welcome. Nor would I fight for her language. I spend
My few pence of Welsh to amuse my friends, to comment
On the weather. They carry no thought that could be mine.

It's the small wars I understand. So now that forty
People lock their gates in Senni, keeping the water out
With frailest barriers of love and anger, I'd fight for them.
Five miles of land, enough small farms to make a heaven,
Are easily trapped on the drawing-board, a decision
Of the pen drowns all. Yes, the great towns need

The humming water, yes, I have taken my rods to other
Swimming valleys and happily fished above the vanished
Fields. I know the arguments. It is a handful of earth
I will not argue with, and the slow cattle swinging weightily
Home. When I open the taps in my English bathroom
I am surprised they do not run with Breconshire blood.

Roland Mathias
A Letter from Gwyther Street

This morning, the rain pucker over,
I crossed Barafundle from the sun rocks
To the leaf bank westward. It was fine
And feathery on the uppish wave. My feet
In lifting sand uncovered an older
Sun and a captured wind dry-beached a decade
Ago. But this is October, the salted-down
Summer of the deckspar, colloped by sea-
Worms, and the indestructible layabout
Plastic of the child engineer.

This evening, such brief spirit sinking. I visit
Friends. And first to the grave-spit at Llanion
Where Siân, her W.V.S. uniform in full
Fold, pairs her ankle-bones to the town. Is there
A message for Elis, tied to his cot like
An idiot, his delicate features clouded

240

Towards a bad-weather eye? Or Doc, cooped up
With his leg off? Or Herbie, lopsidedly
Smiling in the front room, omnivorous,
History and egg slapped on unknowing cheek?.

My footprints this morning on Barafundle
Went in and out of the wave, the fine sand
Darkening at the tide-touch and, as I looked back,
Not a mark of my passing anywhere, only
Sea eating the whiter sift, creaming mouthfuls
Of stick and hampered stone and memory
Trapped there. What remains of companionship
Cannot reach them now. Herbie and Doc
And Elis. No eye-light flickers and signals
Identification on their already buried beach.

Dannie Abse
'The death wind'

This morning [May 4th] an East wind was blowing so vigorously in Ogmore that our wooden gate had been thrust open. From the bedroom window I could see that a ewe with two lambs had trespassed into our garden. They were munching the daffodils and narcissi, a nice, forbidden, wicked breakfast. I rushed downstairs, still in my pyjamas, to shoo them out.

As I closed the gate behind them I thought more of the East wind than the sheep. Probably it was bearing invisible death-seeds from Chernobyl. Perhaps radioactive raindrops were sipped from the daffodil cups by the ewe and the lambs. Information so far is meagre. In any case, who can believe the complacent stealthy reassuring voices of experts and politicians? How much has been covered up before, how much will be told to us now? Will radioactive iodine be taken up by small thirsty thyroid glands? What about my new granddaughter and all those like her from Ogmore-by-Sea to the Ukraine and beyond where Prometheus is still chained to his rock while the vulture eats his liver?

Last Friday in Cardiff, I visited Llandaff Cathedral. I just happened to be nearby, so popped in as I used to as a boy; passing the yellow celandines beneath the yew tree. Inside soaring spaces of worship – Jewish, Moslem or Christian – I feel not just secular but utterly estranged like one without history or memory. Once more, numb, I observed

Epstein's dominating aluminium Resurrected Christ. And it was spring-time, springtime in the real world and all seemingly dead things were coming alive again though a cancer sailed in from Chernobyl.

Inside the Cathedral, I ambled towards the Lady Chapel reredos where, on either side of the sculpted Madonna, six niches are filled with gold-leafed wreaths of wildflowers. In Welsh, dozens of flowers are named after the Virgin, as is proper in a nation that reveres the Mam of the family. The marigold is called Gold Mair – Mary's Gold; the buttercup, Mary's sweat; the briar rose, Mary's briar; the foxglove, Mary's thimble; the monks hood, Mary's slipper; the cowslip, Mary's primrose; and the snowdrop, Mary's taper. Tapr Mair.

If a man believed in a deity, any deity, goddess, god or God, he would in that Cathedral have prayed in English or Welsh or no language at all, for the neutralisation of the death wind. And in Ogmore, this morning, as I stood in my pyjamas, while the opera-dramatic clouds, grey, cream or frowning darker tracked so visibly westwards, my own lips moved.

And I wonder now, once again, in the name of the God others believe in, how much longer will so-called civilised nations absurdly pile up unusable nuclear weapons and to what hell will man be con-signed if, accidentally or purposefully, radioactive winds sail in from places other than Chernobyl.

Tony Curtis
The World

This is how it ends:

a finger slips –
two Russian subs resurrected
from the ocean
retaliate
before they drown.

California
the flat Mid-West
the Great Lakes cities
New York / Washington
– all clouds, acid air.
Europe's on fire.
The Third World eats
itself and starves.

In the far North
the Inuit
listen to their radios.
They move further North and
the North wind sweeps them clean.

This is how it ends

with the last family of Inuit
eating fallen caribou
pushing North
killing sick bears
going West.
Reaching the Bering Straits:
at the edge of the ice
a bloated seal at their feet.

And farther out floating
towards them on a floe
a man, a woman and child
waving spears.

John Tripp
Defence of the West

1. Castlemartin

The long Panzer huts were deserted,
some windows and a chimney smashed.
Soon thistle, nettle and weed
would win back the ranges.
Farmers stumped again through mud,
tractors jerked forward in lines
like peaceful tanks, and sheep
safely grazed. An occasional bang
was the last of the shots out to sea
to use up the shells. I forgot
why they came to this place.

Their markers and targets
were rusted and sodden by rain,
the crossings greasy from track-oil.

Flooded against the blast off the sea
I heard a gun thump, then a short
gutteral command. Red flags drooped,
Achtung said a tilted board
and overhead
the last chopper went for a joy ride ...

2. HMS Felicity in Fishguard

'We have the most
sophisticated gear,' the captain said.
    'Can I see it?'
                'No.'
'Why not?'
        'It's secret.'
'What do you aim at?'
                  'Towed targets.'

She sat in the bay
a frigate of deadly science
that could blow old Fishguard
into the water. The captain's
voice was royal yacht squadron,
his intelligence as crisp as his white
shirt; in blue cummerbund and black
dancing pumps, he gave me
pink gin in the teak wardroom
and produced his handsome young officers
who were ready for World War III
('We could put up a pretty good show,'
a rosy-cheeked boy said to me).

Layers of steel hid technology
that could pinpoint a raft,
knock out a port miles away.
We chugged back to the quay in a launch,
and by dawn Felicity had gone
to shoot missiles at floating planks.

3. Interceptors over Gwynedd

Talking to the shepherd, my eyes
kept on his ginger stubble
and a Woodbine jammed in a hole
in his upper teeth
(it's not often you meet someone who can do that).
He scratched the dog with his stick
My boots slithered in the muck,
it was cold and his breath plumed
as he spoke of sheep and weather
with the nous of centuries behind him.

At first it was a far-off buzz, a sort of
hiss. 'Here they come,' he said.
We stopped talking and listened.
Then out of the west beyond a lattice
of trees, pummelling the ground,
came the hunters suddenly above us
screaming as they bullet-streaked
across the morning sky –
slide-rule perfection in itself
headed out to Menai and the sea.

Two swept over, then one, sluggish
like a slower younger son
still testing its speed; you could see
red-and-white dicing on the nose.
In seconds they had gone
and the trees stopped shaking;
the silence was full of vibrations.

I looked from the sky
to the shepherd, his thin face nutbrown
from years of coastal wind, a weak smile
seaming it as he glanced around the fields.
'They were shifting,' I said.
He lowered the fag to his bottom lip.
'That's progress for you,' he said.

Peter Finch
The Death of King Arthur Seen as a Recent War

On the airwaves we hear that General Belgrano has shells. They are pressed from hot metal, timewarped like black and white photographs, names chalked in shaky hand onto their sides. The governess tricks Menendez, makes him brag about his mirages, makes him think the sea is emulsified with enemy submarines. He sleeps with the girl without being aware of the deception. On awakening he is magnificently triumphant, parades in his quilted combat suit, inspecting troops. The son born of this union, Monsoonon, changes sides like an Italian. He is full of slow strength, his muscles cold, tautened by water.

The opening flights of the Vulcan imagine destruction in debilitating tracks along the runway. Radio messages are vague, trapped by an atmosphere thick as glue. They flew out of here, he says, his disembodied voice roughened, given urgency by it being on its own. I counted them out – Ban of Banoic, Lionel, Bors, Sons of Bors, Sons of Gaunes – and I counted them back.

The full story is bent like soft plastic. It fits the contours of the newscaster's head.

There is a decoy, wrecked by fire, devoid of men. It is a rendezvous for defenders, vulnerable, bobbing in unison around its bulk. They show pictures of it on the screen, radar-smears, smudges like space invaders. When it is hit again they forsake it, leave it and its coffins to the obliteration of the deep.

Menendez's conquering of the castle is his first great exploit after being dubbed a knight. He knows war, his men will tell you, it has stiffened him, given him grit, given him resolve. His enemies flounder, they splash. He has put them in water, darkly, their feet cemented in the coastal sea. His victories are silent, no one mentions them, no one writes them down.

Galahad flickers, sand in his wounds. At sea dark helicopters make themselves huge, stream stripped aluminium in elongated clouds. Nobleness turns to hauteur, hubris, leery smiles.

Towards the end there are references to episodes from history. Older dominions, sieged castles, dawn battles, the war in which Gawain himself has died. Trickles reach us, distortions, exaggerated pride. Sunk trawlers, snapped fuel vanes, looting, garbage, bleeding legs held together with iron-pins. The jumble is a high tide of flotsam, confused nomenclature, bad pictures, their sound dubbed out of sync.

When the sky clears the faces are all still human; well-spoken, weather-beaten men. Their armour is heavy on the bog-land, their boots clank on the sparse metal of the roads. They have not been here long enough for pain to change them, for proximate death to age their eyes. At the end of transmission you can feel history altering. It spreads out with distance; reasons fragment, victories fade.

Tony Conran
Elegy for the Welsh Dead, in the Falkland Islands, 1982

Gwŷr a aeth Gatraeth oedd ffraeth eu llu.
Glasfedd eu hancwyn, a gwenwyn fu.
　　　　- Y Gododdin (6th century)

[Men went to Catraeth, keen was their company.
They were fed on fresh mead, and it proved poison.]

Men went to Catraeth. The luxury liner
For three weeks feasted them.
They remembered easy ovations,
Our boys, splendid in courage.
For three weeks the albatross roads,
Passwords of dolphin and petrel,
Practised their obedience
Where the killer whales gathered,
Where the monotonous seas yelped.
Though they went to church with their standards
Raw death has them garnished.

Men went to Catraeth. The Malvinas
Of their destiny greeted them strangely,
Instead of affection there was coldness,
Splintering iron and the icy sea,
Mud and the wind's malevolent satire.
They stood nonplussed in the bomb's indictment.

Malcolm Wigley of Connah's Quay. Did his helm
Ride high in the war-line?
Did he drink enough mead for that journey?
The desolated shores of Tegeingl,
Did they pig this steel that destroyed him?
The Dee runs silent beside empty foundries.
The way of the wind and the rain is adamant.

Clifford Elley of Pontypridd. Doubtless he feasted.
He went to Catraeth with a bold heart.
He was used to valleys. The shadow held him.
The staff and the fasces of tribunes betrayed him.
With the oil of our virtue we have anointed
His head, in the presence of foes.

Phillip Sweet of Cwmbach. Was he shy before girls?
He exposes himself now to the hags, the glance
Of the loose-fleshed whores, the deaths
That congregate like gulls on garbage.
His sword flashed in the wastes of nightmare.

Russell Carlisle of Rhuthun. Men of the North
Mourn Rheged's son in the castellated vale.
His nodding charger neighed for the battle.
Uplifted hooves pawed at the lightning.
Now he lies down. Under the air he is dead.

Men went to Catraeth. Of the forty-three
Certainly Tony Jones of Carmarthen was brave.
What did it matter, steel in the heart?
Shrapnel is faithful now. His shroud is frost.

With the dawn men went. Those forty-three,
Gentlemen all, from the streets and byways of Wales, .
Dragons of Aberdare, Denbigh and Neath –
Figment of empire, whore's honour, held them.
Forty-three at Catraeth died for our dregs.

Tony Curtis
Friedhof

They are tending the dead at Ypres.
The beech leaves, November bronze,
are lifted and rolled over
into rows between the slabs
by the gardener's blower
while three others follow to rake
the long mound and fork
this harvest into their barrows.

Behind the barbs of squared beech hedge
each yard of peace names its German dead,
twenty by twenty on dark, flat slabs
so that, without the steady sweepers,
you might come to this place as to a park,
tread the leaves in a path to the two figures
– a man, a woman; a father, a mother,
kneeling sharp and hunched before
some undetermined loss.

Years after the war, Kathe Kollwitz,
finding at last her only son's grave,
shaped these two from stone.
Now, his wooden cross a museum piece,
his name is flattened with the others
under this brief quilt of leaves.

At Tyn Cot, The New Irish Farm,
St Julien Dressing Station,
at Sanctuary Wood, at Lijssenthoek,
and a hundred cemeteries more,
the victorious dead, white-stoned, upright,
are ranked in the democracy of death –
Dorset, Welch, Highlander, Sikh,
Six men of the Chinese Labour Force.
The whole world bled through Flanders.

Turning the wet earth, Flemish farmers
still find wire and bones
tangled with the potatoes and beet.
And, occasionally, the local paper
carries at the bottom of a page –
Farmer blinded by shell.
It happens when they remove the detonator
from the rusty casing. The trade is well
established. The explosive is tired
but has a pedigree right enough for the men
of Armagh, Fermanagh, Crossmaglen.

Anna Wigley
Soldier

What did he see in the war, my father?
All I have are the photos – small sharp stills
from a 1940s film: Trevor Howard,
angular, tanned, glancing up handsome
from the shade of a cocked serge cap.
His hands, fine and strong, held compasses, maps;
knew the levers of lorries and the shafts of guns.
The same hands that cupped my head
like an egg when I tripped and fell,
could tell the cool weight of a grenade, the exact bite
of a Stanley knife. Had laid out the dead.

I could well believe he'd been a soldier,
the hardness of his body showed it.
And the way he held the bowl of his pipe,
firmly, with a kind of sure commitment:
this is what I am, these are my tools,
my equipment. There are tasks to be done.
It was there in the weave and cut of his clothes:
things well made, stout for their purpose –
gaberdine and wool, best leather, double-stitched,
double-knotted, built for wear and weather.

What could he do in peacetime
that would compare with those days
deliberate as a bird's or animal's days
when there's food to be found, nests to be made?
The medals meant nothing:
trinkets, he called them. But the men –
ordinary, afraid and brave,
welded to him in the long slow furnace
of shared smokes in canvassed trucks,
nights under desert skies – it was they
who brought up the light in him,
repeating their lines forty years on.

What of the rest could he find to say
to a young girl who knew only
the safe house of his steady arms,
the gentleness of his delphinium eyes;
and the cheerfulness worn casually,
daily, like collar and tie.

R.S. Thomas
The Hearth

In front of the fire
With you, the folk song
Of the wind in the chimney and the sparks'
Embroidery of the soot – eternity
Is here in this small room,
In intervals that our love
Widens; and outside
Us is time and the victims
Of time, travellers
To a new Bethlehem, statesmen
And scientists with their hands full
Of the gifts that destroy.

R.S. Thomas
'The mushroom-shaped cloud'

White skulls, oily with dew in the late moonlight. Rising before dawn, he peered into a field as into a cemetery of white grave-stones. His feet rustling in the wet grass, he moved from one to another like an angel, not to raise but to gather them in a meshed basket. Forty years later he did so again, the sun on his hand. Nature was still bountiful, but man was erecting, beautiful and poisonous, the mushroom-shaped cloud.

★ ★ ★ ★ ★

'Not done yet,' mutters
the old man, fitting a bent
poem to his broken bow.

'Of all the Middle Ages ...'
said Byron. So I refine
my weapons: beams, gases;

composer of the first
radio-active verses. Ah,
me! When I was a child,

innocent plagiarist,
there was dew on the early-morning
mushroom, as there is not now.

Christopher Meredith
Occupied

Shy Ghurkas walking from the camp
smile at my children,
like to say hello.

The young Scot who lives across the road
drinks cans of lager in his livingroom
and, out of battledress,
wears shorts patterned with a union jack.

Doveflutter deepened on an endless loop
is helicopters
some bulbeyed and filmy
other heavy, hung on glimmering blades, the gundecks
slung over Usk,
pinched up at either end
like a canoe.

Apache. lroquois. Chinook.

They name them after beaten people.

Sheenagh Pugh
Two Retired Spymasters

They settled down beside the Suffolk coast,
in the flat lands where men can see for miles
– no hills to hide behind; no tricky forest –
They liked the villagers' polite, closed smiles,

the way a stranger always stayed a stranger.
They used to practice merging with the crowd
of tourists at the festival each summer,
just out of habit; just to show they could.

In the Cross Keys, trying to reminisce
without infringing Acts of Parliament,
they'd talk in hints, pauses, half-sentences.
And sometimes, by the window, they fell silent,

gazing out at the dark, the sundown sea,
and the tired, sunken faces in the glass,
thinking how surely the last enemy
was edging up, for all their watchfulness.

Gillian Clarke
The Night War Broke

the moon stared at the desert
caught the steel of a gun
the eye of a rat

it looked into rooms
at the wideawake in their beds
at their windows
at the whites of their eyes
at their stained faces

it spreadeagled the sea
struck silver for the jet's shadow
lit the deck of the aircraft carrier
for the harrier's foot

struck dumb the sleepless with their radios
in the cities the villages the back of beyond

looked into the pond the bucket the puddle
at the ewes asleep on their shadows
a fox stepping among them
the shepherd's eye
sweeping the pregnant flock

drew blood from the women
drew cries from the babies cut early from their wombs
'to avoid labour in a city at war'
drew afterpains from the uterus
drew milk to the breast on the third day

and somewhere along the line
scrambled language
between lunatic tongue
and the moonstruck
listening in the dark

Tony Curtis
Crane Flies

For Gareth

The foghorns keening in the bay
belie those sultry days.
September's Indian Summer:
our apple-tree's grown sweeter than ever,
hazelnuts ripen and brown,
there's a morning haze across the lawn.

This year so many crane flies
– Daddy-long-legs –
each room in our house has a pair.
They whirr and tick, crucify
themselves in high corners, against lamps.

Yesterday you came from school hurt
that boys were pulling wings apart,
snapping flies' legs like twigs
until you threatened them with worse.
'Crane flies,' you told me,
'the proper name is crane flies.'
Your anger was wonderful,
I could have squeezed you till you cried

All the week the TV has brought us
the phalange massacres in Beirut –
mangled corpses parcelled in sheets.
'Goyim murders goyim, and they hang the Jew!'
Words, gunfire: the tangled lies of hate:
this will be called The September Slaughter.
It will blur into Middle East History.
I would not expect you to distinguish it
from all the other crimes even if you should
some day read it in a book.

Except, maybe the word 'September'
will set your hands fidgeting
and then you'll think of crane flies,

drawn to our lights to die. Remember
how you caught them, held each one
beating in your cupped hands,
learning that sense of life
as a distant, other thing
that would fly if we gave it wing.

Gillian Clarke
The Field-Mouse

Summer, and the long grass is a snare drum.
The air hums with jets.
Down at the end of the meadow,
far from the radio's terrible news,
we cut the hay. All afternoon
its wave breaks before the tractor blade.
Over the hedge our neighbour travels his field
in a cloud of lime, drifting our land
with a chance gift of sweetness.

The child comes running through the killed flowers,
his hands a nest of quivering mouse,
its black eyes two sparks burning.
We know it will die and ought to finish it off.
It curls in agony big as itself
and the star goes out in its eye.
Summer in Europe, the field's hurt,
and the children kneel in long grass,
staring at what we have crushed.

Before day's done the field lies bleeding,
the dusk garden inhabited by the saved, voles,
frogs, a nest of mice. The wrong that woke
from a rumour of pain won't heal,
and we can't face the newspapers.
All night I dream the children dance in grass
their bones brittle as mouse-ribs, the air
stammering with gunfire, my neighbour turned
stranger, wounding my land with stones.

Tony Curtis
From the Hills, the Town

As he talks he rolls an apple in his hands
which with the force of his thumbs
he splits to make two glistening
full-waxed moons of sweet flesh.
Below, the town is a mouth of broken teeth.
In his mind it is geometry, lines form a grid
– the runway, the mosques, the bread shops.
His face is a map of the long year.

Stones and mortars. But now it is a quiet time.
Though the day still has warmth, his men huddle
around a stove, the smoke of bacon, coffee.
He grows hungry, his eyes blink wide.
He fits the two apple halves back together
and bites from one, then the other.

Robert Minhinnick
The Yellow Palm

As I made my way down Palestine Street
I watched a funeral pass –
all the women waving lilac stems
around a coffin made of glass
and the face of the man who lay within
who had breathed a poison gas.

As I made my way down Palestine Street
I heard the call to prayer
and I stopped at the door of the golden mosque
to watch the faithful there
but there was blood on the walls and the muezzin's eyes
were wild with his despair.

As I made my way down Palestine Street
I met two blind beggars

and into their hands I pressed my hands
with a hundred black dinars;
and their salutes were those of the Imperial Guard
in the Mother of all Wars.

As I made my way down Palestine Street
I smelled the wide Tigris,
the river smell that lifts the air
in a city such as this;
but down on my head fell the barbarian sun
that knows no armistice.

As I made my way down Palestine Street
I saw a Cruise missile,
a slow and silver caravan
on its slow and silver mile,
and a beggar child turned up his face
and blessed it with a smile.

As I made my way down Palestine Street
under the yellow palms
I saw their branches hung with yellow dates
all sweeter than salaams,
and when that same child reached up to touch
the fruit fell in his arms.

Sally Roberts Jones
Remembrance Day, Aberystwyth

Spray by the castle hurls across the rail;
The mermaid stares forever across the sea,
Dry-eyed; they lay their poppies at her feet,
But she looks away, to the movement of a sail
Far over breakers; knows not their fallen dead,
Hears not their autumn hymn or the signal guns.

Spray by the castle, spray in November air,
Yearn for the land as she for the empty waves,
(As the dead, perhaps, for their lost and silent home).
Everything empty: castle and crowd and wreaths

Separate beings; and over them, kissing the rain,
The shape of a fish in bronze, without speech, without soul.
On Sundays remember the dead, but not here.
This is another country, another lord
Rules in its acres, who has no respect for love.
Always the sea sucks at the stones of the wall,
Always the mermaid leans to the distant sail;
Already the wreaths are limp and the children wail.

Dannie Abse
Remembrance Day

Unbuttoned at home, last Sunday afternoon,
Violence snored in the armchair.
This week, eyes moist, our neighbour marches
with the veterans, ready to be televised,
his nationalism narrow as the coffin
in which the invented hero lies.

A vision dies from being too long stared at.
Not only songs of the old wars fade but ghosts
on barbed wire, on a bayonet-blade. Yet still
everything is what it is and another thing
as the black-coated ceremonies begin
under a vapour trail in blue cold skies.

2000 men are taking off their hats. Not one cries
'Folly'; not one from somewhere else
when the hollow trumpets toot and the guns
damply thud. Echo of an echo of an echo
vanishing like that vapour trail.
Whatever happened to you, Dolly?

By nightfall, smoke lurks down pub-lit streets
and cheers! cheers! mademoiselle from 'Armentiers';
and did you die of cancer, Lily Marlene?
You have forgotten, cannot touch the pinewood.
So Violence, beery, lonely as an old tune,
lifts his lapel to smell the paper poppy.

Leslie Norris
Autumn Elegy

September. The small summer hangs its suns
On the chestnuts, and the world bends slowly
Out of the year. On tiles of the low barns
The lingering swallows rest in this timely

Warmth, collecting it. Standing in the garden,
I too feel its generosity; but would not leave.
Time, time to lock the heart. Nothing is sudden
In Autumn, yet the long, ceremonial passion of

The year's death comes quickly enough
As firm veins shut on the sluggish blood
And the numberless protestations of the leaf
Are mapped on the air. Live wood

Was scarce and bony where I lived as a boy.
I am not accustomed to such opulent
Panoply of dying. Yet, if I stare
Unmoved at the flaunting, silent

Agony in the country before a resonant
Wind anneals it, I am not diminished, it is not
That I do not see well, do not exult,
But that I remember again what

Young men of my own time died
In the Spring of their living and could not turn
To this. They died in their flames, hard
War destroyed them. Now as the trees burn

In the beginning glory of Autumn
I sing for all green deaths as I remember
In their broken Mays, and turn
The years back for them, every red September.

Edward Thomas
The Owl

Downhill I came, hungry, and yet not starved;
Cold, yet had heat within me that was proof
Against the North wind; tired, yet so that rest
Had seemed the sweetest thing under a roof.

Then at the inn I had food, fire, and rest,
Knowing how hungry, cold, and tired was I.
All of the night was quite barred out except
An owl's cry, a most melancholy cry

Shaken out long and clear upon the hill,
No merry note, nor cause of merriment,
But one telling me plain what I escaped
And others could not, that night, as in I went.

And salted was my food, and my repose,
Salted and sobered, too, by the bird's voice
Speaking for all who lay under the stars,
Soldiers and poor, unable to rejoice.

Biographical Notes

Dannie Abse (b.1923): Poet, novelist and playwright. One of Wales' most significant writers. See the monograph in the *Writers of Wales* series (UWP) and the chapter in *Wales at War*, both by Tony Curtis.

Wilfred Bowden (1888-?): Was a medical orderly in many Great War battles including Mametz Wood. Born in Abercynon, he enlisted at the age of seventeen and served with the Welch Regiment and the RWF.

Gillian Clarke (b.1937): Born and educated in Cardiff. One of the outstanding Welsh poets of her generation, she edited *The Anglo-Welsh Review* in its final years.

Tony Conran (b.1931): Poet, translator from the Welsh and critic. His *Penguin Book of Welsh Verse* became a standard text.

Margaret Davies (1884-1963): She and her sister Gwendoline were the daughters of the industrialist David Davies. Great patrons of the arts, they donated the core of the National Museum of Wales' Impressionist and post-Impressionist paintings. They worked as volunteers in the canteens behind the trenches. Patrons of exiled Belgian artists during the war.

John Davies (b.1944): Poet and woodcarver living in north Wales.

Stevie Davies (b.1946): Novelist and critic born in Swansea where she directs the Creative Writing course at the university. *The Element of Water* was longlisted for the Booker and Orange Prizes and won Welsh Book of the Year in 2002.

Caradoc Evans (1878-1945): Born and brought up in rural Carmarthenshire he was to satirise in his short stories. *My People* and *Capel Sion* brought him literary fame in England and infamy in Wales.

Peter Finch (b.1949): Poet and performer, he is the Chief Executive of the Welsh Academy of Writers.

Raymond Garlick (b.1926): Poet and critic born in London but based for much of his professional life in Wales. Co-edited *The Anglo-Welsh Review* with Roland Mathias.

David Lloyd George (1863-1945): Grew up in Llanystumdwy on the Lleyn Peninsular and became one of the greatest British Prime Ministers. Became Minister of Munitions in 1915 and Prime Minister in 1916.

Robert Graves (1895-1995): Poet, novelist and critic. He was commissioned in the Royal Welch Fusiliers, experiences which led to *Goodbye to All That*. In the Great War he was a close friend of Sassoon. He wrote numerous books, including the novel *I, Claudius* and the highly influential book on myths *The White Goddess*.

Wyn Griffiths (1890-1977): Commissioned in the Royal Welch Fusiliers. *Up to Mametz* (1931) is one of the best accounts of life in that regiment on the Western Front.

Ivor Gurney (1890-1937): Poet and composer born in Gloucester. Gassed in the war, he spent the last fifteen years of his life in a mental hospital.

Nigel Heseltine (1916-1996): Poet, playwright and translator. The son of the composer Peter Warlock; strong Welsh borders connections.

Richard Hughes (1900-1976): Novelist who also wrote poems and plays, including the first radio play ever broadcast, for the BBC in 1924. See also his most successful book *A High Wind in Jamaica*.

Emyr Humphreys (b.1919): Novelist, dramatist, TV producer and poet. A CO in the war. He is a significant and prolific novelist who is concerned with Wales and its non-conformity in a contemporary context.

Siân James (b.1933) Born in Ceredigion. One of the leading novelists of her generation. See especially *A Small Country* and *Love and War*.

David Jones (1875-1974): One of the most significant poet-painters since William Blake. Born in London of Welsh parents, he served with the Royal Welch Fusiliers at Mametz and throughout the war. His poetic novel *In Parenthesis* is one of the most remarkable treatments of war in the English language. See the essay by Duncan Campbell in *Wales at War*.

David Gwenallt Jones (1899-1968): One of the leading Welsh poets of the century. Born in Ponardawe. A conscientious objector, he was imprisoned and wrote about his experiences in the novel *Plasau'r Brenin*.

Elwyn Jones (1909-1989): The son of a steel-worker who became Staff Captain in the Department of Legal Services and, in 1974, Lord Chancellor in Harold Wilson's government.

Glyn Jones (1905-1995): Poet, critic and writer of fiction. Sacked from his teaching job in 1940 after declaring himself a CO. His book of criticism, memoir and autobiography *The Dragon has Two Tongues* is a seminal work.

Gwyn Jones (1907-1999): The son of a miner from Blackwood, he became one of the most notable academics of his generation in Wales. He founded *The Welsh Review* in 1939 and wrote the standard translation of *The Mabinogion*.

Jack Jones (1884-1970): Prolific author from the Valleys who served in the Boer War and the Great War. An active political speaker and broadcaster.

Jonah Jones (1919-2004): A CO who served as a medic with the Parachute Ambulance Corps. Artist, sculptor, calligrapher and novelist. His *A Tree May Fall* deals with the Irish Easter Rising of 1916.

Sally Roberts Jones (b.1935): Born in London but lived and worked in Wales for much of her life. A founder member of the Welsh Academy.

Alun Lewis (1915-1944): Born in Aberdare and educated at Aberystwyth and Manchester, Lewis died in Burma, shot by his own revolver.

Gweno Lewis (b.1920): Born and educated in Aberystwyth, she met Alun Lewis in 1939 and married him in 1941. She has edited much of his work.

Gwyneth Lewis (b.1959): Born in Pontypridd and educated at Cambridge, she is a writer in both languages of poetry and autobiography.

Saunders Lewis (1893-1985): He wrote plays, poems and novels. A founder of Plaid Cymru, he had a profound influence on Welsh politics.

Roland Mathias (b.1915): The son of an army chaplain, he was a CO and briefly imprisoned in 1940. A successful teaching and literary career followed and he was founder editor of *The Anglo-Welsh Review*.

Christopher Meredith (b.1954): Born in Tredegar and educated at Aberystwyth, he is Reader in Creative Writing at the University of Glamorgan. His novels include *Shifts* and *Sidereal Time*.

Robert Minhinnick (b.1952): Editor of *Poetry Wales* for a number of years. An environmental campaigner and travel writer.

T.E. Nicholas (1879-1971): Poet, preacher and dentist. A CO in the Great War and imprisoned in Brixton as a pacifist in the Second World War. A founder member of the Communist party of Great Britain.

Leslie Norris (1921-2006): Poet and short story writer of distinction. Born in Merthyr but taught in England and America, becoming Professor in Utah. See James A. Davies' monograph in the *Writers of Wales* series.

John Ormond (1923-1990): Born in Swansea. Worked on the *Picture Post* as a journalist and became one of the leading documentary and arts BBC filmmakers. See the monograph by M. Wynn Thomas in the *Writers of Wales* series.

Wilfred Owen (1893-1918): Born in the border town of Oswestry. His poems were published posthumously and have come to characterise the horrors, heroism and waste of the First World War.

Sheenagh Pugh (b.1950): Poet, translator and novelist. Reader at the University of Glamorgan.

Goronwy Rees (1909-1979): Educated at Oxford and recruited by MI5. In 1953 Rees became Principal of the University College of Wales at Aberystwyth. Revelations about his relationship with the spy Guy Burgess forced him to resign in 1957. He became a full-time writer and published two volumes of autobiography. At the end of his life he admitted that he had spied for the USSR.

Frank Richards (1883-1961): Fought throughout the Great War in the RWF and was twice decorated, though remained a private. Published *Old Soldiers Never Die* in 1933 with the encouragement of Robert Graves and Siegfried Sassoon.

Kate Roberts (1891-1985): Born and lived in north Wales. She began as a writer after her brother was killed in the Great War. A prolific author and an important influence on Welsh publishing.

Lynette Roberts (1905-1995): The wife of Keidrich Rhys, she was born in South America but brought up in Wales. She published two collections with Faber and was much admired by T.S. Eliot.

Bertrand Russell (1872-1970): One of the leading philosophers, mathematicians and social activists of the twentieth century. Spent much time in Gwynedd.

Siegfried Sassoon (1886-1967): An officer in the Royal Welch Fusiliers. 'Mad Jack' won the MC and then renounced the war. Hospitalised with Wilfred Owen and became his mentor. See *Memoirs of an Infantry Officer*.

Owen Sheers (b.1974): Born in Fiji and brought up in Abergavenny, he was one of the Poetry Society's Next Generation Poets in 2004.

Meic Stephens (b.1938): Prolific critic and editor, formerly Director of Literature at the Welsh Arts Council and Professor at the University of Glamorgan. Co-editor of the *Writers of Wales* series and editor of the *Companion to the Literatures of Wales*. 'Homer' is his translation from his own Welsh.

Caitlin Thomas (1913-1994): Married Dylan Thomas in 1937 and enjoyed a famously tempestuous marriage to him. She is buried by him in Laugharne.

Dylan Thomas (1914-1953): One of the most influential writers of the twentieth century. Although he was determined to avoid seeing action in the war, Thomas wrote some of the most memorable responses to that conflict in his poetry and the autobiographical script *Return Journey*.

Edward Thomas (1878-1917): Born in London of Welsh parents. Encouraged to write poems by Robert Frost just before the outbreak of war. His *Collected Poems* were published in 1920. See the essay in *Wales at War* by Jeremy Hooker.

Gwyn Thomas (1913-1981): One of the most acerbic social observers of the Valleys and the Welsh through his fiction and broadcasts.

Leslie Thomas (b.1931): Born in Newport. *The Virgin Soldiers* was an international success and was filmed. His twenty-eighth novel *Waiting for the Day* was published in 2003 and concerns the D-Day landings.

R.S. Thomas (1913-2000): One of the most significant Christian poets of the twentieth century. Spent almost his entire life in rural parishes in Wales as an Anglican priest.

Lily Tobias (1887 -1994) The pacifist daughter of Jewish immigrants and the aunt of Dannie Abse. An active pacifist who wrote *Eunice Fleet* in 1933 and four other novels.

John Tripp (1927-1986): Poet and broadcaster with a sharp, witty and often dark view of the world.

Wynford Vaughan-Thomas (1908-1987): Educated at Swansea and Oxford, he became a BBC war correspondent in 1943. Later, he was a major force in independent television in Wales.

Sarah Waters (b.1966): Born in Pembrokeshire. She is one of our leading novelists – *Fingersmith* and *Touching the Velvet* being successfully adapted for television. *The Night Watch* was short-listed for the 2006 Man Booker Prize

Vernon Watkins (1906-1967): Born in Swansea and a close friend of Dylan Thomas and Ceri Richards. Watkins served in the RAF in the Second World War. An outstanding neo-Romantic poet.

Harri Webb (1920-1994): Born in Swansea and educated at Oxford. A librarian and editor who joined Plaid Cymru and wrote political and satirical verse.

Anna Wigley (b.1962): Born in Cardiff. Won the Geoffrey Dearmer Prize in 2002.

Raymond Williams (1921-1988): Born to a working-class family in Llanfiangel Crucorney. A hugely influencial academic and cultural critic. He was an active Communist at Cambridge, but interrupted his studies to enlist; he served in the Guards anti-tank division from 1941-45.

The editor, Tony Curtis (b.1946): Professor of Poetry at the University of Glamorgan, where he leads the M. Phil in Creative Writing. He is the author of nine collections of poetry, most recently *Crossing Over*, and has edited several anthologies of poetry and prose. He is also the author of a study of the work of Dannie Abse and editor of *Wales and War* a collection of critical essays which accompanies this book.

Publisher's Acknowledgments

Dannie Abse: 'July 1934' 'Jimmy Ford', 'The night of broken glass' and '"All change!"'from *Ash on a Young Man's Sleeve* (Parthian, 2006); 'Freud, Marx and Sid Hamm' from *A Poet in the Family* (Hutchinson, 1974); 'The sudden shock of battle' and 'The camp' from *Goodbye, Twentieth Century: An Autobiography* (Pimlico, 2001); 'Cousin Sidney', 'Not Beautiful', 'A Night Out', 'After the Release of Ezra Pound', 'The Sheds', 'Remembrance Day', 'Case History' and 'Demo against the Vietnam War, 1968' from *Collected Poems* (Hutchinson, 1977); 'The death wind' from *Intermittent Journals* (Seren, 1994) © Dannie Abse reprinted by permission of the Peters, Fraser and Duncan Group Limited on behalf of Dannie Abse. Wilfred Bowden: 'To encourage the others' from *Abercynon to Flanders and Back* (Starling, 1984). Gillian Clarke: 'Oranges' from *Letting in the Rumour* (Carcanet, 1989); 'The Field-Mouse' from *Selected Poems* (Carcanet, 1985); 'The Night War Broke' from *Making the Beds for the Dead* (Carcanet, 2004) by permission of Carcanet Press Ltd. Tony Conran: 'Elegy for the Welsh Dead, in the Falkland Islands, 1982' from *Theatre of Flowers* (Gomer, 1998) by permission of the author. Tony Curtis: 'From the City that Shone', 'The Portrait of Hans Theo Richter and his Wife Gisela, Dresden, 1933', 'The Death of Richard Beattie-Seaman in the Belgian Grand Prix, 1939', 'Incident on a Hospital Train from Calcutta, 1944', 'Soup', 'A Visit to Terezin', 'The Grammar', 'Veteran, South Dakota, 1978', 'The World', 'Friedhof', 'Crane Flies', 'From the Hills, the Town' from *War Voices* (Seren, 1995); 'Crossing Over', from *Crossing Over* (Seren, forthcoming) by permission of of the author. John Davies: 'Riders, Walkers' and 'Borrowing the Mauser' from *Dirt Roads* (Seren, 1998); 'Pursuit', from *Flight Patterns* (Seren, 1995) by permission of the author. Lady Margaret Davies: 'Those mad British girls', from Eric Rowan and Carolyn Stewart, *An Elusive Tradition: Art and Society in Wales 1870–1950* (University of Wales Press, 2002) by permission of University of Wales Press. Stevie Davies: 'The Fatherland' from *The Element of Water* (The Women's Press, 2001), Copyright ©

Stevie Davies, 2001, by permission of the author and A.M. Heath & Co. Ltd. **Caradoc Evans**: 'Hitler in Aberystwyth', from 'Caradoc Evans, Morgan Bible & Journal 1939-44', *Planet* (2006), pp. 123-65 by permission of John Harris. **Peter Finch**: 'The Death Of King Arthur Seen As A Recent War' from *Selected Poems* (Poetry Wales Press, 1987) by permission of the author. **Raymond Garlick**: 'Looming and sombre' from *Planet* (No.151, November 2002) by permission of the author. **Robert Graves**: 'The Welch Regiment, at Cambrin' from *Goodbye to All That* (Cassell, 1957);'Sospan Fach' [The Little Saucepan] from *Poems about War* (Cassell, 1988) by permission of Carcanet Press Ltd; 'Letter to Siegfried Sassoon, 2nd May 1916' from *In Broken Images: Selected Letters of Robert Graves 1914-1946*, ed. Paul O'Prey (Hutchinson, 1982) by permission of A.P. Watt on behalf of The Trustees of the Robert Graves Copyright Trust. **Wyn Griffiths**: 'Mametz Wood' from *Up to Mametz* (1931). **Ivor Gurney** 'First Time In' from *Collected Poems of Ivor Gurney*, ed. P.J. Kavanagh (Oxford University Press, 1982) by permission of Carcanet Press Ltd. **Nigel Heseltine**, 'Hero of his Village' from *A Book of Wales: An Anthology*, ed. Meic Stephens (J.M. Dent & Sons, 1987). **Richard Hughes**: 'The Nazi Labour Camp' from *The Wooden Shepherdess* (Chatto & Windus, 1973); 'Hitler's coup', from *A Fox in the Attic* (Chatto & Windus, 1961) by permission of David Higham Associates. **Emyr Humphreys**: 'Roll of Honour' from *A Toy Epic*, ed. M. Wynn Thomas (Seren, 1995) by permission of the author. **Siân James**: 'Church and State' and '"Allies advancing"' from *A Small Country* (Seren, 2000) by permission of the author. **David Gwenallt Jones**: 'Dartmoor' from *The Penguin Book of Welsh Verse*, ed. and tr. Tony Conran (Penguin, 1967) by permission of Gomer, translation by permission of Tony Conran. **David Jones**: 'The Queen of the Woods' from *In Parenthesis* (Faber and Faber, 1937). **Glyn Jones**: 'Autobiography' from *The Dragon Has Two Tongues: Essays on Anglo-Welsh Writers and Writing*, ed. Tony Brown (University of Wales Press, 2001) by permission of the University of Wales Press. **Gwyn Jones**: 'Editorial' in *The Welsh Review* (October 1939) from *The Welsh Review* (October 1939). **Lord Elwyn Jones**: 'Margit' from *The Chosen People:Wales & the Jews*, ed. Grahame Davies (Seren, 2002) by permission of Weidenfeld and Nicolson, a division of The Orion Publishing Group. **Jack Jones**: 'The thick of it' from *Unfinished Journey* (Oxford University Press, 1937); 'Letter to the Miners' Lodge, Cross Hands, March 1938' from *Letters from Wales*, ed. Joan Abse (Seren, 2000). **Jonah Jones**: 'His "little war"' from *The Gallipoli Diary* (Seren, 1989). **Sally Roberts Jones**: 'Remembrance Day', Aberystwyth' from *Turning Away* (Gomer, 1969) by permission of the author. **Alun Lewis**: 'All day it has rained', 'Burma Casualty', 'Goodbye' and 'Raiders' Dawn' from *Collected Poems*, ed. Cary Archard (Seren, 1994); 'A fine life', 'The Earth is a Syllable' and 'The duties of the evening' from *Collected Stories*, ed. Cary Archard (Seren, 1991); 'Letter to Gweno Lewis, 30th September 1943' from *Letters to my Wife*, ed. Gweno Lewis (Seren, 1989); 'Letter to Robert Graves, 6th May 1943' from *Alun Lewis: A Miscellany of His Writings*, ed. John Pikoulis (Poetry Wales Press, 1982) by kind permission of Gweno Lewis. **Gweno Lewis**: 'A regular camp-follower' from *Letters to my Wife*, ed. Gweno Lewis (Seren, 1989) by kind permission of Gweno Lewis. **Gwyneth Lewis**: 'The Telegraph Baby 1916', from *Chaotic Angels* (Bloodaxe, 2005) by permission of the author and Bloodaxe Books. **Saunders Lewis**: 'Letter to Margaret Gilcriest, 4th January 1917' from *Letters to Margaret Gilcriest*, eds. Mair Saunders Jones, Ned Thomas and Harri Pritchard-Jones (University of Wales Press, 1993) by permission of the University of Wales Press. **David Lloyd George**: 'Letter to Frances

Stevenson, 4th October 1940' from *My Darling Pussy: Letters of Lloyd George and Frances Stevenson 1913-1941*, ed. A.J.P. Taylor (Weidenfeld & Nicolson, 1975) by permission of Weidenfeld and Nicolson, a division of The Orion Publishing Group. **Roland Mathias:** 'A Letter from Gwyther Street' from *Collected Poems*, ed. Sam Adams (University of Wales Press, 2002) by permission of the author. **Christopher Meredith:** 'My mother missed the beautiful and the doomed' and 'Occupied' from *The Meaning of Flight* (Seren, 2005); 'Averted Vision' from *Planet* 81 (June / July 1990) by permission of the author. **Robert Minhinnick:** 'Yellow Palm', unpublished, by permission of the author. **T.E. Nicholas:** 'To a Sparrow', from *Twentieth Century Welsh Poems*, translation by Joseph P. Clancy (Gomer, 1983) by permission of | Gomer. **Leslie Norris:** 'A Small War' from *Collected Poems* (Seren, 1996); 'Autumn Elegy' from *Selected Poems* (Poetry Wales Press, 1986) by permission of Meic Stephens. **John Ormond:** 'The city split in two' from *Selected Poems* (Seren, 1989). **Wilfred Owen:** 'Anthem for Doomed Youth', 'Dulce et Decorum Est' and 'Strange Meeting' from Collected Poems (Chatto & Windus, 1920). **Sheenagh Pugh:** 'Bolshies' from *Stonelight* (Seren, 1999); 'Two Retired Spymasters' from *Id's Hospit* (Seren, 1997) by permission of the author. **Goronwy Rees:** 'A winter in Berlin' and 'A sinister enchantment' from *Sketches in Autobiography*, ed. John Harris (University of Wales Press, 2001); 'This strange purgatory', from *Where No Wounds Were* (Chatto & Windus, 1950) by permission of Jenny Rees and David Higham Associates. **Private Frank Richards:** (2nd Royal Welch Fusiliers), 'Christmas 1914' from *Old Soldiers Never Die* (Naval & Military Press, 2001). **Lynette Roberts:** 'Swansea Raid' and 'Crossed and Uncrossed' from the *Introduction to Collected Poems*, ed. Patrick McGuinness (Carcanet, 2005) by permission of Carcanet Press Limited. **Kate Roberts:** 'A great shock' from *Feet in Chains*, tr. Idwal Walters and John Idris Jones (John Jones Ltd, 1977). **Bertrand Russell:** 'Letter to Lady Ottoline Morrell, July 1916' from *Letters from Wales*, ed. Joan Abse (Seren, 2000) with kind permission of the Bertrand Russell Peace Foundation Ltd and the Harry Ransom Humanities Research Centre, The University of Texas at Austin. **Siegfried Sassoon:** 'The General' from *Selected Poems* (Faber and Faber, 1970); 'Before Mametz' from *Memoirs of an Infantry Officer* (Faber and Faber, 2000), copyright Siegfried Sassoon by kind permission of the Estate of George Sassoon. **Meic Stephens:** 'Homer', first appeared in its original Welsh in the magazine *Taliesin* (126, Gaeaf 2005). **Owen Sheers:** 'War Wound' from *The Blue Book* (Seren, 2000) Copyright © 2000 Owen Sheers. Reproduced by permission of the author c/o Rogers, Coleridge & White Ltd., 20 Powis Mews, London W11 1JN. **Caitlin Thomas:** 'Drunken Waistcoat' from *My Life with Dylan Thomas*, with George Tremlett (Henry Holt & Co, 1986). **Dylan Thomas:** 'I dreamed my genesis', 'The hand that signed the paper', 'A Refusal to Mourn, the Death by Fire, of a Child in London' and 'Among Those Killed in the Dawn Raid was a Man Aged a Hundred' from *Collected Poems 1934-1953* (Phoenix, 2003); 'Letters to Vernon Watkins, 1940', from *Letters to Vernon Watkins*, ed. Vernon Watkins (J.M. Dent & Sons / Faber and Faber, 1957); 'Knocking down air-raid shelters' from 'The Londoner' in *The Broadcasts*, ed. Ralph Maud (J.M. Dent & Sons, 1991) by permission of David Higham Associates. **Edward Thomas:** 'Recruits', 'Ronville', 'Lights Out', 'Beaurains', 'As the team's head-brass' and 'The Owl' from *Selected Poems and Prose*, ed. David Wright (Penguin, 1981); 'Letter to Merfyn Thomas, April 1917' from **Letters from Wales**, ed. Joan Abse (Seren, 2000). **Gwyn Thomas:** 'Letter to Nana Thomas, Christmas 1940' from *Laughter from the Dark:*

A Life of Gwyn Thomas, Michael Parnell(John Murray Ltd, 1988) by permission of Felix de Wolfe and the Estate of Gwyn Thomas. **Leslie Thomas:** 'The train from Kuala Lumpur' from *The Virgin Soldiers* (Arrow, 2005) reprinted by permission of The Random House Group Ltd. **R.S. Thomas:** 'Welsh History', 'Remembering David Jones', 'Guernica', 'Homo Sapiens, 1941' and 'The Hearth' from *Collected Poems 1945-1990* (J.M. Dent & Sons, 1993) by permission of Weidenfeld and Nicolson, a division of The Orion Publishing Group; 'Local danger' from *Autobiographies*, tr. Jason Walford Davies (J.M. Dent & Sons, 1997); 'Others were brave', 'The mushroom-shaped cloud' and 'The war to end all wars!' from *The Echoes Return Slow* (Macmillan, 1988). **Lily Tobias:** 'The Task' from *Eunice Fleet* (Honno, 2004). **John Tripp:** 'Pay Detachment, Exeter', 'Dering Lines '45', 'Burial Party' and 'Defence of the West' from *Selected Poems*, ed. John Ormond (Seren, 1989) by permission of Jean Henderson. **Wynford Vaughan-Thomas:** 'Anzio' from *Anzio* (Longmans, Green and Co, 1961). **Corporal Ivor Watkins:** (6th Battalion, Welch Regiment), 'Gas!' from *Forgotten Voices of the Great War*, ed. Max Arthur (Ted Smart, 2002). **Sarah Waters:** 'The Blitz' from *The Night Watch* (Virago, 2006), © Sarah Waters 2006, reproduced by kind permission of Virago Press, a division of Little, Brown Book Group. **Vernon Watkins:** 'Sonnet on the Death of Alun Lewis' from *In The Green Tree: The Letters and Short Stories of Alun Lewis* (Parthian, 2006) by permission of Gwen Watkins. **Harri Webb:** 'On Convoy' from *Collected Poems*, ed. Meic Stephens (Gomer, 1995) by permission of Meic Stephens. **Anna Wigley:** 'Soldier' from *Dürer's Hare* (Gomer, 2005) by permission of Gomer. **Raymond Williams:** 'Spain, February 1937' and 'Normandie, July 1944' from *Loyalties* (Chatto & Windus, 1985).

Every effort has been made to contact copyright holders, but if any have been overlooked the publisher will be pleased to make the necessary arrangements.